City Wedding

A guide to the best bridal resources in New York, Long Island, Westchester, New Jersey, and Connecticut

JOAN HAMBURG

with Elise Mac Adam

Illustrations by Sharon Watts

UNIVERSE PUBLISHING

NEW YORK

First Universe edition published in the United States of America in 2003
by UNIVERSE PUBLISHING
A Division of Rizzoli International Publications, Inc.
300 Park Avenue South
New York, NY 10010

Previously published by City and Company.

Text © 2000, 2002 by Maplehill Communications, Inc.
Interior illustrations © 2000 by Sharon Watts
Cover illustration © 2002 by Mary Lynn Blasutta
Cover design by Paul Kepple and Jude Buffum @ Headcase Design
Interior design © 2000 by Don Wise & Co.

2003 2004 2005 2006 2007 / 10 9 8 7 6 5 4 3 2 1
Second Edition
Printed in the United States
Library of Congress Control Number: 2002115722
ISBN: 0-789-308568

Acknowledgments

Thanks to the efforts and contributions of the
following people this book was made possible:

Francine Albert
Ferne Elling
Tracy Guth
Stephanie Iverson
Barbara Kahn
Sandy Prince
Susan Rosenthal
Lindsay Roth
Pat Scanlon
Muriel Sohmer

PUBLISHER'S NOTE

Neither Universe Publishing nor the author has an interest, financial or personal, in the
locations listed in this book. No fees were paid or services rendered in exchange for
inclusion in these pages. While every effort was made to ensure accuracy at the time of pub-
lication, it is always best to call ahead to verify addresses, fees, and other details.

Dear Reader:

Because my mother didn't want to hurt the feelings of her then-unmarried older sister, she and my father eloped. They tied the knot aboard a Holland America Lines ship en route to Bermuda. The bride wore a nautical outfit complete with white deck shoes, and the groom was a vision in baggy shorts. The attendants were fellow passengers dragged in for the ceremony which was presided over by the ship's captain. My mother was definitely a woman ahead of her time.

Since I had no heirloom bridal gown passed on to me, I too rejected a traditional wedding and ended up taking my marriage vows in a glittering gown of blue that I picked out myself. At my direction, the marriage ceremony took place in a small private study surrounded only by immediate family. My husband, dubbed "Long Suffering" by my WOR Radio listeners, claims that even to this day he isn't over the shock of seeing his bride in blue.

Don't forget that when I got married in the early '60s, convention almost always prevailed. Today, anything and everything goes. We recently went to a weekend wedding in Hawaii where the bride and groom walked in bare feet down an empty beach to the accompaniment of the ocean waves and with the assembled guests humming "Here Comes the Bride."

Traditional or not, weddings are a big deal and usually expensive, and brides need to know all the answers: where to find the best places for the reception; where to buy or rent the gown; how to choose the band; how to select the photographer, the caterer, the wedding consultant, the invitations, and everything connected with the wedding—even who will write the toast for the non-verbal best man.

I know the answers. For some 20-odd years as a broadcaster on radio and television, as a magazine article writer and book author, I've collected information on weddings for every level of taste and budget. How is it that I, such an unconventional bride myself with two unmarried eligible children, have become the wedding guru for millions of my listeners?

I was motivated to write this book in response to an almost daily barrage of questions from the audience who are themselves getting married or have a child about to enter into blissful matrimony. So I've included virtually everything that I know and that you need to know, except where to find the groom. And I'm working on that.

How to Use This Book

Read the introduction at the beginning of each chapter carefully. Each is filled with tips on how to save money and how to get the best service possible from each type of vendor.

I have listed hundreds of wedding vendors in this book, from classic wedding locations such as the Plaza to hidden jewels like the Nassau County Museum of Art, and almost any type of florist, wedding gown, or invitation you're dreaming of can also be found in these pages. Use my descriptions as a starting-off point; I encourage you to set up a face-to-face visit with every vendor you are seriously considering.

Remember that prices are always subject to change. Fees are listed for comparison purposes only and may vary depending on the specific services you're looking for.

With all this in mind, take a deep breath, plunge in, and start planning your city wedding.

Getting Started

When you embark on your wedding planning, there are a number of considerations to keep in mind. First, you'll need to draw up a budget that encompasses everything from the wedding gown to the catering, attendant gifts, and favors. Weddings in the tristate area are generally pricier than weddings in most other parts of the country, although it is possible to arrange for a relatively inexpensive wedding. Save the lion's share of your budget for catering, and try to choose a caterer who can supply liquor and wine, or at least arrange for alcoholic beverages (unless you want an alcohol-free reception).

Second, create a planning schedule. There are a number of wedding workbooks and calendars available at bookstores, or you might buy a blank calendar or datebook expressly for the wedding and simply write in your tasks for each month and each week.

You'll have the widest range of options if you start planning your wedding a year or more in advance, but it's not impossible to plan a great party in just six months. Once you decide on a date, arrange for a location immediately (or vice versa). And if you have a favorite rabbi, priest, or other officiant, make sure that person will be available on your date. Once you have these two important aspects arranged, you can start on the details, such as settling on vendors like the caterer, photographer, and florist, and ordering your invitations.

You may want to hire a wedding consultant to save yourself the stress of putting together a party for 100 or more in one of the most expensive cities in the country—or you may decide to take on the challenge by planning the event yourself.

Wedding Planners and Consultants

If a bride and groom are both extremely busy, their parents live out of town, and the wedding is going to be a large affair, it's a good idea to think about hiring a wedding planner. Throughout what can be an extremely hectic event, this professional can truly save the day—and your mind. A good wedding planner can also negotiate better fees with vendors (most have long-term relationships with caterers, florists, photographers, and even reception venues, and can ask for discounts for their clients); make sure your wedding-day decor is delightful; and create a politically correct seating chart that will keep everyone smiling throughout your reception.

Questions to ask

● What types of wedding locations does the planner usually work with?

● If you want an outdoor wedding, has the planner dealt with weather problems and tents in the past?

● What is the average budget of the weddings the planner generally organizes?

● Can you get references?

● Can the planner arrange a wedding outside of the immediate area—if you live in Manhattan but want a vineyard wedding on Long Island, for example, can she arrange that?

● If you're having many relatives and friends fly in from out of town, can your consultant help book hotel rooms and arrange transportation for your guests?

In-the-know tips

● Contacting a planner at least a year before your wedding date is highly advisable.

● Get everything in writing. Be sure you have a contract that spells out exactly how much you'll pay the wedding planner and how much you'll pay for other vendors' services.

● Some planners offer partial planning services. If you'd like to arrange for all the vendors yourself but would like someone to orchestrate the actual wedding day, that can probably be arranged.

● Some caterers act as wedding planners as well and can help you find everything from flowers to invitations to photographers.

● Although you pay a fee for a wedding consultant's services, keep in mind that the consultant may be able to arrange for vendor services at a discount. This may save you money in the long run.

NEW YORK CITY

Marcy Blum Associates

259 West 11th Street • New York, NY 10014
212-929-9814
$: Fee starts at $20,000

Marcy Blum's passion for details has led her to be called "the human wedding Rolodex." The author of the book *Weddings for Dummies,* she can take care of absolutely everything. If the bride and groom don't want to lift a finger, Blum will select the caterer and the reception space, arrange for transportation, hire a cake baker, and even find the wedding dress. If all you want is a simple consultation, she can help you get started on planning your wedding yourself. Blum also organizes and plans destination weddings on occasion, and she helped to invent Walt Disney World's and Sandals Resorts' wedding programs. She also does day-of-the-wedding planning. Those services start at $2,000.

Gourmet Advisory Services

315 East 68th Street • New York, NY 10021
212-535-0005
$: Flat fee or 15 percent commission on the total cost of the wedding

Owner Harriette Rose Katz is known by absolutely everyone in the wedding business. As a full-service wedding consultant, she can arrange for everything from locations and the gown to hotel accommodations for your guests. Katz claims that she will make your wedding dreams come true, and she creates gorgeous events to prove it. She's the perfect planner if you're having a large, extravagant affair, but her services may be a bit more than you need if you're planning an intimate wedding.

Marry Me Productions

222 East 93rd Street • New York, NY 10128
212-426-5776
info@marrymepro.com • www.marrymepro.com
$: 10 percent commission on vendor fees (with some flexibility)

Owner Bridgette Foley has been a wedding consultant for over five years, and she puts together polished, beautiful events. She can plan your entire wedding or provide a simple consultation. She'll help with everything from finding an officiant to choosing your reception site to buying gifts for your attendants.

Wedding Planners and Consultants

Party Artistry

222 Park Avenue South · New York, NY 10003
212-995-2299
and
24 Eisenhower Parkway · Roseland, NJ 07068
973-228-2299
prtyartistry@msn.com · www.partyartistry.ney
$: Fee for complete event planning is $40 per person; $3,500 minimum
Consultations are free of charge and obligation (for event planning)

Party Artistry doesn't just book vendors and a location for your celebration; they create the celebration for you. They have their own in-house floral designer as well as designers who specialize in party decor, and their New Jersey warehouse is stocked with all sorts of props, linens, and tabletop accessories. They also coordinate with outside caterers, photographers, bands, and more. If you want your reception to look absolutely spectacular, call Party Artistry.

Aside from event planning, you can get Party Artistry to design your event decor. They don't charge a fee for their design services. You only pay for the items they use for your event.

Red Letter Events

292 Madison Avenue · New York, NY 10017
212-772-1177
redletny@aol.com · www.redletterevents.com
$: No fee for couple; commission paid by vendors

Red Letter Events doesn't just do weddings—they put together all sorts of large celebrations, including events for MTV, *Billboard* magazine, and Time Inc. The company is a full-service party-planning organization, but they don't charge you a fee: They receive a commission directly from the vendors you use. They have a whole roster of locations you can use, including mansions, lofts, yachts, and private clubs, and they'll also take care of all the other wedding-day details.

The Total Affair

16 West 16th Street · New York, NY 10011
646-230-7991
hmsb5@aol.com · www.thetotalaffair.com
$: Fee is negotiable

For a wonderful party from beginning to end, contact Helaine Bernstein. She's been a party planner for 24 years and has organized thousands of successful affairs, including weddings, bar and bat mitzvahs, corporate parties, and more. Bernstein wants the process to be enjoyable and stress-free for everyone. If you want to be actively involved she'll keep in constant touch, but if you want to delegate everything she'll organize it all, including reception locale, music, flowers, decorations, and photography. She says she can often get services at a discounted price, so her final fee may be less than you originally expected.

Wedding Day Inc.

P.O. Box 300509 · Jamaica, NY 11430
646-246-1922
mchatman@wednday.com · www.wednday.com
$: Flat fee of $2,500 for 15 hours minimum
consultation; additional hours are extra

Wedding Day Inc. owner Mayai Chatman will work within any budget; she can even coordinate weddings for less than $10,000. Her consultation package includes four one-hour consultations with the bride and groom, five hours of in-office coordination, and five hours of wedding-day service. Chatman specializes in designing and coordinating unique and elegant weddings of all sizes, with a touch of your cultural heritage. She is also Royal Caribbean Cruise Line's onboard wedding coordinator, so if you want to sail the seas (or the Hudson) for your wedding, talk to her.

The Wedding Library

50 East 81st Street · New York, NY 10028
212-327-0100
claudiahanlin@weddinglibrary.net
www.weddinglibrary.net
$: Research: Free
Full-Service Wedding Planning: Starts at $15,000
Day-Of-Wedding Planning: Starts at $2,950

Claudia Hanlin founded the Wedding Library as a do-it-yourself center for engaged couples, but her expertise has led her to open up her business to include full-service wedding planning and "day of" wedding planning. She also has an extensive retail business. Doing your own research is free of charge. You can look through hundreds of listings (complete with photos) for photographers, caterers, makeup artists, bakers, calligraphers, stationers, florists, and more. You can also listen to demo tapes from wedding bands and orchestras. Vendors pay a fee to be included in the library, but Hanlin is selective and only includes professionals she has handpicked. You must make an appointment to meet one-on-one with Hanlin to look through her listings. Once you find vendors you're interested in, you can take their business cards and call them directly. In addition, Hanlin's retail business is a one-stop shop for wedding accessories, including a collection of exclusive invitations and bridesmaid dresses, and New York City's largest collection of headpieces, shoes, veils, favors, and more.

Weddings by Amelia

245 West 136th Street · New York, NY 10030
212-283-2106 · Fax: 212-283-2338
weddings_by_amelia@msn.com
$: Fees start at 15 percent of the total cost of the wedding;
for a consultation a few months before, a flat fee ranges from
$800 to $1,500; day-of-wedding consultation
and coordination is $950

Amelia Montgomery does weddings of all types—no budget is too small. She was the bridal consultant for the wedding-planning book *Going to the Chapel: The Guide to Organizing Your Traditional African-Inspired or Totally Unique Wedding,* so if you're interested in having an African-themed wedding, Montgomery is the planner for you. She believes in taking care of the details—she'll even select a dress for the mother of the bride and arrange for your wedding rings to be engraved before the big day.

LONG ISLAND

Annette Babich

212-332-9995 or 516-739-8166
info@annettebabich.com · www.annettebabich.com
$: Fee is usually about 10 percent of the
total wedding budget

Annette Babich's services are truly all-inclusive, covering all the details relating to your wedding, from your engagement through your honeymoon. She'll act as your etiquette advisor, coordinate with everyone from the caterers to the musicians and photographer, and work within your budget. She also claims that, as an unbiased third party, she excels at smoothing over uncomfortable situations or arguments with relatives, attendants, or friends.

The Artist's Wedding Studio
Hampton Wedding

The Artist's Wedding Studio
631-537-8008
www.chuppah.com
$: Chuppahs start at $2,000
and
Hampton Wedding
631-537-3833 · 212-369-3915
info@hamptonwedding.com
www.hamptonwedding.com

Corinne Soikin Strauss has two companies that keep her busy catering to weddings. For the Artist's Wedding Studio, Soikin Strauss designs hand-painted silk chuppahs and hand-designed ketubot that reflect the colors and symbols of the couple. They are designed to be hung on tapestry after the ceremony. The Artist's Wedding Studio also offers creative wedding consultations with particular sensitivity to interfaith and intercultural couples. She excels at combining different religions or cultures to create a beautiful affair. Her chuppah design questionnaire includes inquiries about your favorite artistic school, your taste in music, and design sensibilities.

Hampton Wedding promises to tell you "where to do, who to know, and how to do everything in the Hamptons—and New York City, too." Corinne Soikin Strauss can plan any kind of wedding you can dream up—from beach events to vineyard parties, house weddings, and city weddings. She does full-service and on-site event management and day-of-wedding planning, and can even create save-the-date wedding web sites for you.

WESTCHESTER

Barbara Feldman

P.O. Box 310 · New Rochelle, NY 10804
914-633-7068
$: Flat fee based on scale of wedding

Barbara Feldman has been in business for over 30 years and has been the planner for many an upscale wedding. She'll do everything from finding a suitable location and reviewing contracts to coordinating the menu with the caterer. She'll oversee the rehearsal as well as the wedding reception; assist in selecting music, the photographer, and the floral arrangements; coordinate and mail the invitations; and even arrange hotel accommodations for out-of-town guests.

New Jersey

Elegant Occasions

P.O. Box 86 · Denville, NJ 07834
973-361-9200 · Toll free: 888-361-9177
Fax: 973-361-3309
and
100 Park Avenue · New York, NY 10017
212-704-0048
elegwed204@aol.com · www.elegantoccasions.com
$: Usually 10 to 15 percent of the total wedding budget

Elegant Occasions owner JoAnn Gregoli has been a wedding consultant for 12 years and has been featured on "Good Morning America" and "Weddings of a Lifetime." The head of the New York chapter of the Association of Bridal Consultants, she is one of 16 people in the world with the organization's Master Bridal Consultant degree. Gregoli has planned complicated, original celebrations, including society and celebrity weddings, and even did a wedding on Ellis Island that included the boat upon which the bride's grandfather traveled to America. She offers three types of service: full, partial, and rehearsal and wedding coordination only. For full- and partial-service clients, she does all the research and coordination (with the bride and groom making the final decisions) as well as overseeing the wedding day and rehearsal. For the third choice, Gregoli develops a wedding timeline and then supervises the rehearsal and the ceremony. The rest is up to you.

Grand Luxe International

165 Chestnut Street · Allendale, NJ 07401
201-327-2333
lisa@grandluxeweddings.com · www.grandluxeweddings.com
$: Fees range from $2,500 to $5,000

Grand Luxe specializes in organizing destination weddings to exotic locales, including Italy, Greece, Austria, Denmark, Scotland, and the South Pacific. They'll help you with documentation, your wedding ceremony appointment, and all the reception arrangements (including flowers, photography, music, and food). And once you're abroad, you're not alone: Grand Luxe has English-speaking delegates who can facilitate everything.

CONNECTICUT

Association of Bridal Consultants

200 Chestnutland Road • New Milford, CT 06776
860-355-0464
office@bridalassn.com • www.bridalassn.com
$: Free

This professional group publishes a newsletter and offers seminars and workshops. They're also a great resource for brides and grooms. Call them for a list of member wedding professionals in the tristate area.

Winslow Associates

70 Hamilton Avenue • Greenwich, CT 06830
203-869-6612
winslowjw@hotmail.com
$: Fee starts at $6,000

Each event is unique to Judy Winslow. She organizes everything from destination weddings to garden weddings and will arrange hotels and activities for guests. Winslow and assistant Hilary Houldin's specialty is high-end home weddings, especially tented receptions. Although most couples come to Winslow a year or more in advance, a wedding may be doable in as little as six months.

Newspaper Announcements

You're getting married! Of course you want to tell the world. To list your engagement or wedding announcement, you may have to plan ahead and do some work, but it can be a lot of fun—you get to see your names in print—and you'll get a lot of phone calls from people you forgot you knew.

New York Observer

Engagements Column
www.observer.com • engagements@@observer.com
$: Free

Every week the *New York Observer* publishes a handful of stories about novel New York engagements. Anyone can submit an engagement story to the newspaper, but there are a couple of ground rules: you must be a New Yorker, and you must be engaged but not yet married—so send in your story a little early. Couples have been featured in the column up to a year before the actual wedding date. To submit to the Engagements column, send an email with a brief description of who you are, what you do, how you got engaged, and a couple of details about your wedding plans. If you're picked, someone from the *New York Observer* will interview you. One warning: while the paper rigorously fact-checks the stories to make sure they're accurate, couples do not get to see the article before it runs.

New York Times

Wedding Announcement
Society News
The New York Times
229 West 43rd Street, 5th Floor • New York, NY 10036
www.nytimes.com/weddings • society@nytimes.com
Messages: 212-556-7321
$: Free

For many New Yorkers, having a wedding announcement in the *New York Times* is a rite of passage. Announcements are free, but the *Times* is constantly inundated with requests, so it isn't a given that your story will be selected. The best place to go for information about getting your announcement published is the "How to Submit a Wedding Announcement" page on the *Times* website. (Just go to www.nytimes/weddings and look for a link to the "How to Submit. . ." page.) The newspaper requires that you submit your announcement requests at least six weeks before the wedding, and that your information be typed. The *Times* will also want to know the full names of the bride and groom, when and where they will marry, their professions, parents' names and occupations, and lots of information about the wedding itself. If you're interested, be sure to check out the web site for the complete list of details you'll need to know, and for information about how to submit photographs. If you want to try to get into the big Sunday "Vows" column, you'll have to include a duplicate copy of your submission. Information about "Vows" is also available on the "How to Submit . . ." page.

Reception Locations

Nothing can be more exciting—or confusing—than narrowing your search for wedding reception and ceremony locations. New York City and the surrounding areas have hundreds of sites to fall in love with and to fit every budget and taste. If you've always dreamed of having your wedding in a place with a sense of history, you can choose George Washington's cliffside headquarters in upper Manhattan. If you'd like to start off on your journey together in a yacht on the Hudson, you have several options. Many restaurants can host weddings, or you may be looking for an outdoor location. If you can dream it, you can find it in or near the city. I have included all the locations I really love, from the tried-and-true to hidden gems.

About catering

Many of the spots listed here have their own exclusive caterers, ranging from established New York City catering companies to local restaurants. If you're set on a particular caterer who doesn't usually work at the site, ask whether using an outside company is an option. If you have specific dietary requirements (such as kosher), find out if they can be accommodated when you first contact the location.

In-the-know tips

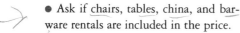

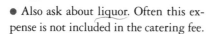

● Ask if chairs, tables, china, and barware rentals are included in the price.

● Also ask about liquor. Often this expense is not included in the catering fee.

● Find out whether the location's caterer can provide the cake as well as the meal.

● Request menu options by fax or email.

● Set up a tasting before the wedding to plan the exact menu.

● Sign a contract before making a deposit. Never pay the whole bill up front; you should pay part of the balance before the wedding and the rest afterward.

● Most caterers can also help you find a location (see the catering chapter).

● Visit the site before you book it. Be sure to walk around, both indoors and out. Do you like the light fixtures, floors, carpets, grounds, and decor? Does the site seem well cared for and clean?

● If you want to save money, think about booking on a weekday evening or a weekend morning or afternoon.

● Consider purchasing cancellation insurance, in case of major weather problems or a natural catastrophe.

NEW YORK CITY

American Park at the Battery

Inside Battery Park, opposite 17 State Street · New York, NY 10004
212-809-5508
www.americanpark.com
$: Sit-down dinner at peak seasons is approximately $125–$160 per person
Capacity: for a sit-down dinner, minimum: 30, maximum: 200

If you want a wedding reception with a fantastic background, you can't do better than American Park at the Battery. The restaurant sits inside Battery Park with spectacular views of New York Harbor, Ellis Island, and the Statue of Liberty. All catering is done in-house by the restaurant and there is a wide range of packages—everything from cocktails to wedding cake and three courses in-between to buffets, and of course you can customize a menu and package to suit your needs. American Park prepares great Continental food and can serve kosher meals.

Americas Society

680 Park Avenue · New York, NY
212-249-8950
www.americas-society.org
$: $5,100 for eight hours
Capacity: maximum 120 people

The Americas Society, housed in a beautiful neo-Georgian building at 68th street and Park Avenue, offers a gorgeous and intimate space for weddings. It has a classical, elegant, "old New York" sensibility, and was even used as a location in the Martin Scorsese movie, *The Age of Innocence*. The fee is for the space rental (your caterer will need to provide furnishings) but the space does come with access to a great kitchen. Be sure to take advantage of the photo opportunities on the main staircase and in the wood-paneled library.

Bateaux New York

Pier 61 at Chelsea Piers · Suite 200A
New York, NY 10011
212-352-9009 · www.bateauxnewyork.com
$: Fees range from $175 to $200 per person for food and location
Capacity: maximum 300

This sleek vessel offers the feel of a bateau cruising down the Seine. Glass walls curve into a glass ceiling, and every seat on the 210-foot boat has an unobstructed view of the city skyline. The food is as breathtaking as the scenery and is created by Noelle Ifshin. The boat, which can be yours for up to five hours, can hold a total of 300 people in its two rooms.

Beekman Tower Hotel, Top of the Tower

3 Mitchell Place · New York, NY 10017
212-355-7300 · www.mesuite.com
$: Fees range from $115 to $140 per person for food and location
Capacity: minimum 75, maximum 110

The view is the star here (along with the bride!). Beekman Tower stands out because of its 26th-floor panoramic view of the Manhattan skyline, East River, and Queens. The hotel was built in 1928 and is a New York landmark. The Top of the Tower isn't as luxurious as some other Manhattan hotel restaurants, but it has an art deco feel and dramatic lighting. Continental-American food is served.

The Boathouse in Central Park

P.O. Box 1357 · Gracie Station · New York, NY 10028
(Located in Central Park at East 72nd Street and Park Drive North)
212-517-2233
$: Fees range from $140 to $200 per person for food and location
Capacity: Weekday & Sunday minimum 100;
Saturday minimum 150; maximum (seated) 250.
Larger parties negotiated on a case-by-case basis

The Boathouse's enchanting dockside setting offers a country feeling in the heart of Manhattan. It's no wonder this Central Park lakeside restaurant is a favorite venue for entertainment industry parties—it's extremely dramatic and very New York. The restaurant is a year-round room facility with floor-to-ceiling windows surrounding eight pairs of French doors that lead out onto an English garden patio and a brand new dock overlooking the Bethesda Fountain. For wedding-day photos, a gondola and gondolier are for hire at $150 per hour. There is no on-site parking for guests, but a complimentary shuttle bus runs between nearby parking lots and the restaurant. The Boathouse is a private venue that only hosts one occasion at a time.

Brooklyn Society for Ethical Culture

53 Prospect Park West · Brooklyn, NY 11215
718-768-2972
www.bsec.org
$: $250 per hour for location only
Capacity: maximum 100

If you are planning a nonsectarian ceremony and a smallish wedding, you should know about the Brooklyn Society for Ethical Culture. This sophisticated turn-of-the-century landmark mansion (originally owned by millionaire William Childs, inventor of Bon Ami cleansing powder) is a delightful place for a nonreligious ceremony. The elegant brownstone is located in the attractive Park Slope section of Brooklyn and features such design elements as Tiffany stained-glass windows, a sunroom leading into a garden, and a mahogany-paneled library. Bring your own caterer, or select from one of the several that the Society recommends. On-street parking can be difficult, but many train lines stop within blocks of the mansion.

The Carlyle Hotel

35 East 76th Street · New York, NY 10021
212-744-1600
www.thecarlyle.com · thecarlyle@rosewoodhotels.com
$: Fees start at $175 per person for food and location
Capacity: minimum 25; maximum 160
for a seated dinner only, 130 for dancing

The Carlyle is one of the best hotels in New York City and is frequented by movie stars and financiers. The hotel has a thoroughly sophisticated yet restrained decor; everything is tastefully done. Large receptions can be accommodated in one of the two Mark Hampton ballrooms on the hotel's second floor: the Versailles suite is done in Louis XIV style; the larger Triannon suite has a more understated elegance. The hotel's wedding coordinators are well connected in the bridal world and, if necessary, can put together a wedding within days. However, you should plan to book over a year in advance—the hotel is extremely popular.

Central Park

www.centralparknyc.org
Permits: 212-408-0226

You can get married in lots of different fabulous locations in Central Park. There's the Bethesda Terrace, the Conservatory Garden, the Shakespeare Garden, Cherry Hill, Bow Bridge, Cedar Hill, and The Mall. For parties of more than 20 people you'll need to get a permit, which you can download off the Central Park website and in some cases (particularly the Conservatory Garden) pay fees for photography and ceremonies. There are a lot of rules to follow for Central Park weddings (no alcoholic beverages may be consumed and no rice, birdseed, or confetti may be thrown, for instance) so confirm all your plans with the Park ahead of time.

The Chemists' Club

40 West 45th Street · New York, NY 10036
212-626-9201
$: $130 per person for food (including cake) and location
Capacity: maximum 120

At the Chemists' Club, you can have an exclusive "club" wedding without a sponsor, since the turn-of-the-century landmark building is open to nonmembers for weddings. It's a charming space, replete with marble columns, a towering fireplace, a living room decorated with English furnishings, and a long mahogany bar. The club also has over 150 sleeping rooms that are available to overnight guests at reasonable rates. Discounted parking is available nearby.

The Empire State Building

350 Fifth Avenue · New York, NY 10118
www.esbnyc.com
212-736-3100

It takes a bit of work, but if you want to have a real New York wedding, consider getting married at the Empire State Building. Each year the Building accepts applications to get married in their observatories, and there is a special annual competition that is staged for Valentine's Day weddings. If you want to take part in the Valentine's Day contest, you have to write an essay explaining why it's important to you to marry at the Empire State Building. Essays are judged for originality and style. For weddings on any other day of the year, call to make arrangements and to discuss fees.

Faculty House at Columbia University

400 West 117th Street • New York, NY 10027
212-854-7192
www.columbia.edu/cu/fachouse
$: Fees range from $140 to $160 per person for food and location
Capacity: minimum 80, maximum 200 with dancing

Those who like faded gentility and the aura of academia should consider the Faculty House at Columbia University. This landmark 1923 McKim, Mead and White building offers two different rooms for weddings, and catering is handled by the experienced Restaurant Associates group. As an added perk, special arrangements can be made with the NYC Parks Department to have the wedding ceremony across from the Faculty House in Morningside Park. Arrangements can also be made with nearby St. Paul's Chapel, with its sweeping Byzantine arches and magnificent acoustics. The Faculty House hosts only one event at a time.

Four Seasons Hotel

57 East 57th Street • New York, NY 10022
212-893-6501
$: Catering starts at about $250 per person, call for additional room fees
Capacity: Grand ballroom minimum 100, maximum 400
Cosmopolitan Room: maximum 165 people for banquet style,
110 people for dinner and dancing

I. M. Pei designed the calm and spacious Four Seasons Hotel, located on a prime stretch of East 57th Street. If you are looking for glamour and luxury, this hotel fits the bill perfectly. It is a favorite of celebrities like Kevin Costner, Oprah Winfrey, Bruce Willis, Sean Connery, and Sylvester Stallone, and the dramatic, terraced Lobby Court makes a wonderful first impression. Guests enjoy cocktails under 30-foot-high ceilings before being escorted into the elegant Cosmopolitan Suite, completed in 2001, for dinner, delicious American cuisine by Executive Chef Brooke Vosica, and dancing. The Four Seasons gets booked quickly so try to make arrangements about a year in advance.

Giando on the Water

400 Kent Avenue • Brooklyn, NY 11211
718-387-7000
www.giandoonthewater.com
$: Fees start at $75 per person for food and location
Capacity: minimum 50, maximum 300

The best river views in New York City aren't necessarily in Manhattan. If you want a great view at a reasonable price, Brooklyn's Giando on the Water offers glittering vistas from its floor-to-ceiling glass windows, in an offbeat location at the base of the Williamsburg Bridge. This is a place where Wall Streeters and local artists alike congregate for dinner during the week. The Northern Italian cuisine may not be fancy, but it is hearty and plentiful.

The Grand Prospect Hall

263 Prospect Avenue · Brooklyn, NY 11215
718-788-0777
www.grandprospect.com
$: Fees range from $80 to $150 per person for food and location
Capacity: minimum 50, maximum 2,000

This century-old landmark building, once a crumbling music hall and ballroom, is Brooklyn's answer to the Waldorf-Astoria. After an 18-year renovation, the building has emerged as a true wedding palace. You'll find dramatic gold-gilded staircases, horseshoe-shaped balconies, lavish chandeliers, Bavarian-style murals, outdoor gardens, and elaborate fountains. If theater has a special meaning for you, this building is also a member of the League of Historic American Theaters. It has been the site of many motion pictures, including *The Cotton Club* and *Prizzi's Honor,* and has been featured in *Vogue* and *Life* magazines. A variety of menus includes French, Italian, Middle Eastern, Asian, Mediterranean, Southwestern, Cajun, and Glatt kosher foods. The Grand Ballroom is a favorite of Orthodox Jews, allowing men and women to sit separately during the celebration. There are many rooms here, so many events take place at once, but only one per room. One drawback: The building is directly off the not-so-scenic Prospect Expressway. On-site parking is available.

Hilton New York and Towers

1335 Avenue of the Americas · New York, NY 10019
212-586-7000
www.hilton.com
$: Fees for the ballroom start at $120 per person for food and location;
penthouse rental fee is $3,100 plus $150 per person for catering
Capacity: Ballroom minimum 120, maximum 1,000;
penthouse maximum 130

A Hilton is a Hilton, but this one has a well-kept secret: there is a spectacular duplex penthouse crowning its towers. The East Penthouse (French decor) occupies 7,500 square feet on two levels. A private elevator goes directly to the 44th floor, where your reception can flow between two floors connected by a spiral staircase. The penthouse has a kitchen, dining room, living room, library, several bedroom suites, and floor-to-ceiling glass walls offering a panoramic view of the city. They are so popular that you'll need to book one year in advance. The hotel also has three ballrooms. One accommodates 150 and is decorated in modern, elegant style; the second has a Versailles theme and will hold 350; the largest will allow for 1,000 guests and has a basic ballroom feel. The Hilton is a favorite of couples marrying at St. Patrick's Cathedral, a short distance away.

Hotel Inter-Continental

111 East 48th Street • New York, NY 10017
212-755-5900
www.interconti.com • newyork@interconti.com
$: Call for rates
Capacity: minimum 30, maximum 160

The Inter-Continental started life as the Barclay in 1926 and is the perfect spot for a sophisticated hotel wedding complete with sumptuous decor and crystal chandeliers. The hotel is very popular with European corporate executives during the week, but on weekends it hosts about 40 weddings per year, attracting uptown couples and their parents. Glatt kosher catering is available.

House of the Redeemer

7 East 95th Street • New York, NY 10128
212-289-0399
$: Dining room is $2,500; dining room and parlour is $3,000;
library is $2,500; first and second floors are $4,000.
Capacity: maximum 150 at cocktail receptions, 100 for dancing

This charming retreat house for the Episcopal Church is also available for weddings. The grand mansion was once the home of the great-grandaughter of Cornelius Vanderbilt and is sumptuously furnished—some antiques date back to the 15th century. You bring your own caterer and arrange for all rentals.

Hudson Waterfront Barge and Garden Pier

290 Conover Street • Brooklyn, NY 11231
718-624-4719
www.waterfrontmuseum.org
$: $1,750 for up to 90 people; $2,000 for 90–130
people with a tent on the pier for an additional fee
Capacity: maximum 130

The riverside barge offers wood floors and walls, dramatic skylights, and a front-row view of the Statue of Liberty. All the decorating and catering details are up to you. During the summer months, receptions can be held outside on the garden pier, and the bride and groom can make a dramatic entrance by boat. Last-minute bookings are sometimes available, so if you've had a whirlwind courtship and can't wait to wed, try here.

The James Burden/Otto Kahn Mansions

7 East 91st Street /1 East 91st Street • New York, NY 10128
$: The James Burden/Otto Kahn Mansions are closed until September 2003.
Call for rates.
Capacity: Call for information

The James Burden and Otto Kahn Mansions are two of the city's most ornate. Both of these venues are extremely popular and have ample experience doing weddings—at a clip of three to four per weekend, year-round. The Otto Kahn Mansion, completed in 1918, was one of the largest private homes in America at that time. In 1934 it was acquired for use as a school by the Society of the Sacred Heart. It features a charming Italianate courtyard with a view across Fifth Avenue to Central Park, an elaborately carved fireplace, and an ornate coffered ceiling. Several rooms are for hire, with the largest accommodating up to 100 guests. There are a few religious fixtures, but if you wish, these can be removed for the day. The James Burden Mansion, a landmark beaux-arts townhouse, has a distinctly French feel, with a ballroom modeled on the Hall of Mirrors at Versailles. Both mansions supply tables and chairs at no additional cost. Catering is not included, so you arrange for your own food service. One drawback is that parties must end relatively early: on Friday by midnight, Saturday by 11 P.M., and Sunday by 6 P.M. The mansions are popular, so book as far in advance as you can.

Lots of Yachts

1 Irving Place • New York, NY 10003
212-505-2214
E-mail: lotsyachts.com
$: Fees start at $90 per person for yacht rental
Capacity: varies

If you've always admired the exquisite boats docked at the World Financial Center, why not charter one for your wedding? Lots of Yachts is a broker for many yachts docked in the city, with a roster of 21 privately owned boats. Whether you're looking for an antique boat with wood trim to accommodate 10 people or an ultra-modern vessel with leather couches to accommodate 500, Lots of Yachts can accommodate you. Most boats will stop near the Statue of Liberty during the ceremony. If you are considering a July 4th wedding, you can even arrange to give your guests the added thrill of being on the river during the fireworks display. You bring in your own caterer or arrange catering with the company.

The Merchant's House Museum

29 East 4th Street • New York, NY 10003
212-777-1089
nyc1832@merchantshouse.com • www.merchantshouse.com
$: $2,500–$10,000 (plus additional charges for staff, tent, etc.)
Capacity: 200 people maximum

The Merchant's House museum, built in 1832, is a perfectly preserved home. It is the only house in New York City whose interior and exterior designs have remained intact since the 19th century and it boasts amazing Greek revival parlors, mahogany doors, marble mantelpieces, and a beautiful garden that can be left open or tented for weddings. Keep in mind that your ability to decorate may be limited because of the site's rules about protecting the antique furnishings and wall coverings. You'll need to bring in your own caterer and furniture, but the Merchant's House does have a modern kitchen (as well as the preserved 19th-century one). The Merchant's House Museum is a great spot if you're looking for an interesting location with history and atmosphere.

The Montauk Club

25 Eighth Avenue • Brooklyn, NY 11217
718-638-0800
www.montaukclub.com
$: Fees start at $95 per person for food (including cake) and location
Capacity: maximum 165

The over 110-year-old Montauk Club was originally built as a gentleman's club; six American presidents have dined there. Brooklyn royalty loves the spot, too: Rosie Perez was married at the club. The Park Slope building is an understated yet elegant location, with imported oak paneling, stained-glass windows, and high ceilings in the second-floor main room, where weddings take place. It's the perfect environment for a wedding with an intimate feel. Parking arrangements can be made at a garage one block away.

Morris-Jumel Mansion

65 Jumel Terrace • New York, NY 10032
212-923-8008
$: $250 per hour for location only, plus an additional
$250 tax-free membership fee
Capacity: seated dinner, 35;
cocktail reception, 100; tented summer event, 250

Set on a rocky cliff in a residential neighborhood of Washington Heights, this stately Palladian villa was once George Washington's headquarters and is currently a museum by day, when visitors travel to this hidden gem to see its period rooms full of priceless furnishings from the 1700s and 1800s. The fee includes only the space; everything else must be rented, including tables and chairs. There are no cooking facilities, so be sure you hire a caterer with his or her own kitchen.

New York Botanical Garden

200th Street and Southern Boulevard · Bronx, NY 10458
718-220-0300
www.abigailkirsch.com
$: Exclusive caterer is Abigail Kirsch (see the catering chapter for more information); fees start at $110 per person for food and location
Capacity: Garden Terrace room holds minimum 100, maximum 350;
Snuff Mill room holds minimum 70, maximum 110

If you love the architectural style of l'Orangerie in Paris, you will adore the Garden Terrace Room at the New York Botanical Garden. The brick building is adjacent to year-round landscaped gardens and private terraces and offers a wonderful sense of space—just the atmosphere that many New York City brides crave. Also consider the Snuff Mill room, an 18th-century stone-and-brick ivy-covered building. The hilltop Bronx location is only a 20-minute car ride from midtown and combines the elegance of fine hotel ballroom dining with a country feeling.

New York Chinese Scholar's Garden

at the Staten Island Botanical Garden
1000 Richmond Terrace · Staten Island, NY 10301
718-273-8200
www.sibg.org
$: Site-rental fee is $1,500; catered exclusively by Catering by Framboise
$95 to $120 per person for food (including cake)
Capacity: maximum 200

If you want to wed in a serene setting with a spiritual feel, look no farther than the Chinese Scholar's Garden on Staten Island. This is the first authentic Chinese garden of its kind built in the United States. It covers two acres, features 80 species of plants and trees native to China, and has three courtyards, a lotus pond, a teahouse, several footbridges, and five Ming dynasty-style pavilions. The tented area accommodates weddings from March through November. On-site parking is available.

New York City Fire Museum

278 Spring Street • New York, NY 10013
212-691-1303
www.nycfiremuseum.org/
$: $3,000 for 8 hours
Capacity: 150 people for sit-down dinner and dancing,
300 for cocktail reception.

The NYC Fire Museum is a beautiful and memorable place to have a wedding and reception. The building was completed in 1905 and was constructed in an Italian Renaissance Palazzo–style with beautiful arches and high ceilings. When you rent the space, you rent the entire museum, so your guests can wander around the amazing exhibits of antique fire engines and then settle down for dinner and dancing in the 3,000-square-foot third floor, which has exposed brick walls, hardwood floors and huge windows. You will need to bring your own caterer and furnishings but there is a catering kitchen. On weekends there is ample street parking in the neighborhood, and the museum is located right next to a parking lot. The New York City Fire Museum is a not-for-profit organization and all funds go to support the museum and its programs, so your wedding will also be helping out a wonderful institution.

New York Marriott Brooklyn

333 Adams Street • Brooklyn, NY 11201
718-246-7000
www.marriott.com
$: Fees start at $100 per person for food and location
Capacity: minimum 50, maximum 1,000 plus

Opened in July 1998, this New York Marriott is located in the heart of downtown Brooklyn, adjacent to Brooklyn Heights, one of the oldest and grandest neighborhoods in the borough. The large ballrooms can accommodate over 1,000 guests, while several smaller rooms are meant for parties of 50. They have a dedicated kosher kitchen and four open-air chuppahs. The New York Marriott can also work out special deals for honeymoons.

The Palm House

at the Brooklyn Botanic Garden
1000 Washington Avenue · Brooklyn, NY 11225
718-398-2400
www.palmhouse.com
**$: Rental fees depend on day of week, time of day, and season: Saturday
and Sunday is $4,000; Monday through Friday is $3,000; daytime is $2,500
Prices vary from November to February
Catering fees range from $100 to $140 per person, including cake
Capacity: varies depending on day of week and time**

You don't have to be a Brooklynite to love the Brooklyn Botanic Garden, a 52-acre paradise only three miles from Manhattan. The Palm House is a replica of the original Garden Conservatory Greenhouse designed by McKim, Mead and White, and it offers casual sophistication. If your dream is to have your ceremony in an outdoor garden, consider the Botanic Garden's magnificent Rose Garden, tranquil Japanese Garden, Cherry Esplanade, or Magnolia Plaza. In warm weather, your cocktail hour can take place around the Lily Pool. One wedding occurs at a time. On-site parking is available.

The Picnic House in Prospect Park

95 Prospect Park West · Brooklyn, NY 11215
718-965-7777
www.prospectpark.org
**$: Rental fee is $2,500 for eight hours
Capacity: minimum 80, maximum 175 for dinner**

This one-of-a-kind natural environment—cherished by couples who love the outdoors—is one of the prettiest wedding locations in Brooklyn. It has a country feel but is conveniently located only 10 minutes from lower Manhattan. The open interior of the brick-and-glass pavilion, which was built in 1927, has hardwood floors, a raised stage for music and the ceremony, a working wood fireplace, and views of Long Meadow. This is a particularly popular venue and weddings are held every weekend, so plan to book at least a year in advance for high wedding season. You select a caterer from one of the 20 recommended by the Picnic House. Limited parking is available.

Pier 60 and The Lighthouse at Chelsea Piers

23rd Street and the Hudson River · New York, NY 10011
212-336-6060 · Fax: 212-336-6417
www.chelseapiers.com
**$: Fees depend on time of year, time of day, and day of week;
a Saturday afternoon wedding in January starts at $110 per person**

Capacity (Lighthouse): minimum 100, maximum 300
Capacity (Pier 60): minimum 150, maximum 1,000

Pier 60 is a favorite of high-profile entertainers and celebrities. This historic pier was where ocean liners, including the White Star Line, entered the United States in the early 1900s. The breathtaking room overlooks the Hudson River and combines the openness of a water location with the amenities of a hotel. The floor-to-ceiling glass windows face the Statue of Liberty and allow for a sweeping view of river traffic. Celebrity caterer Abigail Kirsch, the exclusive caterer at Pier 60, offers a variety of cuisines, including contemporary American, Asian, and kosher. Shuttle buses can be arranged to take guests to pier.

The Pierre

2 East 61st Street · New York, NY 10021
212-838-8000
www.fourseasons.com
$: Fees start at $300 per person for food and location
Capacity: minimum 50, maximum 800

Brides with unlimited resources and scrupulous taste often choose the Pierre as the perfect location for a storybook wedding. If you book here, you'll receive unparalleled service, a stunning environment, and exquisite food. The luxury hotel opened in 1930 with the aim of recreating the atmosphere of a private club or residence, and wedding guests still feel they are entering an exclusive club as they walk in through a private door. The magnificent Grand Ballroom is now decorated in soft hues and features a stunning ceiling with a trompe l'oeil sky, a custom-designed English carpet in tones of aqua, moss green, burgundy, and gold, and custom-made crystal chandeliers. Kosher catering is an option.

The Pioneer **and** *The Peking*

Pier 16 at South Street Seaport · New York, NY 10038
212-748-8786
www.southstseaport.org
$: Fees start at $1,050 for *The Pioneer*,
$5,000 for *The Peking*, for two-hour set-up and three-hour party
Capacity: maximum 40 for *The Pioneer*,
200 for *The Peking*

If you love a cool harbor breeze and want a casual wedding for a small group of guests, consider *The Pioneer.* This restored two-mast, iron-hull schooner is available for private charter. You can take your guests on a two-hour sunset cruise past the Statue of Liberty and other landmark sites. Bring your own caterer and a sense of adventure—there is no shelter on the ship (although there is a restroom). *The Peking* is permanently moored at Pier 16; it can accommodate up to 200 guests for a formal seated dinner and offers spectacular views of the lower Manhattan skyline, the Brooklyn Bridge, and New York Harbor. During the evening, the ship's 17-story-high masts are illuminated by spotlights, creating a very dramatic environment. The ships are available April through October.

The Plaza

Fifth Avenue and Central Park South • New York, NY 10019
212-759-3000
www.fairmont.com • newyork@fairmont.com
$: Fees for the Grand Ballroom start at $300 per person
($250 during off-season)
Other rooms start at $250 per person ($230 during off-season)
Capacity: minimum 10, maximum 450

The Plaza is the crème de la crème of New York hotels. Set against the background of Central Park, the hotel has been the site of some of the most glamorous and historic social events of the century. Donald Trump and Marla Maples had a Plaza wedding and Joan Rivers walked her daughter, Melissa, down the aisle here to the tune of "Hey Big Spender." At the Plaza, the average wedding costs upwards of $75,000, but you need not spend this much. If you are set on a Plaza wedding but want to save some money, you can save at least $50 per person if you book your wedding during the off-season. With 14 different rooms, the Plaza is always bustling, but it can also accommodate weddings with as few as ten guests.

The Puck Building

295 Lafayette Street • New York, NY 10012
212-427-2818
www.puckbldg.com/
$: Prices start at $6,000 for the rooms (but are subject to change) and catering starts at approximately $120 per person
Capacity: Skylight Ballroom 250, Grand Ballroom, 750

The Puck Building is a gorgeous landmark built in the late 19th century, and it offers two wonderful rooms for wedding ceremonies and receptions. The Skylight Ballroom is the smaller of the two rooms and it is splendid, with wonderful views and fabulous skylights. The Grand Ballroom is huge and can easily handle a big crowd. The building has a few caterers it regularly works with, but you can negotiate to bring your own. If you want a place that is elegant and sophisticated but still full of character, look no further.

St. Regis Hotel

2 East 55th Street • New York, NY 10022
212-753-4500
www.starwoodhotel.com
$: Fees start at $300 per person for food and location
Capacity: minimum 120, maximum 225

The St. Regis is the perfect location for the bride who wants a classic and luxurious hotel wedding with a dash of tasteful opulence. The hotel is located in a 1904 beaux-arts building and is known for its Roof Ballroom on the 23rd floor as well as the Versailles and Louis XIV Suites. You'll find lavish details, such as high ceilings, mahogany walls, and Oriental rugs. This was John Jacob Astor's home in the early 1900s, and today it's a favorite of celebrities and world leaders. Unlike other large, top-tier hotels, only one wedding is held at a time here.

Sky Studios

704 Broadway • New York, NY 10003
212-533-3030
www.skystudios.com • info@skystudios.com
$: 10,000 per penthouse (2 penthouses total)
Capacity: 150

Sky Studios is a truly remarkable location. It is an enormous private home with two penthouses and gorgeous rooms that you can use to create amazing environments. You can have a garden ceremony on the roof garden, then have an indoor sit-down dinner, and while you're eating, the roof can be transformed into a swank lounge setting for cake-cutting, dessert, and dancing. If you time it right, you can be dancing on a beautiful rooftop as the sun sets. The space is gorgeous and is often a location in movies and TV shows (the rooftop pool was featured in an episode of "Sex and the City"), and has hosted celebrity weddings. Jerry Seinfeld married Jessica Sklar in front of a fireplace. If you're looking for an amazing, romantic location that can change moods over the course of your wedding day, consider Sky Studios.

The Stanhope Hotel

995 Fifth Avenue · New York, NY 10028
212-774-1234
www.theparkhyatt.com
$: Fees range from $130 to $185 per person for food and location
Capacity: minimum 10, maximum for dinner and dancing 85

The Stanhope is often the choice of sophisticated couples who appreciate its understated elegance; its quiet, exclusive location across from the Metropolitan Museum of Art; and its exquisite catering. The hotel specializes in small receptions for 60 to 80 guests. In-house Curt Sassak lends his contemporary American touch to the hotel's restaurant-quality party menu. You may bring in your own kosher caterer.

The Supper Club

240 West 47th Street · New York, NY 10036
212-921-1940
www.thesupperclub.com
$: Fees start at $150 per person for food and location
Capacity: maximum 350

Couples who love swing music should take a look at this traditional New York club. Your guests will feel that they've traveled back in time to a 1930s big-band club. Wedding ceremonies and receptions can take place seven nights a week. The restaurant serves Continental-American dishes at private events.

Tavern on the Green

67th Street and Central Park West · New York, NY 10023
212-873-2466
www.tavernonthegreen.com
$: Fees start at $150 per person for food and location
Capacity: minimum 30, maximum 1,200

Tavern on the Green is embraced by New Yorkers as an over-the-top fantasy setting for major celebrations. Built to house sheep in 1870, the building became a restaurant in 1934. Couples who consider themselves true New Yorkers, even if they originally hail from Iowa, love the Tavern. The glass-enclosed Crystal and Terrace rooms feature rococo touches like stained glass, etched mirrors, interior trees, paintings, antique prints, and crystal chandeliers. The outdoor garden space is very romantic, with thousands of tiny lights and lanterns strung on the trees. Unless you book the entire restaurant, which accommodates 1,200 guests, you will share the facility with other diners, who will be in different rooms.

Top of the Times

255 West 43rd Street · New York, NY 10036
212-768-8989
www.commonground.org
$: Site rental fee from $200/hour
Capacity: maximum 150

If you're looking for a truly unusual rooftop site and are not afraid of doing something outside the box, Top of the Times may be for you. The building is the largest supportive housing program in the country, providing single-room residences for low-income folks; the rooftop rental fee goes to job-training programs for residents. Be assured that this is a fabulous and secure outdoor space in the middle of the city. A dedicated elevator with a security guard brings guests directly to the 15th floor, where there are several indoor rooms and a number of terraced gardens. Top of the Times has an exclusive contract with Ark Restaurants, which can handle all styles (vegetarian, kosher, etc.).

Tribeca Rooftop

2 Desbrosses Street · New York, NY 10013
212-625-2600 · Fax: 212-625-2606
www.tribec.com · Billy.Reilly@tribec.com
$: Prices start at $180 per person
Capacity: Minimum 125, maximum 400

If you're looking for a big beautiful space with fabulous views, be sure to check out the Tribeca Rooftop. The space is a 15,000-square-foot penthouse that offers incredible panoramic views of Manhattan, from lower Tribeca up to the Empire State Building and across the Hudson River. It has a cherry-wood dance floor, a 65-foot-high skylight and mezzanine balcony from which you can catch fabulous sunsets, dreamy night skies, and bright days. If you're having a big wedding, think about bringing your crowd downtown. There is a lot of parking in the neighborhood and there are plenty of hotels within walking distance.

200 Fifth Club

200 Fifth Avenue · New York, NY 10010
212-675-2080
www.200fifth.com
$: Fees range from $130 to $180 per person for food
(including cake) and location
Capacity: minimum 130, maximum 350

By evening, this turn-of-the-century marble lobby, with its beautifully carved ceiling, is the passageway to the 200 Fifth Club, where over 80 weddings are held each year. There is an atmosphere of old-world elegance in the baroque-style ballroom, which has mirrored columns, antique chandeliers, and a touch of gold in the woodwork. The room lends itself to formal receptions—80 percent of all Saturday-night weddings held here are black-tie events. There is a even a dressing room for the bride. The location hosts only one event at a time.

United Nations Delegates' Dining Room

First Avenue and 46th Street • New York, NY 10017
212-963-7098
www.restaurantassociates.com
$: Fees range from $175 to $225 for food and location;
security and building fees additional
Capacity: minimum 150, maximum 450

The United Nations Delegates' Dining Room of the United Nations offers a sweeping view of the East River through its floor-to-ceiling windows. The space is designed in the same 1960s modernist style as the rest of the U.N. The international menu is very good and features entrees from around the world, including New Zealand leg of lamb, blinis and caviar, and sushi. Since the United Nations is considered international territory, wedding ceremonies are not permitted on site; you may, however, marry at the U.N. Chapel across the street.

The Waldorf-Astoria

301 Park Avenue • New York, NY 10022
212-355-3000
$: Fees range from $300 to $350 per person for food and location
Capacity: minimum 40, maximum 1,000

As one of the world's most famous landmark hotels, the Waldorf-Astoria has played host to presidents, royalty, industry leaders, and movie stars. Its fame has even attracted wealthy European couples, who charter entire 747s to fly in their wedding guests for the weekend. The two-tiered Grand Ballroom seats 1,000, but there are 24 less-enormous ballrooms to consider. For example, the Conrad Suite, once temporary home to Grace Kelly, comes complete with a marble fireplace. If you are planning a reception for 500, the Starlight Room, the Waldorf's former supper club, has been recently restored to its original romantic splendor. The room features French doors opening onto a terrace, lush plants, a retractable roof (to let the stars shine in), and estate furniture. Kosher catering is available.

The Water Club

500 East 30th Street • New York, NY 10016
212-545-1155
www.thewaterclub.com • waterclub@aol.com
$: Fees range up to $200 for food and location
Capacity: minimum 20, maximum 200

For couples who are looking for a fine dining experience with a heavenly view from every seat, the Water Club is a superb choice. There are several outdoor spaces for ceremonies and dining, including a deck overlooking the East River. The menu features grilled meats and fish from local markets, or you may bring your own kosher caterer. The club also offers valet parking. You should book three to four months in advance.

Wave Hill

675 West 252nd Street • Riverdale, NY 10471
718-549-3200
www.wavehill.org
$: Site rental fee ranges from $3,500 to $6,000 (all but $1,000 is tax deductible); the exclusive caterer is Great Performances (see the catering chapter for more information) and starts at $200 per person
Capacity: minimum 100, maximum 200

The gardens at Wave Hill are beyond exquisite. This unspoiled, 28-acre estate will be a welcome surprise to guests who have never visited the magnificent public garden, cultural institution, and Victorian mansion. Originally built in 1843 as a country home overlooking the Palisades and the Hudson River, Wave Hill's guests have included natural scientists Thomas Huxley and Charles Darwin. The site was also a favorite of Theodore Roosevelt's family, who rented it during the summers of 1870 and 1871. If you love nature, you will adore this year-round oasis of serenity a short drive from midtown Manhattan. All private events take place after 6:15 P.M., when Wave Hill closes to the public. On-site parking is available.

World Yacht

Pier 81, West 41st Street and the Hudson River · New York, NY 10036
212-630-8800
www.worldyacht.com
$: Four-and-a-half-hour-cruise charter fees, which cover captain, crew,
and fuel, range from $500 to $6,500 depending on the day
and season; food starts at $125 per person
Capacity: minimum starts at 50, maximum 500, call for details

When Billy Joel and Christie Brinkley married in 1985 on *Riveranda*, one of five vessels in World Yacht's fleet, the company became an overnight sensation. Their yachts vary in size, with *Cabaret*, the smallest, holding 150 guests, and *Dutchess*, the largest, accommodating 500. *Riveranda*'s three decks recently underwent a million-dollar renovation, and the yacht was rechristened *Inamorata*. No matter which boat you rent, you and your guests should bring a spirit of adventure and expect some rocking, especially at the pier.

LONG ISLAND

Coindre Hall

101 Browns Road · Huntington, NY 11743
631-277-7800
www.lessing.com · ben@lessing.com
$: Site rental fee ranges from $1,500 to $2,750; the preferred
caterer is Lessing Caterers, $70 to $250 per person
Capacity: maximum 250

A favorite of young professionals, Coindre Hall is one of the oldest Gold Coast mansions in Suffolk County, overlooking a lovely view of Huntington Bay. The 1912 French-style mansion features a dramatic gabled dormer flanked by a copper dolphin, and its medieval facade encloses a charming sun porch. Coindre Hall was a private home until recently, when the county bought it as a recreation venue. Lessing Caterers is the hall's preferred caterer, but you can make arrangements to use a different caterer if you wish.

The Harbor Club at Tee T's Landing

95 New York Avenue • Huntington, NY 11743
631-271-5600
$: Fees start at $65 per person for food (including cake) and location
Capacity: minimum 100, maximum 240

The Harbor Club offers an outstanding North Shore harborside location at a very reasonable price. The club has European decor, with yards of highly polished marble, and lovely outdoor areas, including a waterfront garden, patios, decks, and a veranda. You can have an outdoor ceremony on the upper deck, with the water sparkling behind you. Continental cuisine is the club's specialty, but Italian, German, French, Portuguese, Asian, and kosher cuisines are also available.

Harrison House

Dosoris Lane • Glen Cove, NY 11542
516-674-2955
www.harrisonhouseglencove.com
$: Fees range from $120 to $190 per person for food and location
Capacity: minimum 125, maximum 250

A summer home of the Pratt family in the early 1900s, this Gold Coast Georgian mansion offers a posh setting for a fantasy wedding. During the week, Harrison House is a center for corporate retreats; on weekends, the mansion is host to the unions of many influential Long Island families. The in-house catering staff offers a five-course meal of new-American cuisine. In temperate weather, outdoor wedding ceremonies take place beneath a majestic copper beech tree, surrounded by 55 acres of landscaped gardens. A bridal suite is available, and if your guests need overnight accommodations, there are approximately 200 rooms. The hotel extends a wedding discount.

Nassau County Museum of Art

One Museum Drive • Roslyn Harbor, NY 11576
516-484-9338
www.nassaumuseum.com
$: Site rental is $5,300 for museum and tent, $3,300 for museum
only ($1,300 of the fee is deductible)
To simply have guests in the garden for the ceremony, fee is $750
Catering fees vary depending on which of the site's three caterers you use
Capacity: maximum 175

Set on 140 acres of lawn and formal gardens with a magnificent outdoor sculpture collection, Nassau County Museum of Art is a refined location for couples who love art. This museum is an undiscovered treasure for sophisticated, cultivated parties.

The 20th-century galleries remain open during wedding receptions, which may be held outdoors under a climate-adjusted tent from March to November. For small receptions of 50 people or less, be sure to look at the wood-paneled library, complete with a cozy fireplace. You may be able to reserve space as little as two to three months in advance.

Oheka Castle

135 West Gate Drive · Cold Spring Hills, NY 11743
631-692-2707
www.oheka-castle.com
$: Site rental fees range from $4,000 to $10,000; catering ranges from $180 to $400 per person, including cake
Capacity: minimum 125, maximum 700 for a tented wedding

Oheka Castle is over the top. This home was built in the early 1900s as a summer residence for banking tycoon Otto Hermann Kahn (Oheka is an acronym of Kahn's name) and was the site of lavish parties during the Roaring Twenties. You'll find formal gardens, reflecting pools, fountains, turrets, horseshoe staircases, fireplaces, a wood-paneled library, and a cobblestone courtyard, not to mention a red carpet for your guests. The Grand Ballroom features tapestry wall coverings, polished wood floors, and two huge crystal chandeliers. Newlyweds are invited to spend their first night in the mansion's enormous bridal suite, which has three bathrooms. Catering encompasses a variety of cuisines and they can have kosher food brought in from an outside caterer.

The Swan Club

Shore Road · Glenwood, NY 11547
516-621-7600
www.swanclub.com · info@swanclub.com
$: Fees start at $65 per person for food and location
Capacity: minimum 40, maximum 230

The Swan Club, known for its lush, landscaped gardens and picturesque waterside environment, provides a photographer's paradise on the North Shore's Gold Coast. There are beautiful outdoor picture spots, including a bride's walk, wishing-well bridge, gazebo, waterfall, and dancing-water fountain. The ballroom, where receptions take place, is a traditional room with wood floors and a fireplace. The swan motif is used throughout, even in the floral landscape, and is etched onto the glass doors. More than one event may be held at a time.

Vanderbilt Mansion at Dowling College

Idle Hour Boulevard · Oakdale, NY 11769
631-244-3131
www.vanderbiltmansion.com
$: Fees start at $95 per person, including cake
Lovin Oven is the exclusive caterer
Capacity: minimum 100, maximum 200 for cocktails

The reception space at this small liberal-arts college is a well-kept secret. The early-1900s Vanderbilt Mansion sits on the Connetquot River and offers a traditional, elegant setting; it's no wonder the site is a favorite with Long Island politicians. This large and spacious venue offers many different areas for your guests to enjoy, including the Grand Ballroom, which has stunning French doors leading out to a riverside veranda, a large foyer with stained glass and a spiral staircase, and a courtyard with a fountain and a garden. Bookings are accepted no more than one year in advance.

WESTCHESTER

The Castle at Tarrytown

400 Benedict Avenue · Tarrytown, NY 10591
914-524-6366
Toll free: 800-616-4487
www.castleattarrytown.com
$: Fees start at $160 per person for food (including cake) and location
Capacity: minimum 85, maximum 150

The Castle at Tarrytown is a true castle, with 31 sleeping rooms, located in nearby suburban New York and overlooking the Hudson River and the Manhattan skyline. A stone wall encloses the castle grounds, which feature rare and beautiful varieties of trees and flowers. Other castle touches are Tiffany-style stained-glass windows and a musicians' balcony. While castles aren't known for being cozy, this one definitely is. Even the service is relaxed and friendly. You can expect excellent French cuisine served on Eschenbach china, either in the Caramai Ballroom or the Great Hall. This location is very popular, and weddings are hosted seven days a week, one event at a time. Rooms are available for overnight guests.

The Culinary Institute of America

1946 Campus Drive • Hyde Park, NY 12538
845-451-1223
www.ciachef.edu
$: Call for rates
Capacity: minimum 50, maximum 275

If you want your reception to feature first-rate gourmet fare in a country setting, at a price that won't break the bank, take a trip to the Culinary Institute of America. CIA is a hidden gem. Two spaces are available: St. Andrew's Cafe, an airy room with French doors, a wall of windows, and a small terrace; and the Alumni Hall, formerly the school's chapel, which has stained-glass windows and a vaulted ceiling. Your menu will be custom designed after a consultation. You can reserve on short notice, but keep in mind that the school is closed for the month of July and on holiday weekends.

Dolce Tarrytown House

East Sunnyside Lane • Tarrytown, NY 10591
914-591-3105
www.dolce.com
$: Rates vary depending on time of day, time of year, and number of guests
Capacity: Varies depending on time of year, call for information

This Great Gatsby-like mansion, located in Washington Irving country, is a popular site for Westchester weddings. Originally home to several millionaires—including railroad magnate Thomas King, tobacco entrepreneur William Harris, and Duke University founder Benjamin Duke's daughter, Mary Duke Biddle—the mansion is now used as a conference center during the week. Picturesque surroundings include 26 acres of grass and woods with Hudson River views. There are several different ballrooms to choose from, depending on the size of your reception. Be sure to see the Winter Palace room, with its floor-to-ceiling windows overlooking the river. It may be possible to book a date only six months in advance. All catering is done in house, although kosher caterers may be brought in. More than one wedding may be held at a time.

Estherwood

49 Clinton Avenue • Dobbs Ferry, NY 10522
914-693-3322
www.estherwood.com
$: Site rental fees range from $500 on weekdays to $1,400
plus $10 per person on weekends; catering ranges from
$100 to $160 per person
Weekday capacity: minimum 75, maximum 200
Weekend capacity: minimum 120, maximum 200

Estherwood is a neo-Renaissance mansion, built in 1894 for millionaire inventor James Jennings McComb and his new wife, Esther Wood. It stands on the campus of the Masters School, a coed boarding school. You can have your ceremony in one room (or outside in warm weather), then have your guests adjourn to the dining room, dance in yet another room, sit by the fireplace in the library, and stroll through the manicured gardens. The stone mansion is stunning and contains myriad charming details, including a wide wraparound veranda with vaulted tile ceilings and mosaic floors; an octagonal library paneled in mahogany with stained-glass windows; a dramatic, two-story entrance hall with a marble staircase; and an oak paneled dining room with decorative motifs. Catering arrangements are made through the mansion exclusively.

Hudson Valley Resort and Spa

400 Granite Road • Kerhonkson, NY 12446
845-626-8888 • Toll free: 888-684-7264
www.hudsonvalleyresort.com • info@hudson
$: Call for prices and packages for food and location
Capacity: maximum 600

The Hudson Valley Resort was originally called the Granite Hotel and was a popular "Borscht Belt" hotel in the 1960s. Now, after a $25 million renovation, the state-of-the-art hotel attracts several weddings per month. The ballroom is quite nice, and the menu features excellent Hudson Valley regional cuisine. The hotel also offers many opportunities for recreation—a European-style health spa, an 18-hole golf course, indoor and outdoor pools, tennis, horseback riding, hiking, full-court basketball, and boating—making it perfect for a weekend wedding. Special room rates are offered for out-of-town guests; call to discuss wedding packages.

The Lodge at Catskill Corners

5368 Route 28 • Mt. Tremper, NY 12457
845-688-2828 • Toll free: 877-688-2828
www.catskillcorners.com • thelodge@usa.net
$: Rates vary according to season
Capacity: minimum 60, maximum 120

The three-year-old Lodge is a luxurious, 52-room, country-style inn. If you love nature and are looking for a chic wilderness wedding, this is the location to consider. The surrounding country is largely untrammeled, with a large French community, low weekend traffic, many fine French-country restaurants, and myriad activities, such as river tubing, hiking, and antiquing. If you want to get married outdoors, the hotel has a pavilion overlooking the crystal-clear Esopus Creek. Call for information about wedding packages.

Onteora, the Mountain House

96 Piney Point Road · Boiceville, NY 12412
845-657-6233
www.onteora.com · info@onteora.com
$: Fees start at $100 per person for food, location, and some flowers
Capacity: minimum 50, maximum 175 (for tented weddings)

Onteora offers a breathtaking, panoramic view of the Catskills's Esopus River Valley. This elegant, hillside bed and breakfast was built in 1928 and is filled with an eclectic collection of Asian and American antiques. The inn has a great room with a cathedral ceiling and massive stone fireplace, a 40-foot covered dining porch with tree-trunk columns and railings, and five guest rooms. Weddings from May to October are held outdoors under a tent; during the winter, celebrations can take place in the great room. Catering is by Catskill Rose Restaurant, a local four-star eatery, featuring cuisine that is a mixture of classic French and Californian, or New World Home Cooking. As part of your wedding package, it is required that you take the bed-and-breakfast's five guest rooms for two nights.

Tappan Hill

81 Highland Avenue · Tarrytown, NY 10591
914-631-3030 · Fax: 914-631-5399
www.abigailkirsch.com
$: Fees start at $110 per person for food and location;
see the catering chapter for information on exclusive caterer Abigail Kirsch
Capacity: minimum 80, maximum 260

If your dream is a country-estate wedding close to the hustle and bustle of the city, Tappan Hill (just 45 minutes away) may fit you to a T. Situated on a spectacular hilltop, Tappan Hill was once the home of Mark Twain. The landmark location offers spectacular Hudson River views, a marble entrance rotunda, handsome rooms, terraces, and delicious food. In addition to catering parties for celebrities, exclusive caterer Abigail Kirsch has catered for Presidents Clinton, Reagan, and Ford, the queen of Thailand, and the president of Turkey. The environment is warm, elegant, and traditional, and outdoor ceremonies are possible in stone or grass courtyards. Two events may occur at the same time, but there are separate facilities.

New Jersey

Crossed Keys Inn

289 Pequest Road • Andover, NJ 07821
973-786-6661 • Wedding line: 973-829-9922
info@crossedkeys.com • www.crossedkeys.com
$: Call for information
Capacity: Call for information

This charming, 200-year-old inn and country estate is filled with beautiful antiques. It's classically romantic, with a great history, too. Celebrities like Groucho Marx and Mae West stayed and performed here during summer-stock tours. Guests have access to the entire 12-acre estate—complete with a babbling brook—and can stay in a restored 18th-century house. Your ceremony can take place in a beautiful garden setting, followed by dinner and dancing in a magnificent grove of 110-year-old oak and weeping beech trees. Catering is provided by nearby Celsos Catering. Only one wedding at a time is held on the site.

The Crystal Plaza

305 West Northfield Road • Livingston, NJ 07039
973-992-8100
www.crystalplaza.com • info@crystalplaza.com
$: Fees range from $100 to $350 per person for food and location
Capacity: minimum 100, maximum 400

If you're dreaming of sparkling chandeliers, mirrors galore, and a grand ballroom atmosphere, consider the Crystal Plaza. Inspired by Newport mansions, Stanford White built the European-style estate as one of his personal residences at the turn of the century. Just about any cuisine, including Indian, French, and Italian, can be created by the venue's 21 chefs.

Highlawn Pavilion

Eagle Rock Reservation • West Orange, NJ 07052
973-731-3463
www.highlawn.com
$: Fees range from $80 to $129 per person for food (including cake)
and location
Capacity: minimum 100, maximum 170

It's difficult to find a better skyline view of New York from New Jersey than the one from Highlawn Pavilion. The 1909 Florentine-style building is set high on a cliff in the 400-acre Eagle Rock Reservation. Egyptian-born chef Sam Mikhail oversees the award-winning European-American menu. The wine cellar can be used for a private cocktail reception for the bridal party. The reservation is gorgeous any time of year, but especially during the fall; if you are thinking of marrying in September or October, book more than a year in advance.

Lake Mohawk Country Club

21 The Boardwalk • Sparta, NJ 07871
973-729-6156
www.lakemohawk.com
$: Fees range from $65 to $75 per person for food
(including cake) and location
Capacity: minimum 125, maximum 250

Lake Mohawk Country Club sits on one of the most beautiful man-made lakes in New Jersey. This 1929 landmark building overlooks an 800-acre lake, which is surrounded by luxurious homes. The half-mile-long boardwalk is excellent for photo ops. During warm weather, the ballroom's French doors open to a lakeside tented area where wedding vows can be exchanged. Catering options include wedding standards like filet mignon, prime rib, veal Marsala, and chicken Francaise.

The Manor

111 Prospect Avenue • West Orange, NJ 07052
973-731-2360
www.themanorrestaurant.com
$: Fees start at $75 per person for food (including cake) and location
Capacity: minimum 40, maximum 200

Although the Manor is a bit less opulent than some of the other halls listed here, it is a good value for the money and well suited to the budget of many young couples. It sits on a stunning 20-acre estate and has formal gardens, fountains, a grand lobby fireplace, a glass atrium, and four reception rooms. If you'd like to have your ceremony

outside in the garden, a minimum of 120 guests is required. Be aware that more than one wedding or party may take place at once.

New Jersey Performing Arts Center

One Center Street • Newark, NJ 07102
973-242-6000
www.njpac.org
$: Site rental fees range from $1,000 to $11,500; Restaurant Marketing
Associates is the exclusive caterer; fees start at $106 per person
Capacity: minimum 50, maximum 400

The New Jersey Performing Arts Center offers magnificent, unusual reception spaces. The Donor's Lounge, with room for 70 guests, is decorated in the style of a traditional, cozy living room, complete with a fireplace and an outdoor deck, while the stage at Prudential Hall is a unique place to gather 400 of your closest relatives and friends (the fee for the stage, which includes tables and chairs, is $11,000). Of course, the availability of the spaces is contingent upon the performance schedule.

The Newark Club

The Metropolitan Room
One Newark Center, 22nd Floor • Newark, NJ 07012
973-242-0658
www.newarkclub.com
$: Fees start at $90 per person for food and location
Capacity: minimum 100, maximum 310

This is a glamorous, sophisticated venue. Located on the 22nd floor of One Newark Center, the Metropolitan Room offers a breathtaking, panoramic view of New York City. The elegant environment, with its cherry-wood armchairs and mauve-colored carpet, is an executive dining club that, during the week, serves lunch to politicians, corporate leaders, and deans from the nearby New Jersey Medical and Dental College. On weekends, those in the know host receptions at the club. The inlaid dance floor is one of the most beautiful we have seen, and the first-floor lobby can be used for the wedding ceremony. Valet parking in an indoor garage is available.

Pleasantdale Chateau and Conference Resort

757 Eagle Rock Avenue · West Orange, NJ 07052
973-731-5600
www.pleasantdale.com
$: Fees range from $199 to $229 per person for food and location
Capacity: minimum 125, maximum 350

Set on the grounds of a 40-acre estate, this French Normandy chateau is distinctive enough to impress the most seasoned wedding guest. Pleasantdale Chateau can supply all the elements of a beautiful, traditional wedding. The mansion has antique-appointed rooms, 15th-century Spanish floor tiles, formal gardens, rolling lawns, shaded ponds, an indoor Roman-style pool (great for photos), an octagonal ballroom with a 45-foot-high skylight dome, and even a private heliport. White-glove service and well-prepared food match the superlative environment; special dishes include thyme-marinated filet mignon and sesame seed-crusted Chilean sea bass. Luxurious overnight accommodations are available for the bride and groom.

Stony Hill Inn

231 Polifly Road · Hackensack, NJ 07601
201-342-4085
www.stonyhillinn.com
$: Call for prices
Capacity: minimum 50, maximum 300

Stony Hill Inn, a Dutch Colonial mansion dating from 1818, is a favorite of New Jersey's political elite. On weekends, the restaurant is a lovely place to host an elegant wedding. There are several rooms available for receptions, including the Aviary Room, a beautifully appointed formal dining room. The inn specializes in Italian-continental cuisine and does not have any overnight guestrooms.

CONNECTICUT

Manhattan Yacht Charters

P.O. Box 308 · Fairfield, CT 06430
203-256-8730 or 212-995-5470
www.manhattanyachtcharters.com · mary@manhattanyachtcharters.com
$: Fees start at $100 per person
Capacity: Boats can accommodate any size party up to 600 guests

Manhattan Yacht Charters has been arranging yacht parties for over a decade. The company represents three dozen different boats, all with a different decor and style, which can accommodate groups up to 600 people. All catering is in-house.

Stonehenge Inn and Restaurant

35 Stonehenge Road · Ridgefield, CT 06877
203-438-6511
www.stonehengeinn/ct.com
$: Fees range from $79 to $95 per person for food and location
Capacity: minimum 60, maximum 130

Stonehenge is a charming French inn, like the kind you'd expect to find in Provence. With a tranquil, lakeside country setting, its highly regarded, four-star restaurant serves authentic French cuisine and hosts elegant parties. Specialties include salmon in pastry, braised leg of veal, and tenderloin Wellington. Newlyweds are offered a complimentary room at the inn for their wedding night.

Waveny House

677 South Avenue · New Canaan, CT 06840
203-966-0502
$: $2,650 for seven hours, for location only
Capacity: maximum 160

Set on the gorgeous grounds of a 300-acre estate in the Connecticut countryside, Waveny House is a traditional English stone mansion, built in 1912. The gardens and grounds were laid out by well-known landscape architect Frederick Law Olmstead. Nowadays, the mansion is a community recreation area for the residents of this posh Connecticut community; it is also rented by many in-the-know, cost-conscious brides. You can bring in your own caterer, florist, and party planner, but the site will only communicate with one primary contact—usually the couple. Non-residents must take part in a lottery and book a year in advance. Call for details.

Notes

Notes

Ceremony Officiants

If you regularly attend a church or temple, or are a member of a mosque or another kind of congregation, you may already have a relationship with a member of the clergy who will be able to perform your wedding ceremony. And if you've already chosen a religious setting, you will probably be required to use the clergy at that location. (In some cases you can bring in another officiant, but this isn't standard.) However, if you are having an interfaith wedding or are not especially religious, finding an officiant may be a bit more challenging. If you want to be married by a judge, you can get lists of judges available for weddings from the clerk's office of your local city or village hall. If you'd like to be married in a spiritual ceremony by a nondenominational officiant or by co-officiants from different religions, consult the listings in this chapter. Fees for a clergymember's time generally start in the low hundreds. Please contact the individual officiants listed here for their rates. (Since many officiants work from their homes, I've chosen not to include their addresses.)

JUDGES/JUSTICES OF THE PEACE

Information about ceremonies to be held at a clerk's office within New York City's five boroughs is included here. If you are in Long Island, New Jersey, or Connecticut, contact your local city or village hall for information. Both people must appear in person to get the license and bring proof of I.D. (passport, driver's license). For more information, you can look on the website: www.nyc.gov.

MANHATTAN
Municipal Building
1 Centre Street, 2nd Floor
New York, NY 10007
212-669-2400

BROOKLYN
Municipal Building
210 Joralemon Street, Room 205
Brooklyn, NY 11201
718-802-3585

QUEENS
Borough Hall
120-55 Queens Boulevard
Kew Gardens, NY 11424
718-286-2829

BRONX
Supreme Court Building
851 Grand Concourse at 161st Street
Ground Floor
Bronx, NY 10457
718-590-5307

STATEN ISLAND
Office of the City Clerk of New York
Borough Hall
10 Richmond Terrace, Room 311
Staten Island, NY 10301
718-816-2290

$: $25 for the ceremony (you must bring a money order payable to "City Clerk of New York") and $30 for the license, which must be obtained at least 24 hours (but not more than 60 days) before the ceremony.

If you have parents and stepparents and don't know who's going to walk you down the aisle, you may choose to have a City Hall wedding. Or maybe you're even eloping! If so, getting married in New York City is a snap. Only Staten Island requires an appointment; in the other boroughs, you can just show up. You should have at least one witness, although you can bring as many as will fit into the judge's chambers.

St. Paul's Chapel

Columbia University
Corner of 117th Street and Amsterdam Avenue • New York, NY 10027
212-854-1487
www.columbia.edu/cu/earl/stpauls
$: Ranges from $600 to $900

This 1904 nondenominational chapel on the Columbia University campus is perfect for interfaith or nonreligious couples. Its Northern Italian Renaissance architecture features a columned portico entrance with a Guastivino tile ceiling. The chapel is laid out on a Latin cross plan.

OFFICIANTS FOR INTERFAITH CEREMONIES

NEW YORK CITY

Brooklyn Ethical Culture Society

53 Prospect Park West • Brooklyn, NY 11215
718-768-2972
www.bsec.org

The Brooklyn Ethical Culture Society can provide you with the names of rabbis, ministers, and judges that perform an interfaith or other type of ceremony. Ask to speak with Lisel Burns.

Dovetail Institute for Interfaith Family Resources

800-530-1596
www.dovetailinstitute.org • di-fr@bardstown.com

Ask for Joan Hawxhurst to receive information about clergy for interfaith weddings.

New York Society for Ethical Culture

212-874-5210
office@nysec.org • www.nsyec.org

Because the ceremonies performed at New York Society for Ethical Culture are based on nonsectarian philosophy, it may be particularly appropriate for those without a traditional religious affiliation or for couples of different faiths. There is an application process; call for details.

Rabbi Marcia Rappaport

212-741-7378

Blessed with a cantorial voice, Rabbi Rappaport offers warm, sacred, funny, and personal ceremonies. She does Jewish, interfaith, nondenominational, and civil ceremonies and is willing to co-officiate; she says that she particularly enjoys working with another officiant. She's also willing to travel—once she went as far as Mexico—and believes that since anywhere people gather together for ritual is holy ground, all locations are appropriate for wedding ceremonies.

LONG ISLAND

Reverend Susan Marlan

516-487-2447
www.interfaithceremonies.com

Rev. Marlan specializes in weddings of all faiths in any combination, as well as same-faith couples who choose not to be married in a traditional setting. She also marries couples who have no defined faith. Her attitude is wonderfully positive, and she truly believes she's blessed to have the job of joining couples in marriage. She's officiated at unusual weddings, including one during which the groom, a fan of Groucho Marx, carried a rubber chicken in his pocket, and many in which dogs were included as beloved family members. Rev. Marlan has also worked with rabbis, cantors, and other officiants. She can travel throughout the tristate area. She also performs commitment ceremonies.

Interfaith Clergy

Toll free: 877-779-0017

Rabbi Shimon Berris is the director of this organization, based in Cherry Hill. It's a group of more than 50 rabbis, priests, and ministers who conduct Jewish, Catholic, Protestant, and interfaith ceremonies. Some of the clergy are retired, while others are still working in their temples or parishes. Their basic belief is that all marriages should be celebrated and blessed, and that it is important for the bride and groom to have a religious, spiritual connection. The officiants are willing to travel.

Wedding Officiants & Religious Objects

Creative Wedding Ceremonies

Deborah Roth, Interfaith Minister
212-665-9660
www.spiritedliving.com

Reverend Deborah Roth is a relationship and life transition coach who performs a wide variety of creative wedding ceremonies. She works with couples who come from different faith traditions and with couples who are interested in creating a personal ceremony. Roth draws on a wide range of wedding traditions from many cultures to build an original, unique ceremony. In addition to weddings, Roth also provides pre-marital coaching; leads Bridesmaid Celebration Circles where the bride and her bridesmaids celebrate their relationships; and creates Magical Bridal Showers. Roth's work has even been featured in a one-hour special on TLC's "A Wedding Story." Roth doesn't believe in cookie-cutter wedding ceremonies, and she is happy to work with you to make your vows perfect.

Heritage Chuppah

Madlyn Dickens
www.heritagechuppah.com • madlyn_dickens@hotmail.com
718-884-6214
$: Up to 20 photographs $3,000, each additional photo is $45

Madlyn Dickens is a graphic designer who created her first "Heritage Chuppah" for her niece's wedding. It was such a success that it has turned into a business. Couples bring collections of family photos to Dickens, who then scans them and transfers them onto fabric. She then calligraphs the names of all the people in the photos onto the fabric transfers, cuts the cloth into leaf shapes, and appliques the pieces together to create a "family tree" image which she then sews onto an oversized tallit or white striped damask. The final chuppah gives the sense that the couple is getting married underneath a canopy of family, smiling down on them. Dickens also sews drapery rings into the chuppah so that after the wedding it becomes a family heirloom that can be reused and rehung. If you'd like a Heritage Chuppah you should gather your photographs and contact Dickens 6 to 8 weeks before the wedding. She can work faster with a 10 percent rush charge (and she warns that for rushes you must have all your pictures ready to go).

The Wedding Ladies

Joan Katz and Margery Langner
Judaic Art & Crafts
Norshon Road • Merrick, New York 11566
516-868-5572 • Fax: 516-623-6392
j.katz@mindspring.com
$: Ketubot start at approximately $100

For over ten years, Joan Katz has represented over 30 ketubot artists from around the United States and Israel. She knows the history and meaning of each piece of work, and can even help you find an artist who can do custom work if you want something truly unique. Her partner, Margery Langner, designs beautiful, colorful chuppahs. The Wedding Ladies love to work with couples to help them build the perfect materials for their weddings, but be sure to allow enough time. Katz asks for 4 to 6 weeks for ketubot, and custom ketubot take 8–14 weeks.

Notes

Catering

When planning your reception, finding a caterer is the next important step after settling on a location. There are a few basic questions to ask yourself. First, how much are you willing to spend? Second, what kind of food do you want to serve? Third, where is your wedding taking place? (Many reception locales have their own catering departments and won't let you work with outside companies.) Fourth, do you want a casual event or a truly upscale party? After you've answered these questions, you can start looking at the options. Make phone calls and ask questions. When you finally decide on a caterer, be sure to ask what the company will supply in addition to food: Ask about wait staff, tables, chairs, linens, china and other tableware, and serving equipment. What about floral centerpieces? (Some caterers also do flowers.) If you're having a tented wedding, can the caterer procure the tent? You may be charged a set amount for liquor, no matter how much or how little guests drink, or you may pay based only on how much people actually imbibe. Some caterers don't have liquor licenses but can contract out your booze order, or your reception site may take care of the drinks.

In general, find out what to expect and what you'll need to supply. Don't be shy about bombarding your caterer with questions—no professional will be offended. Most caterers are excited to work at weddings and will do the utmost to supply you with the best food, staff, and rental equipment that your budget will allow. If your caterer seems unwilling to spend a lot of time working with you or acts annoyed when you ask questions, find a new one.

Our list features the best the tristate area has to offer. Remember that because many caterers will travel, a Manhattan caterer may be the perfect choice for a suburban Connecticut wedding.

In-the-know tips

● Make sure your caterer has a license. You don't want to be financially responsible if something goes wrong. A licensed caterer is insured for any injury to their wait staff or to your guests.

● Ask to see photos of previous weddings the caterer has done—this will give you an idea of the caterer's food presentation skills and will let you know whether you are on the same wavelength when it comes to decor. (One person's idea of elegant can be another's idea of tacky!) All reputable caterers will also supply you with sample menus, letters of recommendation or references' phone numbers, and a contract. Make sure to read the contract carefully, and be sure you are satisfied with all the terms before you sign.

● Many caterers have websites, where you can view sample menus, read letters of thanks, and see photographs of weddings the company has catered in the past.

- Some caterers can supply wedding cakes in addition to the reception meal. Purchasing dinner and cake from the same vendor may save you money. Some caterers actually require that you use one of their cakes.

- Transportation is generally an extra fee if your caterer must travel more than 20 miles to get to your reception site. Ask during your initial conversation.

- If you find that many caterers are outside your price range, consider going ethnic. Ghenet, one of the caterers we've listed here, is actually an Ethiopian restaurant that also caters weddings. Their price per person is much lower than many French- or American-style caterers, and the food is delicious. (However, they don't supply rentals or service, so you'll have to arrange for those on your own.) Your local Indian or Italian restaurant may be willing to cater your wedding, as well. Call around the neighborhood where your reception will take place to see what nearby restaurants have to offer.

- Finally, book your caterer at least six months in advance. If you plan to wed in the high season (May through October), you may need to reserve even earlier. If you wait until the last minute, you could be stuck with take-out from the corner pizza parlor.

NEW YORK CITY

Acquolina Catering and Event Management

2191 Third Avenue, 4th Floor • New York, NY 10035
212-994-9300
www.acquolinacatering.com
$: Prices start at $80 per person for food only

If you want show-stopping food at your wedding, look no further than Acquolina. This caterer, specializing in fabulous Northern Italian cuisine, can create wonderful, memorable meals that will satisfy all of your guests. (Their amazing pasta dishes are perfect for vegetarians.) While Acquolina's first interest is in good, elegant food, they can also provide specialty linens, flowers, complete silverware and furniture rental, as well as a complete staff. In addition, they can also help with general party organizing and planning. Among the offerings that will get your guests talking are their amazing risottos, a fantastic frittini misti (lightly fried bites of sage, fennel, Portobello mushroom, and asparagus tips), mouth-watering filet mignon, and a spectacular assortment of desserts.

Arthur Avenue Caterers

2344 Arthur Avenue • Bronx, NY 10458
Toll free: 866-2-SALAMI
info@arthuravenue.com • www.arthuravenue.com
$: Call to discuss menu options and prices

This Italian caterer started life over 50 years ago under the moniker Mike's Deli in New York's "real" Little Italy, on Arthur Avenue in the Bronx. If you're looking for an Italian feast capped off with a multitiered white ricotta wedding cake, this is the caterer for you. A typical Arthur Avenue menu includes passed hors d'oeuvres with an antipasto buffet and old-world-style entrees ranging from rigatoni with sausage to filet mignon with porcini mushrooms and truffle oil. They even serve a traditional Italian wedding soup of tortellini and meatballs in broth.

Dan Barber

26 West 17th Street, 11th Floor • New York, NY 10011
212-647-1713
irene@barberinc.com
**$: Cocktail receptions start at $28 per person, excluding alcohol,
service, and rentals; seated dinners start at $80 per person,
excluding alcohol, service, and rentals; Barber can supply rentals,
bar service, lighting, invitations, flowers, and more for an additional fee.**

One of my personal favorites, Dan Barber is a seasoned wedding professional who has even done a New York Public Library fundraiser at my home. He's not only a caterer, but also an event planner who can supply virtually everything you need for the perfect wedding. Barber is willing to travel for weddings and has created wonderful events from the Hamptons to the Berkshires. He remembers one amazing wedding he catered on an island off the coast of Maine: Everything—from the food to the 250 guests—was boated over. Barber orchestrated a Friday-evening rehearsal dinner, a Saturday wedding, and a Sunday brunch. His signature cuisine includes heirloom tomato and watermelon soup, roasted organic hen, and steamed local trout. He is willing to create organic and kosher menus.

Serena Bass

404 West 13th Street • New York, NY 10014
212-727-2257
serenabass@earthlink.net
$: Call to discuss menu options and prices

Serena Bass is known for her simple but "up a notch" presentation of familiar food. Her menus are generally American with international flair. For example, the menu for Sarah

Jessica Parker and Matthew Broderick's wedding in May 1997 included an oyster bar; purple figs wrapped in prosciutto; red snapper with charmoula sauce and preserved lemons; and chicken with Moroccan spices and glazed quinces. Bass is willing to cater events outside New York City and has worked in New Jersey, Connecticut, and the Hamptons.

The Cleaver Company

Chelsea Market • 75 Ninth Avenue
New York, NY 10011
212-741-9174
www.cleaverco.com • cleaver@cleaverco.com
$: Buffets start at $135 per person;
seated meals start at $150 per person

Mary Cleaver, who's been in the catering business for 20 years, considers herself an event planner as well. Her company is very nearly full-service—her staff can do everything, even help you choose a location. Cleaver loves doing weddings; her goal is to give each couple the party they want while staying within their budget. The Cleaver Company's cuisine is eclectic and seasonally based, using the best of local produce. Cleaver tries to buy organic whenever she can. Besides buffets or seated meals, Cleaver can do tasting stations and meals in which the first course is seated and the rest are buffet-style, to let guests mingle and dance. The Cleaver Company has an "environmental policy" that includes recycling as much as possible as well as donating leftovers to City Harvest, which then brings food to shelters and soup kitchens across the city. To boot, Cleaver and her staff are incredibly friendly.

Creative Edge Parties

110 Barrow Street • New York, NY 10014
212-741-3000 • Fax: 212-741-3888
parties@creativeedgeparties.com • www.creativeedgeparties.com
$: Seated meals start as $60 per person; an all-inclusive wedding
(with staff, rentals, and drinks) starts at $185 per person

Creative Edge Parties works for the best in New York—the caterer supplies the food for Martha Stewart events. The cuisine could be described as "new American multi-culti" and includes appetizing treats such as Maine lobster bites with artichokes, lemon aioli, and caviar and seared, cubed foie gras with balsamic-glazed Granny Smith apples. And those are just the hors d'oeuvres! For main courses, Creative Edge offers scrumptious fare such as grilled veal medallions with shallot balsamic sauce and braised capon filled with figs, apricots, and coriander. If you're looking for a four-star dining experience comparable to what you'd enjoy at a fine restaurant, Creative Edge is among Manhattan's best. These people even handled parties for the Pope with aplomb.

Feast & Fêtes Catering

60 East 65th Street · New York, NY 10021
212-737-2224 · Fax: 212-327-4020
jeanchristophe@feastandfete.com · www.danielnyc.com
$: Call to discuss menus and prices

Feast & Fêtes is the catering arm of New York City's world-famous French restaurant Daniel. You can bring the best of fine restaurant fare to your wedding: Everything is prepared by Daniel's 28 chefs. If you choose Feast & Fêtes, make sure your budget is large—they're at the very high end of caterers. Owned by Jean-Christophe Le Picart and Daniel Boulud, Feast & Fêtes provides sumptuous cuisine and attention to detail, attracting some of the most influential people in New York: They supplied the culinary treats for the society wedding of Alexandra Miller to Alexandre Von Furstenberg, as well as the wedding of George Stephanopoulos to Alexandra Wentworth. Each guest at a Feast & Fêtes–catered event can choose from Daniel's menu, which includes such treats as roasted cod with squid-ink bow-tie pasta, cockles and clams in a saffron bouillon, and roasted monkfish and lobster with cured bacon.

Fletcher Morgan

432 West 19th Street · New York, NY 10011
212-989-0724
www.fletchermorgan.com
$: Seated meals start at $175 per person; buffets start at $125
per person. This includes food, rentals, service, and wine.

Fletcher Morgan co-owner Gregory Barreta has described his culinary style as "sophisticated but bam! in your face at the same time." This bold attitude has attracted high-profile clients from the fashion and art worlds. The company still has time to devote to creating highly personalized weddings, however, and the caterers are willing to travel outside of Manhattan; they've catered weddings in the Hamptons, Connecticut, and New Jersey.

Fletcher Morgan menus vary by the season and the theme of the wedding, with a focus on French cuisine that incorporates elements of Asia, South America, and the Middle East. Selections include fare such as grilled sea scallop vermicelli salad; Filipino chicken adobo with coriander pommes purée; crispy-skin salmon with baby vegetables in a tamarind carrot jus; and gibelotte of rabbit in a red and white wine sauce with toasted pistachios.

Food in Motion

148 Chambers Street • New York, NY 10007
212-766-4400 • Fax: 212-766-4402
$: Seated meals start at $150 per person; buffets start at $135
per person. This includes food, rentals, service, and open bar.

Food in Motion offers catering with a fresh twist. Husband and wife owners Lloyd Zimet and Michelle Lovelace carefully design menus only after talking to their clients—they don't have set "wedding fare." They've done everything from Moroccan-themed weddings to parties with a 1930s theme (if you want a swinging wedding, this may be the catering company for you), and they're famous for their vodka fruit drinks, such as lime rickies with Midori. The company is willing to work outside New York—they did one stunning lakeside wedding in Connecticut for a pair of Hollywood producers. Zimet remembers the scene as extraordinarily beautiful; two of the waiters even went into the lake in rowboats to distribute floating candles.

Food in Motion can prepare anything from a raw oyster bar to a down-home barbecue and offers dishes such as toasted polenta with deep-fried sage leaves; Welsh rarebit in toast cups with bacon; seared tuna with sushi rice tea sandwiches; and rack of lamb with red wine and olive sauce.

Ghenet

284 Mulberry Street • New York, NY 10012
212-343-1888
$: Meals start at $13 per person; call to discuss menus and prices

Workye Ephrem was running Ghenet, her amazing Ethiopian restaurant in Soho, when she decided to cater her daughter's 350-guest wedding in 1998. Since then, Ephrem has been doing both large and small parties. Although the catering arm of Ghenet is not full-service (they supply food and service only), they're a great option if your budget isn't huge but you want an exotic, truly delicious menu. Ghenet's traditional Ethiopian dishes include doro wat, a stew made with chicken and hard-boiled eggs that is seasoned with berberi, a blend of red chili peppers, onions, garlic, and other spices. Entrees are eaten by hand with spongy injera bread. Dessert in Ethiopia (and at Ghenet) is generally a simple selection of fresh fruit, so you'll have to get your wedding cake elsewhere.

Glorious Food

504 E. 74th Street · New York, NY 10021
212-628-2320 · 212-988-8136
info@gloriousfood.com · www.gloriousfood.com
$: Call for prices

This upscale caterer has handled parties of all kinds—from huge art-world functions to private weddings. Their food is delicious and the service is absolutely impeccable. Their prices are high, but you're paying not only for fabulous food, but for peace of mind and terrific presentation.

Gracious Thyme

2191 Third Avenue · New York, NY 10035
212-873-1965
$: Seated meals range from $50 to $85 per person.
This includes food only, but Gracious Thyme will provide everything else you
need for an additional fee. Cakes range from $5 to $20 per person.

Gracious Thyme specializes in high-end, full-service event planning and catering. The company can suggest unusual locations such as museums, nightclubs, outdoor venues, galleries, and historical landmarks. Founded in 1986 by Judy Hundley and Mark Cummings, Gracious Thyme is also the place to go if you're looking for simple, elegant French-influenced food. A sample menu includes seared sea scallops with orange chive beurre blanc; chilled jumbo lump crabmeat; herb-crusted baby lamb chops with roasted fennel and tomatoes and truffled potato souffle; and medallions of veal with madeira sauce.

Great Performances

287 Spring Street · New York, NY 10013
212-727-2424
www.greatperformances.com · info@greatperformances.com
$: Seated meals start at $200 per person, which includes food,
rentals, service, and bar setup.

This catering star has partnered with some of New York's prime party locations, including the Asia Society and Wave Hill. The company also has a service that will help you choose a location for your wedding—anything from the unusual to the grand. Great Performances has catered events for Hillary Rodham Clinton and Mayor Rudy Guiliani. (If those two can agree on one caterer, you've got to check it out.)

Great Performances serves Modern American cuisine "with a difference," which includes Pacific Rim, Caribbean, and Mediterranean delicacies. Menus often include fare such as Hudson Valley foie gras ravioli with braised royal chard and fennel in an herbed beet broth, and yummy hors d'oeuvres range from miniature veal burgers topped with melted fontina cheese to grilled swordfish tacos with guacamole and pico de gallo. Their ice cream bar has become a staple at Great Performances weddings—it seems to be all the rage with clients.

JJM Distinctive Catering Inc.

159 East Houston Street · New York, NY 10002
212-353-8848
$: Call for prices

JJM Distinctive Catering is an old-fashioned caterer. They prepare delicious, affordable menus that are inventive and guaranteed to please a wide range of palates.

Mark Fahrer Caterers

391 Second Avenue · New York, NY 10010
212-727-1700
www.markfahrer.com
$: Buffet or seated meals start at $80 per person for food only. Service is an additional $37 per hour, and rentals range from $20 to $30 per person. Fahrer can also supply wedding cake at $5 to $15 per person and can also arrange for liquor and wine.

Mark Fahrer starts with the reception site—he has dozens of great location ideas—then plans a distinctive wedding around it. He also considers his clients' ethnic heritage. For example, for the wedding of a Jamaican groom and a bride from Guyana via England, he created a menu combining English and Jamaican fare. He traveled all the way to North Africa to research food for a Moroccan-themed party and created a South African feast for the premiere of the film *Mandela.*

Fahrer uses the best ingredients he can get his hands on: sea salt, extra virgin olive oil, organic eggs. He goes from there to create mouthwatering dishes such as paillard of chicken marinated in mango-infused oil, boneless breast of duck framboise, and cold poached salmon with green yogurt sauce. Fahrer has been in the business for 20 years and is direct and outspoken—he'll definitely let you know his opinion. He now has a food bar and tasting room and a fully insured liquor license. If you want a wedding planner/caterer who will come up with ultra-creative ideas for your celebration, give him a call.

Mood Food, Ltd. Cuisine with Atmosphere

263 West 12th Street · New York, NY 10014
212-243-4245
$: Seated meals start at $70 per person.
This includes food only, but service, rentals, flowers, cakes,
and location scouting are available for an additional fee.

Mood Food owner Tinker Boe has traveled as far as Bangkok to do an event, but she's also a willing visitor to such nearby locales as Connecticut, Long Island, and New Jersey. A self-taught chef, Boe launched her company in 1985 and has since honed her skills on some of New York's most influential citizens. She craves a culinary challenge and likes to create custom events; she claims that no two are the same. Boe has created menus based on the bride or groom's ethnic heritage—for example, she combined Western and Southern Indian cuisines for a couple of Indian descent. She has also worked on themed weddings, creating a shimmering, opalescent affair for a couple who met while scuba diving and putting together a pop-art extravaganza for a couple whose parents were collectors. And her creativity doesn't stop at the wedding: Boe also creates miniature replicas of wedding cakes for anniversary celebrations.

Olivier Cheng Catering and Events

495 Broadway, 2nd Floor · New York, NY 10012
212-625-3151
www.ocnyc.com · franck@ocnyc.com
$: Seated meals start at $175 per person

Olivier Cheng, formerly of Matthew Kenney's catering company, offers delicious, inventive food and puts together great parties. His ideas are exciting, lively, tasty, and are sure to get people talking. The company has a global menu that mixes American cuisine with all kinds of influences from Europe and Asia. Everything from Olivier Cheng is fabulous, from his cool summer soups to hearty tuna dishes. Cheng also does event execution and design, so if you like you can put everything in his hands. If you do, you can be certain his work will be clean, elegant, totally customized, and comfortable.

Robbins Wolfe Eventeurs

521 West Street · New York, NY 10014
212-924-6500
The Hamptons: 631-537-1926 · Locust Valley: 516-671-2127
www.robbinswolfe.com
$: Call to discuss menu and prices

Robbins Wolfe is a fun and original caterer. The company plans each wedding according to the couple's instructions and dreams and can arrange everything from invitations to lighting, decor, and floral design. They attract a celebrity clientele, including Uma Thurman and Ethan Hawke. For their wedding, Robbins Wolfe created a seven-course meal, featuring a tasting plate of beluga caviar and smoked salmon, black-truffle ravioli in a saffron cream sauce, and roasted Dover sole. For other events, the company has done everything from arranging for Arabian dancers to creating a multicolored martini bar.

Saffron 59

59 Fourth Avenue • New York, NY 10003
212-253-1343
www.saffron59.com • saffron59@safron59.com
$: A custom menu is created for each wedding, so prices vary.
Generally, hors d'oeuvres and a buffet meal or tasting stations range
from $85 to $155 per person. This includes service but not liquor.
Decorations and cakes are also available for an additional fee.

Irene Khin Wong, Saffron 59's Burma-born owner, is considered the city's leading Asian-food caterer and offers delicious cuisine that's mainly Thai and Vietnamese. After founding and running a Burmese restaurant in Soho, Road to Mandalay, Wong took a three-year sabbatical to travel through Vietnam, Indonesia, Malaysia, Thailand, and the former Burma (now Myanmar). While there, she filled a culinary journal with exotic recipes, which now inspire Saffron 59's catering menu. Now, Wong aims to "share the riches of these extraordinary world cuisines." This philosophy shows in delectable dishes such as classic Thai green chicken curry with tomatillo, Vietnamese-style charred steak with lemongrass and soy, and grilled sea bass wrapped in banana leaves. Wong also offers a large selection of vegetarian items, such as braised baby bok choy with sherry and ginger and Asian water spinach with tofu and black-bean garlic. Even the waiters can get into the mood: They'll sport Mao jackets or bright sarongs if you like. Saffron 59 has catered weddings from Amsterdam to Tuscany, and from the Hamptons to upstate New York.

Seasons Distinctive Catering

146 Allen Street • New York, NY 10002
212-420-6045
$: Plated meals range from $45 to $85 per person.
Cocktails $15 to $23 per person.

Seasons Distinctive Catering is a great young catering company that prepares inventive, contemporary American cuisine that often draws on ethnic, especially Asian, food traditions. The chef-owners Marc Tessitore and Robert Zimmerman love to meet couples at their Allen Street store so they can show off their food's freshness and style. Seasons, as its name implies, works hard to emphasize produce at its ripest and most fresh, so the menu shifts throughout the year. That said, they are still careful to tailor their food to your needs and can even come up with menus that fit into pre-conceived themes (Southern food, for instance). Since Seasons is a full-service cater-er, they can provide everything from the food and liquor to rentals and tuxedoed waiters. Seasons likes to start working on weddings about six months in advance, but in a pinch, they can do great work on short notice (two months) as well. By appoint-ment only.

Special Attention

333 East 30th Street · New York, NY 10016
212-477-4805
spattention@aol.com
$: Seated meals start at $200 per person.
This includes food, service, rentals, and full bar service.

Special Attention has catered parties for all sorts of New Yorkers, including execu-tives at such stylish publishing giants as *Elle Decor* and *House Beautiful*. The full-serv-ice company can put together the entire wedding, recommending florists, musicians, bakers, and more. Owner Ellen Gelb is a mistress of organization—she successfully catered weddings during every major snowstorm of the 1990s. Perhaps fewer guests than expected made it to the events, but the food and service went off flawlessly!

Special Attention's food has an Asian flair: sushi stations and accents such as sesame-crusted tuna and dumplings lace the menus. Gelb also excels in American fare such as Maryland crab cakes and carving stations, and she tosses in some French, Italian, and Moroccan specials, like French chicken with a cabernet demi glas, Bolognese Ragu, and Moroccan stew with couscous. She'll work with the bride and groom to create the perfect wedding menu; for one of her "snowstorm" weddings, she put together a veg-etarian menu for 125.

Spoonbread

364 Cathedral Parkway · New York, NY 10025
212-865-0700
www.spoonbreadinc.com · darden343@aol.com
$: Seated meals start at $30 per person; service and rentals are extra.
Liquor is available in conjunction with Embassy Wine & Liquor,
a company that charges only for what's consumed.

Former Wilhelmina model Norma Jean Darden and her sister run this down-home catering company. Darden fell into catering after her book *Spoonbread and Strawberry Wine: Reminiscences and Recipes of a Family* was published in 1980. Since then, she's been going great guns and has clients such as Whitney Houston, Bill Cosby, and Mike Tyson. Spoonbread will travel to do weddings; the company has catered events in Philadelphia, New Jersey, Long Island, Westchester, and Connecticut.

Darden's specialty is a combination of Caribbean food, soul food, and mainstream Continental-American. Since she's from North Carolina, Southern influence is also apparent in all Spoonbread offerings. Such specialties as African fish stew and pecan chicken with white-peach sauce are sure to whet everyone's appetite. Spoonbread's special "Silver Stars" wedding menu includes boneless chicken breasts stuffed with crab in champagne sauce. Your guests will be thanking you for decades.

Susan Holland & Company

142 Fifth Avenue • New York, NY 10011
212-807-8892 • Fax: 212-243-5667
$: Buffet and seated meals start at $175 per person,
which includes food, rentals, and service

This full-service catering firm can do everything from supplying invitations and booking the band to decorating the venue and finding a photographer. Susan Holland believes that food and decor should go hand in hand, forming one cohesive sensibility to create a memorable event, and she takes pains to create just the right ambience for each wedding. She's a firm believer in what she calls "casual elegance" and likes to say that her company combines old-world service with a downtown aesthetic for hip, well-put-together weddings. Her attention to style and detail obviously works: her clients have included Liza Minelli, Diana Ross, and k.d. lang.

"The chef defines the food," Holland says, so she works with only the best. Her American/Global cuisine encompasses such disparate delights as asparagus salad with quail eggs, roasted beets, and pistachios, Moroccan-spiced rack of lamb with tagine of tart fruits, and crab salad with Thai green curry, grilled pineapple, and papadums.

Zarela Catering

953 Second Avenue • New York, NY 10022
212-644-6740 • Fax: 212-980-1073
www.zarela.com
$: Seated meals range from $55 to $125 per person for food only

Dubbed "one of the best caterers in New York City," Zarela Catering is an extension of the famed Mexican restaurant Zarela, founded by Chihuahua native Zarela Martinez 11 years ago. Her daughter, Marissa Sanchez, heads the catering operation and can supply almost everything, including liquor for an additional fee. The caterers will travel anywhere in the tristate area. Menus can be traditionally Mexican or "pan-Mexican eclectic," including such delights as manchamanteles de pollo (chicken braised with tomato, red chili, and dried fruit sauce), camarones in salsa verde (shrimp sauteed in tomatillo sauce), and even make-your-own tacos. The folks at

Zarela can also liven up the decor of your wedding, dressing up tables with brightly colored serapes and woven, multicolored fabrics.

LONG ISLAND

The Art of Eating

P.O. Box 3232 · East Hampton, NY 11937
631-267-2411
www.hamptonsartofeating.com
$: Seated and buffet meals start at around $50 to $75 per person for food only. Service, bar setup and liquor, and rentals are additional.

Featured on both the Food Network and on *Martha Stewart Living*, The Art of Eating is a full-service caterer and event planner. They can do everything from booking a band to hiring floral designers and arranging for transportation to and from the wedding. However, eating is their number one concern, and they offer all sorts of treats—including grilled striped bass stuffed with leeks and fresh herbs, Long Island duck salad, and pan-roasted poussin with garlic.

Corinne's Concepts in Catering

845 East Jericho Turnpike · Huntington Station, NY 11746
631-351-6030 · Toll free: 800-919-9261
www.corrinescatering.com
$: Seated meals start at $50 per person

If you're interested in using a Long Island vineyard as your wedding location, call Corinne's right away. Corinne Futerman and her son Keith have organized dozens of weddings at the Island's best vineyards, including the Gristina, Pellegrini, and Sag Pond Vineyards. You'll by no means be limited to a wine motif at a Corinne's wedding, however; the company also caters events all over Long Island, New Jersey, Connecticut, and Manhattan.

As a full-service caterer, Corinne's can arrange for all aspects of the wedding, including a tent, flowers, and the entertainment. A unique menu is created for each wedding, but examples of culinary creations include poached salmon with sauce verte, jumbo shrimp scampi, grilled rack of lamb, and baby lamb chops with mint sauce. Corinne's also offers many pasta varieties and carving stations.

Culinary Architect Catering

475 Port Washington Boulevard · Port Washington, NY 11050
212-410-5474 or 516-883-7885 · Fax: 516-883-7867
$: Seated meals start at $105 per person
for parties of 100 or more; for fewer than 100 guests,
seated meals start at $115 per person. This includes food,
service, rentals, mixers, cake, and nonalcoholic drinks.

Long Island's 19-year-old Culinary Architect Catering specializes in unique venues and prides itself on elegant and unusual parties. The company can suggest unusual sites, such as the New York Hall of Science in Flushing Meadows and the Manhasset Preserve, a private mansion overlooking Long Island Sound. Clients ranging from Gregory Hines to *Bride's* magazine have been drawn to Culinary Architect for tasty dishes such as lobster in phyllo dough, flaky cheese straws, crab shumai with apricot dipping sauce, chateaubriand with truffle sauce, and grilled salmon with lemongrass. The caterers can also create your cake; most come decorated with a miniature nosegay made to match the bride's bouquet.

WESTCHESTER

Abigail Kirsch Culinary Productions

81 Highland Avenue · Tarrytown, NY 10591
914-631-3030
www.abigailkirsch.com
$: Prices depend on location, season, and day of the week.
At the company's exclusive locations, buffet and four-course
seated meals generally start at $110 per person in high season and
$100 per person in low season. This price is all-inclusive.

Abigail Kirsch is a consummate professional, catering more than 500 weddings a year in Westchester County. Her food is outstanding, and the service is excellent. She is a great choice for large weddings—with big budgets. Her exclusive venues include Pier 60 at Chelsea Piers, with huge picture windows on the Hudson; Tappan Hill, a stunning historic mansion once owned by Mark Twain, in Tarrytown; and the New York Botanical Gardens in the Bronx, which boasts an amazing glass-walled greenhouse. She can also cater at other locations; her team will bring everything with them.

Kirsch's menus include macadamia nut–crusted mahi-mahi with brown sugar pineapple glaze and boneless braised shortribs of beef with caramelized root vegetables. Her staff is famous for first-rate service. A word to the wise: Kirsch doesn't usually do kosher weddings (although she can bring in a kosher caterer), and her cocktail hour is sometimes extra-long—be specific about how long you'd like yours to last.

NEW JERSEY

Epicure Catering

124 Greenwood Avenue · Midland Park, NJ 07432
201-445-2776
www.epicurecatering.com · celiam@prodigy.net
**$: Seated and buffet meals range from $50 to $60 per person for
food and rentals. The company can also provide service
and bar setup for an additional fee.**

Epicure is a family-run caterer that can create a wedding as formal or casual as you are. From a grazing party with pasta stations and carving boards to an elegant seated dinner, they can work with you to create a celebration that matches your style. Entree selections include Mediterranean chicken with artichokes and mushrooms in a lemon basil sauce, filet with red-wine pistachio sauce, veal chops with crab meat and white asparagus, and pork loin with apricot chamomile sauce. They can also accommodate vegetarians and vegans. Epicure also creates fantastic, fresh-flower-trimmed cakes, and can coordinate everything from rentals to flowers and horse-drawn carriages.

Fabulous Foods Catering,
Party Planning & Special Events

55 Moonachie Avenue · Moonachie, NJ 07074
800-365-4747
$: Seated and buffet meals start at $25 per person

Fabulous Foods is a full-service caterer and can travel anywhere within the tristate area. They've worked at all sorts of unique locations, from yachts to mansions, and can work within any theme. The company offers a wide range of items on their menus, including miniature crab fritters with Cajun tartar sauce, herb-marinated chicken skewers with macadamia dipping sauce, and mesquite-grilled vegetables.

CONNECTICUT

Cabbages & Kings

58 Saugatuck Avenue • Westport, CT 06880
203-226-0531
www.cabbagesandkingscatering.net
$: Seated meals range from $40 to $150 per person for food only.
Service, rentals, liquor, and cakes are additional.

Cabbages & Kings owner Sarah Gross is known as much for how her parties look as for how her food tastes. After working with Martha Stewart for five years, Gross set out to found her own catering and event planning company and now specializes in eclectic ethnic food. She says she absolutely loves doing weddings. She's willing to get creative in the kitchen to please her clients and has done everything from a vegetarian wedding to a personalized castle cake. One wedding Gross conceived and created was set up as a picnic, with individual picnic baskets—complete with flatware, china, bread, and wineglasses—on blankets, and a menu that included skewered lemon-dill salmon, grilled swordfish and tuna, and a series of sauces including mango salsa and spicy tomato salsa.

Fjord Catering and Yacht Charters

143 River Road • Coscob, CT 06807
203-622-4020
Toll free: 800-9CLAMBAKE
www.fjordcatering.com • general@fjordcatering.com
$: Clambakes start at $65 per person;
other meals range from $55 to $95 per person for food only.

At one summer wedding in Connecticut, the bride wore a sheath, the groom wore a tux, and the guests enjoyed an old-fashioned clambake in the groom's backyard. This feast was catered by Fjord. Run by a Norwegian family led by "Pappa Fish" Nygaard, this cozy catering firm specializes in—you guessed it—seafood. The company owns a whole fleet of boats (well, at least four) and can take couples and their guests for a cruise out on Long Island Sound or provide a reception with a nautical feel on a docked boat that can accommodate up to 100 people.

Fjord is full-service and can do everything from food to decor and music. They're willing to accommodate any budget. The company's fortes are clambakes, excellent raw bars, Hawaiian luaus, Scandinavian smorgasbords, and just about any seafood-oriented fantasy you can dream up. Some delectable specials include sea scallops with roasted garlic sauce; gravlax sliced thick with scalloped potatoes; boneless salmon steaks, poached and served the Norwegian way; and fresh lobster.

J ewelry

N ew York City has an entire universe of wonderful jewelry stores and your choices are almost unlimited. Before you start shopping, try to narrow down what kind of pieces you're looking for. If you're shopping for an engagement ring, do you want a modern piece, an estate piece, or something designed for you? If you're looking for a diamond, do a little bit of research before you set out. (Tiffany & Co. has a useful brochure called "How to Buy a Diamond" that you can download from their website.) If you're looking for presents for bridesmaids and attendants, consider giving them simple jewelry pieces. They are versatile, beautiful, and don't have to be expensive. Enjoy shopping. Buying jewelry is one of the most pleasurable parts of the wedding planning process.

1,873 Unusual Wedding Rings

800-877-3874 · 212-944-1713
4 West 47th Street, counter # 86 · New York, NY 10036
www.unusualweddingrings.com

Another Diamond District prize, 1,873 Unusual Wedding Rings is a terrific jewelry resource. Established in 1947, the shop has a long history taking care of generations of jewelry. They carry many hundreds of rings in tons of styles, including Claddagh, Celtic, and Hebrew, and in a wide assortment of metals and karats. If you're looking for your dream ring, they can often find exactly what you're looking for if you bring them a photograph, and since they're also a full-service shop, they can repair and restyle almost any "problem ring" you bring in.

Asprey

725 Fifth Avenue · New York, NY 10022
212-688-1811 · 800-883-2777
www.asprey.com

Asprey is a classic British jeweler and is famous for designing pieces that have gone to the Oscars, including the famous "Titanic Necklace." Madonna wore a vintage Asprey tiara, with 767 diamonds in it at her wedding, but you can wear something a little simpler to yours. Asprey has several ring collections including a series featuring their famously brilliant-cut diamonds. Other designs work with a wide variety of stones and colors that make glamorous, lively engagement rings.

Boucher Jewelry

9 Ninth Avenue · New York, NY 10014
212-807-9849 or 866-623-9269
www.boucherjewerly.com · info@boucherjewerly.com

If you're looking for beautiful wedding jewelry and attendant presents, Laura Mady's beautiful jewelry designs, lively with color and light-catching shapes, can be made to order for an entire bridal party. Mady can design different pieces that use the same pearls or stones for each member of the bridal party (from mothers of the bride and groom all the way to junior attendants) so that the look is consistent, but people get to wear jewelry that matches their personalities. You can go into either of Boucher's two stores (in Manhattan and Cold Springs, NY) with swatches, or you can place orders online and have pictures of the pieces emailed to you. Earrings or a basic necklace can start at about $40, so you can easily give your bridesmaids great presents for a reasonable price. Boucher can work with any budget, offers discounts for large orders, and can even put together wonderful pieces in a rush.

Cartier

653 Fifth Avenue • New York, NY 10022
212-753-0111
www.cartier.com

Cartier is home to famously fantastic jewelry, expensive and beautiful. Their rings run the gamut from traditional classic diamonds in prong settings to ultra-modern clusters of diamonds. Many of their signature pieces make wonderful wedding bands, and their inventive designs might be the perfect thing if you're looking for something a little unusual. Browse through their collections and get inspired.

The Clay Pot

162 Seventh Avenue • Brooklyn, NY 11215
800-989-3579
www.clay-pot.com

This Park Slope institution started in 1969 as a ceramics studio, but it has been selling engagement and wedding rings since 1989. The store is friendly, comfortable, and has a wide selection of wonderful rings designed by over 75 artists. They also have two GIA-certified diamond consultants on site to answer any questions you might have and help you decide what ring is best for you.

The Diamond Co.

62 West 47th Street • New York, NY
888-825-1233 • 212-819-0336
info@thediamondco.com • www.thediamondco.com

Visit New York City's famous "Diamond District" on West 47th street, and you can be easily overwhelmed by the sheer number of diamond stores. The Diamond Co. has been around since 1968 (and has sold jewelry to the public since 1997), sells classic, simple styles, and has great prices. The Diamond Co. sells diamonds that have been appraised by independent appraisers (mostly from the Gemological Institute of America—GIA), and makes sure you understand everything about your purchase. They carry great, traditional diamond engagement rings, earrings, and necklaces. For more information, browse through their informative website.

Doyle & Doyle

189 Orchard Street · New York, NY 10002
212-677-9991
endolye@doyledoyle.com · www.doyledoyle.com

For amazing estate jewelry, pay a visit to Orchard Street. This small store carries Georgian, Victorian, Edwardian, art deco, and art nouveau pieces and displays them in elegant small cases throughout the store. Co-owner Elizabeth Doyle has an amazing eye, a degree from the Gemological Institute of America, and an ability to find gorgeous jewelry for her store. You're guaranteed to see amazing, one-of-a-kind pieces.

DVVS Fine Jewelry

263A West 19th Street · New York, NY 10011
212 366-4888 · Fax: 212 366-4949
www.dvvs.com

If you're looking for reasonably priced, funky jewelry, visit this small shop. They carry hip modern rings by a range of designers in gold, platinum, and sterling silver. They also do Celtic designs and custom work.

Eric Originals & Antiques

4 West 47th Street · New York, NY 10036
212-819-9595

Visit Eric Originals for wonderful vintage pieces. You'll find work by designers like Cartier and Van Cleef & Arpels in addition to pieces with old-fashioned cuts of diamond. They are reasonably priced and their collection is a treat to browse through.

Fortunoff

681 5th Avenue · New York, NY 10022
212-758-6600 · 1-800-367-8866
www.fortunoff.com

OTHER NEW YORK STATE LOCATIONS:
The Mall at the Source
1300 Old Country Road · Westbury, NY 11590

NEW JERSEY LOCATIONS:
Woodbridge Center Drive · Woodbridge, NJ 07095
and
**Paramus Park Mall,
Paramus, NJ 07652**
and
**250 Wayne Towne Center
Wayne, NJ 07470**

CONNECTICUT LOCATION
499 Post Road · Westport, CT 06880

Fortunoff has been a jewelry standby for over 80 years and they've expanded their wedding collection to include everything from engagement rings and wedding bands to bridal jewelry (tiaras, pearls, necklaces). They also have a huge line of presents for the groom, bridesmaid presents, and gifts for the rest of the bridal party (even ringbearers). Fortunoff also lets you order a lot of these items online, so you don't have to run around town if you don't want to.

Fragments

107 Greene Street · New York, NY 10012
212-334-3955
and
53 Stone Street · New York, NY 10004
212-269-3955

Fragments is a super-hip jewelry store that caters to a fashionable, celebrity clientele. They carry work by a wide selection of designers. Visit the stores to find unusual, striking pieces, not at all your typical wedding bands. The jewelry is lively and with such an array of design sensibilities to choose from, you're sure to find something wonderful.

Frank Pollack & Sons

608 Fifth Avenue, Suite 903 · New York, NY 10020
800-DIA-DUST
customerservice@diadust.com · www.diadust.com

If you're looking for interesting estate pieces, be sure to visit Frank Pollack & Sons. This shop is the largest buyer of antique and estate jewelry in the United States and the pieces they find are beautiful and different. The store is by appointment only but they are a wonderful resource for jewelry with history.

Fred Leighton

773 Madison Avenue · New York, NY 10021
212-288-1872

The windows at Fred Leighton often have gorgeous estate pieces in them that look like they might show up on the Oscars someday, but if you dare to step inside you can find fabulous, elegant engagement rings in plenty of styles. At Leighton you'll also find wedding bands (including some very thin, stackable ones) and a wide selection of diamonds in a variety of cuts—antique and modern.

Graff

721 Madison Avenue · New York, NY 10021
212-355-9292
www.graffdiamonds.com

The website claims Graff has "the most fabulous jewels in the world" and it's hard to disagree, given people's reaction to their Madison Avenue storefront. Looking into the windows is like looking at the incredible jewel displays at the Museum of Natural History. Brilliant, enormous white and yellow diamonds flash out at you as you walk past. All of Graff's jewelry is handmade and the metal work tends to be subtle, not to distract from the beauty of the stone. If you're looking to dazzle and have the cash, Graff can show you something amazing.

Harry Winston

718 Fifth Avenue · New York, NY 10019
212-245-2000
www.harrywinston.com

Marilyn Monroe sang about Winston; both Carrie and Samantha from "Sex and the City" received (and returned) baubles from Winston—what better credentials do you need? The jewels in Harry Winston's landmark store are absolutely amazing and come in a wide range of styles. The pieces are pricy, but classy and gorgeous.

James Robinson

480 Park Avenue · New York, NY 10022
212-752-6166
www.jrobinson.com

The James Robinson shop is a wonder. Look around and you will see unbelievably beautiful 19th- and 20th-century jewelry, exquisite silver flatware, antique porcelain and glass pieces, and all manner of singular and amazing objects. Ask to see some rings and the knowledgeable staff will bring out an assortment to suit your taste and tell you the history of jewelry making as you admire the pieces on your fingers. They have everything from lockets and pins to amazing cufflinks, and their antique porcelain collection is really incredible. If you're looking for estate pieces don't miss a chance to go in.

Michael C. Fina

545 Fifth Avenue · New York, NY 10017
800-289-3462

A traditional place for couples to register, Michael C. Fina is also a reliable source for all kinds of jewelry and presents. Come here to find a wide variety of engagement rings and wedding bands at reasonable prices. They also have a great selection of pearl jewelry to complement wedding gowns. Michael C. Fina is also a terrific resource for presents for attendants and can supply you with everything from cufflinks and key rings, to delicate jewelry for bridesmaids.

Mikimoto

730 Fifth Avenue · New York, NY 10019
212-457-4600 · 800-701-2323
www.mikimoto.com

Mikimoto is considered by many to be the first and last word in pearls. Their website even contains extensive discussions of how pearls are made and things to consider when you buy them. Pearls from Mikimoto are luminous, gorgeous, and expensive, but they'll last a lifetime.

Norman Landsberg, Inc.

66 West 47th Street · New York, NY 10036
212-391-1980 · Fax: 212-730-4853
info@normanlandsberg.com · www.normanlandsberg.com

Norman Landsberg is a fantastic 47th Street find. They have hundreds and hundreds of engagement and wedding rings to choose from by over 25 designers in a huge array of prices. They've been in business since 1948 and are prepared to answer any question you have for them. Since they specialize in diamonds with GIA grading reports, you can be assured of getting what you pay for.

Push Jewelry

420 Mulberry Street · New York, NY 10012
866-349-7874
info@pushjewelry.com · www.pushjewelry.com

Take a trip to Nolita and check out Karen Karch's stylish, original designs. In 1997 she premiered a line of engagement and wedding jewelry called "Til Death Do Us Part," which features powerful, unusual designs and beautiful stones and metals. Push Jewelry has new collections once or twice a year and also has a growing signature collection. Custom work is available by appointment only. Karch's work is eye-catching and beautiful.

Reinstein Ross

29 East 73rd Street · New York, NY 10021
212-772-1901
and
122 Prince Street · New York, NY 10012
212-226-4513

Step into the Reinstein Ross stores and you'll be amazed by the color and sparkle of the stones. All of the pieces are handmade and if you're looking for something a little different than the standard diamonds-in-prong-settings, stop by. You'll find plenty of diamonds, in beautiful and unusual settings, but you'll also find juicy-looking rubies and a huge spectrum of sapphire colors. Reinstein Ross has 3 different "colors" of gold, in addition to white gold, from which you can pick the best color for your stone and skin tone. If you want friendly, personalized service and custom pieces, look no further. While you're in, check out their wonderful earrings that have changeable "drops" which you can purchase in literally hundreds of colors and patterns. Men should ask about their cufflink and shirt stud sets, which are also fantastic.

Stardust Antiques

38 Gramercy Park North · New York, NY 10010
212-677-2590 · 888-434-5530
www.stardustantiques.com

Stardust Antiques is a comfortable store that sells lots of things besides jewelry (including bridal party presents), but for unusual, one-of-a-kind engagement and wedding rings, you should look in. Owners Ken and Esther Gold travel all over the world looking for estate collections and individual pieces to bring back to their store, so it is always interesting to stop in and see what they have. They also carry contemporary wedding bands styled after antique pieces, if you prefer to order a new one.

Tiffany & Co.

Fifth Avenue at 57th Street · New York, NY 10022
212-755-8000

MANHASSET
1980 Northern Boulevard · Manhasset, New York 11030
516-869-0800

WHITE PLAINS
125 Westchester Avenue · White Plains, New York 10601
914-686-5100

EAST HAMPTON
53 Main Street · East Hampton, NY 11937
631-324-1700

CONNECTICUT
140 Greenwich Avenue · Greenwich, CT 06831
203-661-7847

NEW JERSEY
The Mall at Short Hills
1200 Morris Turnpike · Route 24 & JFK Parkway
Short Hills, NJ
973-467-3600

www.tiffany.com

For many, Tiffany & Co. is the first and last word in wedding jewelry and presents. They are famous for their engagement rings, classical, elegant, and entirely tasteful. Their most famous ring, the Classic Tiffany six-prong platinum set engagement ring, which was introduced in 1886, remains one of the most popular engagement ring designs in the world. If you're new to the jewelry game, Tiffany even published a pamphlet: "How to Buy a Diamond" (which you can download from their website) that teaches you all the basics. Tiffany & Co. also carries a fantastic selection of necklaces, chains, wedding bands, earrings, cufflinks, and other perfect presents for the wedding party.

VanCleef & Arpels

744 Fifth Avenue · New York, NY 10019
212-644-9500

The place is legendary, and its jewels have shown up on the hands and throats of awards show attendees. Their jewels are gorgeous, expensive, and extremely classy. Their rings have an old-fashioned glamour to them but they also carry a line of equally fancy but lighter designs.

Wedding Ring Originals

674 Lexington Avenue • New York, NY 10022
800-522-1175 • 212-751-3940
www.weddingrings.com

For a huge selection, check out Wedding Ring Originals. They carry thousands of custom-made rings and can even customize their own wedding bands to match your engagement ring. Wedding Ring Originals has work by many designers in designs ranging from "Victorian" to contemporary, at extremely reasonable prices.

Bridal Gowns

We all know that the bride is the center of attention at every wedding, and as she walks down that aisle, hundreds of eyes snap to—the dress. Shopping for a wedding gown can be an exhilarating experience, one that fulfills all your childhood dreams of being a princess bride. Then again, when you're schlepping off to a bridal warehouse sale with your mother, it doesn't seem so glamorous. Keeping certain key factors in mind as you're shopping will help you remain in control of the situation—and have a good time, too.

Dress basics

● A gown can't magically transform you into another person. It won't make you taller or make your neck longer. Don't go shopping expecting a miraculous transformation. Keep an open mind and ask your salesperson or bridal consultant to help you choose a gown that flatters your figure and accentuates your best features.

● Listen to everyone's advice, but pick a gown you really love. If you choose the cream puff your mother likes you may spare her feelings, but you may end up feeling uncomfortable on your wedding day.

● Start looking for your gown early. Some custom bridal salons require that you order your gown nine months to a year in advance. Remember that you'll most likely need at least two (and maybe as many as four or five) fittings before your gown is ready to sweep down the aisle. Give yourself plenty of time to find your dress; then avoid rush fees by giving the salon plenty of time to get it ready.

● Don't forget about accessories. After you purchase your gown, you're going to need shoes, a headpiece, a veil (optional), gloves (also optional), and the right lingerie (mandatory!). Save some cash for these extras.

● Most shops require a 50 percent deposit when you order your gown. The balance is generally due at the first fitting or when you pick the gown up.

● Pay with a credit card. This gives you more rights as a consumer. You can get a receipt no matter how you pay, but some credit cards offer insurance if your gown turns out to be flawed.

Questions to ask before you buy

● If you're having a gown custom made, will the designer create a "muslin" (a practice gown) first to make sure you love the style?

● Will they alter an off-the-rack gown (one that wasn't custom made for you but was perhaps a sample in the shop) so it will fit you? If so, how much will it be for alterations?

● Do they have seamstresses available on site? (Most salons do.)

● What do they charge for a rush job?

In-the-know tips

● Most gowns run small—about two sizes smaller than street clothes.

● Alterations can take a month to complete after your first fitting.

● Keep an open mind when looking at gowns. You just might surprise yourself with the gown you ultimately choose.

● Don't buy the first dress you try on—until you've tried on others and you're sure it's the one.

● Get everything in writing. You're probably paying more for this gown than you've ever paid for any article of clothing, so have the shop write down exactly what you're getting. This is especially important for custom gowns.

● Keep in mind that bridal-shop appointments take one to two hours.

Space them out: You don't want to try to do six in one day.

● If you can, go shopping during the week to avoid the weekend rush.

● When you go to your fittings, bring the exact undergarments (bustier, control-top hose, etc.) and shoes you'll wear on your wedding day. They make a big difference in the way the gown fits and is altered.

● If you buy bridesmaids' gowns at the same shop where you buy your gown, you may be able to get a group discount.

● Tell the shop that your wedding is a few weeks before it really is so your gown will definitely be ready on time.

NEW YORK CITY

Amsale

625 Madison Avenue · New York, NY
212-583-1700
www.amsale.com
$: Gowns start at around $2,500

Amsale Aberra designs strong, classical, elegant bridal and evening gowns that, if you haven't seen them on brides, you have spied in celebrity snapshots or in the movies (Julia Roberts wore an Amsale dress in *Runaway Bride)*. Her work is fresh and sophisticated and wonderfully structured. A terrific feature on the Amsale website is a collection of photographs of real brides wearing her dresses, so you can get a sense of how they look "in action." Amsale does eveningwear and bridesmaid collections as well. By appointment only.

Barneys Bridal Salon

660 Madison Avenue • New York, NY 10021
212-826-8900
$: $3,000 to $12,000

The Barneys bridal salon carries the type of gowns you'd expect from the legendary department store, including haute couture designs from Richard Tyler, Pamela Dennis, Yohji Yakamoto, Lucy Barnes, as well as offbeat designers like Olivier Theyskens, and others. The salon also carries dresses from bridal designers such as Vera Wang.

Bergdorf Goodman

754 Fifth Avenue • New York, NY
212-872-8957
$: Gowns start at $2,500

Bergdorf's gives brides the ultimate New York experience: a deluxe bridal salon, lots of personal attention, and a wonderful selection. It's expensive, but Bergdorf's is a great resource for one-stop-shopping. Among the designers they carry are: Amsale, Angel Sanchez, Ines diSanto, Melissa Sweet, Ulla Maija, Carolina Herrera, Steven Stollman, and Badgeley Mishka. The bridal salon also offers a couture service that starts at $15,000. Some of the designers Bergdorf's carries are available to work directly with brides, making one-of-a-kind gowns for them. The salon also sells headpieces, veils, and shoes, and through the department store can recommend a personal shopper and cosmetics assistance. The salon recommends that brides start looking nine months to a year before the wedding. By appointment only.

Blue

125 St. Mark's Place • New York, NY 10009
212-228-7744
$: 1,300 to $2,500

Owner Christina Kara takes one look at her customers and pulls the perfect dress from her overstuffed racks every time. Even if you think you know what looks good on you, Kara knows better! Her shop contains a number of samples, but Kara custom designs all of the gowns, so any dress can be altered to your specifications: If you like the neckline of one gown and the skirt of another, no problem. Be prepared, though, for Kara's strong opinions. She's not shy about telling you what you should wear. Her gowns are sometimes funky, usually on fashion's cutting edge, but with a princess air. The tiny store is often mobbed, so make an appointment. Kara appreciates six months to design a dress; if you come earlier, she may suggest that you come back closer to the wedding date.

The Bridal Atelier by Mark Ingram

1227 East 56th Street, 3rd Floor • New York, NY 10022
212-391-6778 • Fax: 212-319-6774
www.bridalatelier.com
$: Gowns start at about $2,200

Put all your fears about fussy bridal salons behind you when you go to the Bridal Atelier. Mark Ingram, who managed the former Wearkstatt store in Soho, has created a wonderful, comfortable, friendly bridal shop specializing in beautiful gowns. Among the designers carried at the Bridal Atelier are Peter Langner, Anne Barge, Monique Lhuillier, Angel Sanchez, and Judd Waddell, and they are the only shop in Manhattan to carry the complete Wearkstatt collection of bridal gowns. The Bridal Atelier can also help you with accessories: headpieces, veils, and wraps. The staff is friendly, well informed, very helpful, and will provide you with excellent advice. By appointment only.

The Bridal Buildings

1385 Broadway and 1375 Broadway • New York, NY 10018
www.bridalbuilding.com
$: Varies, depending on what's available and which showrooms are open

The Bridal Buildings house a slew of bridal designers' showrooms and sales offices. It's a little-known secret that some of these are open to the public on Saturdays. Expect some chaos, but you may walk away with a deal. Ask for prices before you agree to alterations, though—sometimes fees can be exorbitant. Some showrooms are only open from 9 A.M. to 2:30 P.M., but some are open all day.

The Bridal Garden

122 East 29th Street • New York, NY 10016
212-252-0661
www.bridalgarden.org
$: $295 to $2,695

Sheltering Arms Children's Service, one of New York City's premier nonprofits, runs this bridal shop. They've been helping disadvantaged children since 1823. Most of their gowns are from designers who have donated their overstocked or sample gowns. Dresses are sold at approximately 65 percent off their original prices. Designers available include Vera Wang, Amsale, Wearkstatt, Badgley Mishka, One of a Kind Bride, and many more. You can shop by appointment only. Seamstresses are on hand to do alterations for an extra charge.

Cynthia C. & Company

414 West Broadway • New York, NY 10012
212-966-2200
www.cynthiac.com
$: $2,000 to $5,000

Cynthia Corhan began designing sophisticated wedding gowns 17 years ago, and finally had the opportunity to design a dress for her own wedding in 1999. She uses fine silk fabrics from around the world (including organza, charmeuse, satin, and more) to create designs with a clean, elegant simplicity. Many are finished with hand embroidery and beadwork. Recently she's had many calls for strapless gowns as well as gowns in subtle hues such as silvery gray and light yellow. Gowns generally take six months to create; in emergencies, a simple sheath can be completed in as little as a week, and other rush gowns can be had within six weeks for an extra charge.

David's Bridal

General phone: 800-399-2743 • Brooklyn, NY: 718-238-1633
Long Island City, NY: 718-784-8200 • Yonkers, NY: 914-779-1366
Carle Place, NY: 516-741-9898 • Springfield, NJ: 973-921-9090
Paramus, NJ: 201-587-9774 • East Brunswick, NJ: 732-249-6552
Danbury CT: 203-778-4499 • Manchester, CT: 860-645-7883
Orange, CT: 203-891-8300
www.davidsbridal.com
$: $99 (during $99 sales) to $1,000

David's Bridal claims to have everything the bride needs except the groom, so if you're interested in one-stop bridal shopping, check out the David's nearest you. With 150 stores across the United States, this is the largest bridal-gown retailer in the country—which has its pros and cons. David's combines the variety of choices of a superstore (thousands of gowns and dresses) with personalized boutique service (bridal consultants work with you). Gowns for maids, moms, and flower girls are available, as well as accessories from tiaras to shoes and even gown-preservation services. David's generally carries sizes from 2 to 26, and in-house seamstresses can do alterations. The stores are famous for $99 sales, but the gowns are generally samples and can be fairly worn by the time they're sold. David's also carries a number of "house" brands, including Oleg Cassini, Gloria Vanderbilt, and Enzio. The company has bought the rights to use these designer labels; be aware that the gowns are designed by David's, not by the designers themselves. Check out the website for specific location information and for dozens of images.

Gene London's Fan Club

22 West 19th Street • New York, NY 10011
212-929-3349
$: Custom gowns range from $500 to $2,000;
vintage gowns start at $300

This amazing vintage store carries all sorts of antique gowns (many of which were used in films) that can be altered for the perfect fit. The shop also offers dresses designed and manufactured in house—their signature 1930s form-fitting gowns are extremely popular. Custom gowns are ready three months from the ordering date; vintage gowns are available immediately.

The Gown Company

312 East 9th Street • New York, NY 10003
212-979-9000
www.thegowncompany.com

The Gown Company Atelier
Alterations and Custom Work
333 East 9th Street • New York, NY 10003
212-979-7800

$: Starting price for samples: $800 to $1,500; custom orders: $1,300 to $4,500; average price is $2,500. Custom-designed gowns start at $2,000.

The Gown Company started as a sample sale company, producing sample sales for wedding gown designers and gradually began selling both samples and excess inventory by designers like Peter Langner, Lazaro, Helen Morley, Marianna Hardwick, and others. All of their off-the-rack dresses are discounted at least 50 percent from what you would pay at bridal salons. The Gown Company also can custom order gowns (at full price) directly from designers the same way bridal stores do, so if you're having a hard time finding the gown you've set your heart on, the Gown Company may be able to help you get it. Go to the Atelier, the Gown Company's "sister store" across the street for alterations, or you can have a gown custom made to your own specifications right there.

Ilana

Dressmaker and Seamstress
150 East 69th Street · New York, NY
212-570-9420
$: Depends on the amount of work you need, the fabric costs, and style

Ilana is a great dressmaker and tailor who can do everything from restructuring your dress to creating something from scratch. If you want her to make your wedding gown, Ilana asks that you bring in not only pictures of your dream dress, but a favorite piece of clothing from your own closet, so she can see what you like to wear and what your style really is. She will do a series of fittings and, if the dress is complicated, will put together a muslin model for you. In addition to making wedding gowns, Ilana does alterations and can make non-wedding clothing. She works by appointment only and for wedding dresses, she says it's best to allow four to six months.

Jana Starr

236 East 80th Street · New York, NY 10021
212-861-8256
$: $500 to $2,800

Jana Starr has been in business for 27 years, and her motto is: "I never put a bride in something she doesn't belong in." Her shop sells original gowns, usually fashioned of antique handmade lace and silk, from every decade from 1900 to 1970, and she takes care to customize each dress for the wearer. Starr's brides send her photographs from their weddings, which she keeps in albums so you can see how the antique gowns look when they get updated for modern weddings. Jana Starr also consults and works with a dressmaker in the restoration and modification of family heirloom or archive dresses. She's accustomed to discriminating clientele—she's sold gowns to Phoebe Cates and Amy Carter. One big plus is that turnaround time is minimal, since the dress is being modified, not built from scratch. Walk-ins during store hours are welcome and evening appointments can be arranged. Call for more information.

Jane Wilson-Marquis

155 Prince Street · New York, NY
212-477-4408
and
130 East 82nd Street · New York, NY
212-452-5335
www.bridalgowns.net
$: Ready-to-wear gowns for $1,000 to $2,000

Jane Wilson-Marquis is an Englishwoman who has been designing beautiful clothing in Soho since 1985. While she does couture eveningwear and even has a ready-to-wear evening line, she has earned a wonderful reputation for her bridal lines. Her work is exquisite, romantic, and utterly unique. First and foremost, she is concerned with fit and tailoring her dresses to her brides. She works in rich European fabrics and all of the details are imaginative, elegant, and complement the structure and silhouette of the dresses. Wilson-Marquis does couture wedding gowns and has an ever-growing line of ready-to-wear bridal dresses as well. In addition, she does terrific bridesmaid and flower-girl dresses and carries gorgeous headpieces, spectacular veils, and other accessories. By appointment only.

Karin Yngvesdotter Couture

24-31 41st Street · Astoria, NY 11103
718-278-9295
www.yngvesdotter.com · kyngvesdotter@nyc.rr.com
$: Simplest gown starts at $1,000

Karin Yngvesdotter offers so many options to her brides it is hard to know how to describe her. She is a wonderful designer and puts together inspired collections. Her strengths are in cut and fit, and she creates architectural, sleek gowns with clean, carved lines. Her work draws inspiration from many sources: Hollywood glamour of the 1930s, Celtic culture, contemporary fashion, and most important, the bride. Yngvesdotter prides herself on her custom work and she likes to work with the bride to create a gown that is truly unique. For each gown, she puts together muslin models and does many fittings to ensure that the dress has a perfect fit; she can embellish the final dress with hand embroidery, beadwork, and lace. When you go to Yngvesdotter, you visit her at her home and the casual, warm environment will make you happy, relaxed, and able to think about creating your dream dress. You can also bring a dress you already have to Yngvesdotter for complicated alterations and restructuring. She is a pleasure to work with.

Kleinfeld

8202 Fifth Avenue · Brooklyn, NY 11209
718-765-8500
www.kleinfeldbridal.com
$: Dresses start at $1,800; average is $3,000

A New York institution, Kleinfeld is the ultimate NYC bridal salon, featuring 900 wedding dresses, plus every accessory imaginable to complete your wedding ensemble. Co-owner Mara Urshel says the store carries the best of American and European designers, and staffs over 50 alteration specialists. Kleinfeld claims to be the biggest bridal salon in the city and the selection here is definitely very upscale. Brides work with a personal gown consultant, so call for an appointment. One tip: If your consultant isn't bringing you the gown you're seeing in your mind's eye, ask if you can cruise the racks solo. Kleinfeld recommends coming in 6 to 12 months before the big day, although some stock and sample gowns can be ready more quickly.

Lestan Fashion Headquarters

1902 Ralph Avenue · Brooklyn, NY 11234
718-531-0800 · Fax: 718-531-0005
$: $400 to $3,000

This family-run Brooklyn shop has a huge selection of bridal gowns in sizes 2 to 30 and carries a range of American designers, including Eve of Milady, Diamond Collection, Maggie Sottero, Mori Lee, and more. Service is extremely personable, and appointments are recommended. Lestan suggests that you contact the store six to eight months before your wedding. There is a rush charge for quick turnarounds.

Mary Adams, The Dress

138 Ludlow Street · New York, NY 10002
212-473-0237
www.maryadaamsthedress.com
$: $1,500 to $3,500

Mary Adams's gowns are elaborate and whimsical, yet very feminine. They focus largely on back details, including beautiful bustles. Adams has a wide range of customers, including stylish, funky, feminine women who want something different. In fact, she rarely makes a traditional white gown and often works in color: all-red gowns, white dresses with colored coats, an ornate pink-and-gold gown. Adams also works with all sorts of silks and does some hand beading. She has a seamstress on the premises to do alterations. Adams generally requires six months to deliver a gown but is sometimes willing to do rush orders.

Michael's, The Consignment Shop for Women

1041 Madison Avenue · New York, NY 10021
212-737-7273 · Fax: 212-737-7211
info@michaelsconsignment.com · www.michaelsconsignment.com
$: $350 to $1,200

A New York City institution for almost 50 years, Michael's specializes in the resale of pristine, preowned designer clothing and accessories. Michael's offers high fashion and the best designer-name brands, including Vera Wang, Yumi Katsura, Christian Dior, Amsale, Carolina Herrera, in sizes 2 to 14. However, no alterations are available on site.

Michelle Roth

24 West 57th Street, Suite 203 · New York, NY 10019
212-245-3390
www.michelleroth.com · info@michelleroth.com
$: $2,900 and up

The Michelle Roth atelier houses her amazing collection, along with a small selection of European wedding gowns. Her work is exquisite, chic, and, since she really focuses on providing the finest possible fitting, the level of customer service is very high. Wedding dresses by Michelle Roth are all made of fine silk fabrics and decorated with delicate embellishments and beading. She believes that there should be no limits to the bride's gown: "Two things must never know any boundaries—love and the wedding dress." Roth's work has been featured on "Martha Stewart Living" and "Oprah," and in magazines such as *Vogue, Elle,* and *Town and Country.*

Miri Designs

501 Seventh Avenue, Suite 506 · New York, NY 10018
212-869-3844 · Fax: 212-869-3849
$: wedding gowns start at $3,100; mother-of-the-bride suits start at $1,970

Miriam Urbach, the designer of Miri creates lavish and opulent dresses that make brides absolutely glow. She works in luxurious fabrics and adorns them with hand embroidery, inventive beading, handmade fabric flowers, and French lace. Miri Designs are wonderfully feminine, emphasizing the figure with built in bustiers and impeccable tailoring. If you're looking for wonderful haute couture wedding gowns, evening gowns, or suits, visit Miri Designs. By appointment only.

New York Wedding Center

118 Bowery · New York, NY 10013
646-613-9800
$: $100 and up

New York Wedding Center is a New York legend. The store carries stock gowns from designers such as Alfred Angelo and Mon Cheri and does custom work as well. On-site tailors and designers will even copy dresses from pictures you bring in. And with the purchase of a bridal dress of $500 or more, you get a bridesmaid's gown free. The shop requires 8 to 12 weeks for custom designs but can rush an off-the-rack gown in two weeks.

One of a Kind Bride Designs by Candace Solomon

89 Fifth Avenue · New York, NY 10003
212-645-7123
$: 1,500 to $12,000 for ready-to-wear separates for brides;
$4,500 to $12,000 for couture collection. Store has a year-round
sample rack with reduced-price dresses in sizes 2 to 10.

Owner Candice Solomon's designs have been featured in *Martha Stewart Weddings.* Her best-sellers are strapless styles and halter gowns with fitted bodices and full skirts. One of a Kind requires 4 to 10 months to create a gown, depending on the design and the amount of embroidery or beading. Any gown ordered less than four months in advance of the wedding will include a rush charge of 10 percent of the total price of the gown. Her dresses are available only in her showroom; shopping is by appointment only.

Penny Babel Couturier

19 East 69th Street · New York, NY 10021
212-879-5844
$: Custom, $2,000 to $6,000; heirloom gown restyling, $300 to $1,000

If you're looking to flex your design skills, Penny Babel will work with you to dream up and create an original wedding gown. The end result is extremely high quality, often with an old-world couture look. Babel works only in fine fabrics. Depending on the time of year, she requires four months to design and create a custom gown; she can do rushes only when her workload is light.

Babel also restyles vintage gowns. She ususlly adds new elements, and even takes gowns completely apart and virtually redesigns them. (She doesn't do any reweaving of worn fabric or lace.) She can remain true to the gown's original feel or completely reinvent it. For example, one customer needed an heirloom gown made dramatically larger. Babel created a completely new bodice and used the embroidered lace of the original dress to create the skirt of the new dress. She has also taken 1930s sleeved gowns and made them off-the-shoulder, and has made 1950s gowns more modern by taking out extra crinolines for a more streamlined look. Babel usually requires four months for gown restyling as well.

Quentzal Haute Couture

Greenwich Village
888-605-5988
$: ready to wear, $900 and up; custom, $1,600 and up

Designer Lourdes Currie has been in business for over 20 years. She started out creating Mexican wedding dresses, then turned to designing replicas of Victorian gowns. Now she designs for the sophisticated bride and specializes in art deco—era gowns. Her 1930s collection has sheer, sexy designs in silk chiffon adorned with chantilly lace, bugle beads, crystals, freshwater pearls, and natural seashells. Many of her designs have been worn to the Academy Awards. Her European collection—formal, structured, and elegant designs—can be made as separates as well. Currie generally needs three months to create a gown, although six-week rushes are sometimes possible. Shopping is by appointment only.

Randi Rahm

407 East 58th Street, New York, NY 10022
Moving to: 574 Fifth Avenue, New York, NY 10036
212-223-7187 / 212-869-2296
www.randirahm.com
$: Bridal gowns are custom couture and start at $5,000;
evening, everyday, and wedding separates can cost less

Randi Rahm's wedding gowns are powerful, timeless, and 100 percent original. Her work is classic, and she subtly reworks and innovates vintage styles to give them a modern twist. Her gowns are all made in-house, from the sewing to the beading; nothing is sent out, so the work is carefully supervised from start to finish. One of Rahm's particular strengths is that she makes clothes for real women, using design tricks that can transform and enhance your body. She also likes to create gowns that can be reused after the wedding. Bustiers can be detached from ballgown skirts so they can be worn later as separates. In addition to wedding gowns, Rahm designs everyday clothing, evening gowns, and children's dresses. Allow 4 to 6 months to work with Randi Rahm on your dress. Rahm works by appointment only.

Reem Acra

245 Seventh Avenue, Suite 6B · New York, NY 10001
212-414-0980
www.reemacra.com
$: Dresses start at $3,000; custom couture gowns start at $12,000

Reem Acra specializes in simple, elegant A-line gowns in silk satin, silk crepe, and silk organza that are embellished with exquisite hand embroidery and beadwork. Her gowns are always sophisticated and beautifully ornate. Acra also carries an amazing selection of matching tiaras. She works by appointment only and generally requires six months to create most bridal gowns, but she can work more quickly for a rush fee.

Reva Mivasagar

28 Wooster Street • New York, NY 10013
212-334-3860 • Fax: 212-334-3861
$: $2,000 to $5,000

Reva Mivasagar offers both eveningwear and bridal gowns in his Soho shop, with an emphasis on clean, sophisticated lines. Alterations are done on the premises. Mivasagar has 72 choices in his "fabric library," including silk charmeuse, silk organza, silk chiffon, satin-faced organza, and nine types of duchess silk satin. Mivasagar will make as many muslin practice dresses as needed to get the sizing perfect and then creates your custom gown. Expect anywhere from five to seven fittings. Customers can walk into his shop, but appointments are recommended.

You can also purchase shop samples at a discount, but you must pay at least $100 in alteration charges and $50 in dry-cleaning charges.

RK Bridal

318 West 39th Street • New York, NY 10018
800-929-9512
www.rkbridal.com
$: $300 and up

RK Bridal crams a lot into a small space, carrying over 450 gowns by designers such as Jim Hjelm, Marisa, House of Bianchi, Eve of Milady, Jasmine Bridal, the Diamond Collection, and more—all at discount prices. The store also carries gowns for maids and flower girls as well as accessories. They will make custom changes to some gowns. It generally takes up to four months for gowns to come in (depending on delivery from the manufacturer); if the manufacturer doesn't have your gown in stock, you can pay a rush charge for quicker delivery.

Saks Fifth Avenue, The Bridal Salon

611 Fifth Avenue • New York, NY 10022
212-753-4000
$: $2,800 and up; average cost is approximately $3,200

Saks Fifth Avenue's bridal salon carries over 100 sample gowns, all of them available on special order; they don't sell samples except during special sales. Saks designers include Badgley Mischka, Ulla-Maija, Vera Wang, Carolina Herrera, Amsale, and more. Shopping is by appointment; each bride is matched with a consultant for an hour. The salon also has its own alteration staff, which is meticulous about getting you a perfect fit. It generally takes four to eight months for a Saks gown to be ready, but rushes can be done for a fee and usually take a month, depending on the designer.

Selia Yang

328 East 9th Street • New York, NY 10003
212-254-9073 • Fax: 212-393-1126
www.seliayang.com • info@seliayang.com
$: Wedding gowns start at $1,800; bridesmaid dresses start at $275

Visit Selia Yang's tiny, elegant East Village shop and you'll be swept away by her exquisite designs. Yang has been designing wedding and bridesmaid gowns for over five years and began bridal work at the request of her clients who were looking for simple, sophisticated designs. She uses beautiful materials in inventive ways: layers of organza create a soft, structured look, and silk satin glows behind hand beading and embroidery. Her bridesmaid dresses are inventive, wearable, and make fabulous cocktail dresses. Yang's work is clean and modern and will make you feel beautiful.

Sposa Bella

8207 Fifth Avenue • Brooklyn, NY 11209
718-680-9665
$: $2,000 and up

All bridal gowns are completely custom made at Sposa Bella. There are no gowns in stock; instead, you'll find albums full of photos of gowns the store has made in the past. Describe your dream gown and they'll whip it right up. The most frequent requests are gowns with tight bodices, ball-gown skirts, and extremely long trains. Turnaround time is three to four months.

Vera Wang

991 Madison Avenue • New York, NY 10021
212-628-3400
www.verawang.com
$: $3,000 and up

Vera Wang is one of the best-known bridal designers in the world, having created a classic and elegant style that has become her trademark. She works with a wide variety of fine fabrics, satin, twill, tulle, and matte jersey. The detailing on her dresses, which can include long sashes, fancy trims, fabric corsages, and lace-up backs, is exquisite and romantic. Wang has a large celebrity clientele and her work has become the prototype of sophisticated, modern style. Wang also designs some accessories and has teamed with shoe designer Stuart Weitzman to produce a line of fabulous wedding shoes.

Yumi Katsura Bridal House

907 Madison Avenue • New York, NY 10021
212-772-3016
www.yumikatsura.com
$: Dresses start at $3,000

East meets West in Japanese bridal house Yumi Katsura's sensual bridal gowns. Designer Erisa Katsura, who also designs couture gowns, uses amazing silk fabrics (including crepe and chiffon) to create gowns that drape the body and seem to float as the bride moves. Katsura's dresses are extremely modern, perfect for the high-fashion bride. It generally takes about three to four months to create a gown, but work can be done faster for an additional rush charge. Shopping is by appointment only.

LONG ISLAND

Antique Costume and Prop Rental

709 Main Street • Port Jefferson, NY 11777
631-331-2261 • Fax: 631-331-9692
www.antiquecostume.com
$: $100 to $600 (rentals)

This antique costume and prop-rental shop is housed in a Victorian mansion. Each room is set with period furniture and a costume outfit for the bride, so she can experience an actual setting for her wedding. (She can even have her wedding photos taken here.) Brides come here from all over the country and Europe to be outfitted for historic weddings. In fact, Antique Costume and Prop Rental is one of the biggest outfitters for historic weddings in the country, offering medieval to modern bridal gear. The store can outfit the entire wedding party for less than what a bride normally pays for an inexpensive wedding gown. Accessories are available, and all alterations are done on site at no cost to the bride. Shopping is by appointment only.

Bridal Couture of Manhasset

1663 Northern Boulevard · Manhasset, NY 11030
516-365-8455
$: $1,000 to $7,000

Bridal Couture of Manhasset has been in business for over 12 years and carries a large selection of gowns in all sorts of styles. Designers include Jim Hjelm, Vera Wang, Richard Tyler, Bob Mackie, Marisa, and more. The store can also create custom gowns. Full-service alterations are available for an additional charge. Custom gowns take approximately eight months.

The Bridal Suite

2449 Middle Country Road · Centereach, NY 11720
631-585-6040 · Fax: 631-585-3156
www.thebridalsuite.com
$: $500 to $2,500

In business for over 27 years, this Centereach bridal salon has gowns for the bride, bridesmaids, mothers of the bride, and some flower-girl dresses. It boasts a large selection of designers, including Jim Hjelm, Marisa, Eve of Milady, Illisa, and Jasmine and carries sizes for both petite and full-figured brides, plus more than 40 lines of dresses for moms and maids. Six seamstresses work on site. The average price of a gown sold here is $850, so stop in if you're looking to get a great gown at a low price. Orders should be placed from six months to a year in advance of the wedding.

Lillettes

861 Merrick Road · Baldwin, NY 11510
516-546-5660 · Fax: 516-546-5651
$: $800 to $2,500

This Baldwin salon has been in business for 50 years and carries gowns by designers such as Mori Lee, Paloma Blanca, Illisa, and the Diamond Collection in sizes 2 to 30. The most requested style is a simple, classic Audrey Hepburn/Grace Kelly look. The shop says that each bride is a celebrity to them: If you buy a gown from Lillettes, they'll even give you a "Down the Aisle in Bridal Style" video. Lillettes is happy to do custom work for plus-size brides, up to any size. They can also make alterations to gowns, such as adding sleeves to a strapless gown. The shop also sells shoes, jewelry, purses, and they are great about finding the perfect bra for you. Turnaround time is six to eight months depending on the style of the gown; rushes are possible for an extra charge. Shopping is by appointment only.

Lynbrook Bridal Center

416 Sunrise Highway · Lynbrook, NY 11563
516-599-1151 · Fax: 516-887-5260
$: $400 and up

If you're looking for a wide selection of plus-size bridal gowns (as well as a variety of styles in other sizes), check out the Lynbrook Bridal Center. The store sells gowns by designers including Eve of Milady, Illisa, Mon Cheri, Mori Lee, Alfred Angelo, Moonlight Design, and more. In-stock gowns can be ready in as little as four days; gowns ordered from manufacturers take five to six months. No appointment is necessary.

My Daughter's Wedding III

37 South Middleneck Road · Great Neck, NY 11021
516-773-7778
$: $1,000 to $5,000

My Daughter's Wedding III carries designer gowns from Scassi, Rose Taft, and Steven Yeurich, but owner Yon Kim can custom design any gown you desire. She has an incredibly loyal customer base and is known for excellent alterations. A custom gown can be ready in as little as eight weeks; it takes at least three months for designer gowns.

Nancy Sinoway

595 Willis Avenue · Williston Park, NY 11596
516-873-7377 · Fax: 516-873-6031
$: $1,600 and up

Nancy Sinoway is a former production manager for Vera Wang and has run her own bridal studio for 15 years. She designs each custom gown herself, favoring traditional styles with tulle skirts and satin bodices. Sinoway also offers "alternative" bridal gowns for older brides, brides marrying for the second time, or anyone who wants something a little different. In fact, she'll make any gown you can imagine. Gowns can take anywhere from three days to three months to be ready, depending on the fabric and styling.

New Jersey

Bridal and Costuming by Lady Gwendolyn

17 South Broadway • Pitman, NJ 08071
856-589-4344 • Fax: 856-589-4344
www.ladygwen.com
$: Call for prices

Lady Gwendolyn stocks historically accurate gowns for theme weddings, with an emphasis on the medieval period. Owner Gwen Lowe also offers contemporary wedding gowns (discounted at 20 to 40 percent) and gowns on consignment. She carries veils, headpieces, gloves, jewelry, and more to complete your ensemble.

Lady Gwendolyn can also outfit men in historic costumes or traditional tuxedos. Check out the store's website for examples. You may just get inspired to have your own historic wedding! Turnaround time is 16 to 18 weeks for contemporary designer gowns. Custom period gowns take about two months. Rentals can be taken home the same day.

Bridal Salon

534 West Side Avenue • Jersey City, NJ 07304
201-433-1884
$: $199 and up

Owner Patricia Foo has been in business for over 11 years and does all the designing for this Jersey City bridal salon. All gowns are made to measure, and Foo says her most popular designs are A-line with beading and embroidery. A basic gown takes six weeks to create; Foo needs twelve weeks or longer during her busiest months, February through August. She also designs bridesmaid dresses. Shopping is by appointment only.

Elegant Brides

175 Center Avenue • Westwood, NJ 07675
201-666-6669
$: $500 and up

Elegant Brides carries designers such as Richard Glasgow, Tomasina, Jasmine, and Mon Cheri. The most popular designs are halter bodices, strapless dresses, and A-line gowns. Turnaround time is four to six months, or three months with an added rush charge.

Irene's Bridal of Short Hills

9 Roosevelt Avenue · Chatham, NJ 07928
973-701-7337 · Fax: 973-701-7339
www.irenesbridal.com · www.irenesbridal@hotmail.com
$: $1,500 and up

You could say that Irene's is the "first bridal salon" of New Jersey—its designers created both of New Jersey Governor Christine Todd Whitman's inauguration gowns. Irene's carries designer gowns but can also create custom styles. In addition, the shop carries gowns for mothers, so you can gussy up the whole bridal party in one spot. Turnaround time is five to nine months; custom gowns take nine months to a year. Rush work is available (call for information). She also does accessories, flower-girl dresses, and eveningwear.

Piera's Bridal

1104 Main Street · Belmar, NJ 07719
732-280-1977
$: $350 and up

This Belmar bridal salon has a corner on glamour: They've made evening gowns for Mrs. New Jersey and several Miss Americas. The shop's signature style is simple, elegant, and traditional, with little embellishment. Custom gowns are made of high-quality fabrics such as silk, and Piera's also stocks gowns by designers such as Demitrios, Victoria, and Eden Bridal. On-site seamstresses will also do alterations on gowns purchased elsewhere. Delivery on gowns in stock can be immediate; custom gowns take about six months.

CONNECTICUT

Cameo Bridal Boutique

270 Federal Road · Brookfield, CT 06804
203-744-8359 · Fax: 203-775-6195
$: $700 and up

Cameo Bridal Boutique specializes in elegant, understated gowns with clean lines. The shop carries a range of gowns, including Angelique, Jasmine, and Dimitrios, as well as a full line of accessories. Cameo created the gown for Kiss band member Ace Frehley's bride, so you know they know how to rock! Turnaround time ranges from four to six months. However, if you order a stock gown, delivery can be much faster.

Razook's

45 East Putnam Avenue · Greenwich, CT 06830
203-661-6693 · Fax: 203-661-9115
$: Call for prices

Razook's carries ready-to-wear and custom gowns. The store also carries designs by outside designers in addition to its own private label. The store is known for its hands-on fitting. Custom designs take at least six months; off-the-rack selections are available more quickly. Rush charges depend on the gown selected.

Veils and Headpieces

Most bridal boutiques and salons also offer veils, but if you're looking for a very specific style or are wearing an heirloom gown and want to add contemporary veiling, these shops may be a godsend for you. You can also try taking a stroll through Manhattan's garment district; you'll find plenty of shops that offer veiling supplies, including fabrics by the yard, trim, cloth flowers—and even tiaras.

NEW YORK CITY

Chloe's Crown

46 Hicks Street · Brooklyn, NY
212-769-7643
www.chloescrown.com · Katie@chloescrown.com
$: Prices for custom work start at $250

If you're looking for a nontraditional headpiece that still has a vintage feel, try on some of the Chloe's Crown tiaras. Designer Katie Schmidt Feder started designing headpieces for her own wedding. Her work took off and now her pieces show at the Brooklyn Artisan's Gallery, at Stardust Antiques in Gramercy Park, and at Jane Wilson-Marquis's high-end bridal shop. Schmidt Feder's work is delicate and unusual, combining fine twisted wire with vintage beads, Swarovski crystal, and semi-precious stones to produce singular headpieces. She also loves to do custom work and can incorporate sentimental elements—pieces of family jewelry, like an earring or a broach—into the piece to give it extra significance. She even structures her pieces so that they can be worn after the wedding as chokers. Headpieces from Chloe's Crown take about two to six weeks to create.

Cinderella Division of Margola Corporation

48 West 37th Street • New York, NY 10018
212-564-2929
$: $40 and up

The veil department of this garment-district retailer offers both veils and headpieces. You can buy them together or just one or the other. They carry beautiful, ready-made long veils complete with silk-flower wreaths and will create custom veils as well. Their biggest call is for headpieces incorporating ceramic flowers and hand-wired beading. They can copy most magazine styles; bring in a photo and they'll work their magic. Cinderella has a new line of tiaras from Europe that can be purchased alone or with matching earrings and necklace. The store appreciates brides who give them three to four weeks to create a veil and/or headpiece, but they will do emergency rushes.

Fenaroli

501 7th Avenue, Suite 416 • New York, NY 10018
212-764-5924
www.fenaroli.com
$: Veils start at $100; handbags: $65 and up;
headpieces and tiaras: $200

Fenaroli's Manhattan showroom is packed with bridal accessories. They sell everything from veils and tiaras to shoes, handbags, jewelry, and flower-girl dresses, living up to their motto: Everything but the Gown. They have beautiful headpieces and hair combs finished in seed pearls and Swarovski crystals, and dyeable satin shoes. Their work is traditional and elegant, and they are happy to work with brides on custom pieces. Fenaroli is by appointment only.

Justine by Design

1-866-842-7277
www.justinebydesign.com
$: Tiaras start at $200

Justine, a transplanted Englishwoman, has been designing her exquisite tiaras and headpieces for several years and does a lot of work with the bridal-gown designer Jane Wilson-Marquis. The work touches on Greek, Elizabethan, and medieval designs, but there is a simplicity and an elegance to the headpieces that make them wonderful, imaginative complements to contemporary wedding dresses. "My brides want to feel like princesses for a day but still feel comfortable, like themselves." All of Justine's tiaras, headpieces, and jewelry are made of hand-soldered silver or gold, not wound wire, and decorated with precious and semi-precious stones. Justine works by appointment only, and it usually takes her from two to six weeks to create a headpiece.

Manny's Millinery

26 West 38th Street · New York, NY 10018
212-840-2235
$: Headpiece "frames" start at $3 each; polyester flowers are $4.50
and up; silk flowers are $10.50 and up; 72-inch-wide veiling is $4/yard;
108-inch-wide veiling is $5.50/yard.

For the do-it-yourself bride, Manny's Millinery comes to the rescue will all sorts of bridal veiling supplies. You can pick up a range of silk and polyester flowers, as well as headpiece frames and several types of veiling.

Paul's Veil & Net

28 West 38th Street · New York, NY 10018
212-391-3822
$: Wholesale and retail; prices vary

You'll find friendly and knowledgeable service at Paul's, one of the largest bridal headwear shops in New York. They carry just about everything you'll need, including ready-made headpieces and veils, veiling by yard, headpiece frames, and tiaras. If you're looking to make your own veil or to have one made for you, you'll find it all here. Most of their work is custom veils.

Sposabella Lace and Veils

252 West 40th Street · New York, NY 10018
212-354-4729
www.sposabellalace.com
$: Veils range from $35 to over $500; average price is $150

An appointment is suggested at this veil emporium. Their philosophy is that the veil is a separate proposition from the wedding gown, so there's no need to bring photos of your gown with you to your appointment. They like to have three months to create a veil, although they can create some simple styles in as little as 24 hours.

The Wedding Library

50 East 81st Street · New York, NY 10028
212-327-0100 · Fax: 212-327-1069
www.weddinglibrary.net
claudiahanlin@weddinglibrary.net

Claudia Hanlin's Wedding Library sells amazing headpieces, veils, and other bridal accessories, in addition to providing a host of wedding planning information. See "Wedding Planners" for details.

Bright Ideas

74 East Ridgewood Avenue • Ridgewood, NJ 07450
201-652-0944
www.brightideas.com
$: Headpieces are $50 to $399; veils are $20 to $150

If you're looking to have a custom headpiece made in New Jersey, check out this bridal accessory retailer. They carry dyeable shoes—great for matching to those bridesmaids' dresses!

Sew and Show

401 North Avenue • Garwood, NJ 07027
908-789-2115
sewandshow@aol.com
$: $75 and up

Not only can you have a custom headpiece made here at a reasonable price, but you can also have alterations made to your bridal gown.

Tammy Darling
1 Henry Street • Basking Ridge, NJ 07920
908-696-8484
www.tammydarling.com
$: Hairpins start at $125; veils start at around $110;
tiaras average between $200 and $400

Tammy Darling makes fabulous headpieces, hair ornaments, and veils that are lively, sophisticated accents for almost any kind of wedding ensemble. While she does create beautiful white, sparkly pieces (one of which was featured on "Ally McBeal"), she is really known for her use of color. Darling's website shows off her wonderful pieces, but you should really visit her store where you can get a lot of personal attention and lots of help matching the perfect headpiece to your dress. In addition to tiaras, Darling also sells work by other designers, including Lori London, Kristina Eaton, Malis Henderson, and veils by Jennifer Lee, and is always expanding her bridal accessories—she also carries bags, jewelry, and shoes. Her shop is open Monday through Saturday; Thursday evenings by appointment.

Personal Gown Shoppers

NEW YORK CITY

Constance Breslin

212-988-2829
$: 20 percent of the total cost of the gown

Constance Breslin is a retired Bloomingdale's divisional merchandise manager and loves working with couture. She works with the newest and best-known designers and specializes in nontraditional wedding gowns. Her customers are generally career-oriented women in their thirties who are sure of what they want. Breslin can find an elegant couture gown, created especially for her client, at the right prices. But whether the dress costs $1,800 or $18,000, Breslin offers the same amount of personal service. She can also assist in finding suitable outfits for bridesmaids, the mother of the bride, even the groom. Contact her six months before your wedding.

Gail Kittenplan

212-348-8401
$: 20 percent of the total cost of the gown

Gail Kittenplan does both special-occasion and bridal personal shopping. She works with high-end designers and generally takes about two to three hours to find the perfect gown. Contact her four to six months before your wedding.

Marjorie Stokes

212-629-8889 · Fax: 212-239-9445
$: 20 percent of the total cost of the gown

Freddie Johnson is the new owner of the late Marjorie Stokes's business. She works exclusively with very expensive high-end American designers. She can generally choose a gown within three hours and goes with the bride to all fittings afterward. Fallen in love with a gown from a magazine or website? Johnson can locate it and often purchase it at a discount. Contact her six to eight months before your wedding.

NEW JERSEY

Jean Wyman, Inc.

Jean Wyman Buying Service
973-258-1236
$: 20 percent total cost of the gown and/or $300 per day

Jean Wyman has been in business for 30 years and works exclusively with top designers. She can generally find you the perfect gown within two days. Wyman can also find special-occasion dresses for the rest of the wedding party. She recommends that you contact her three or more months before your wedding.

Dry Cleaning and Preservation

NEW YORK CITY

Chris French Cleaners

57 Fourth Avenue • New York, NY 10003
212-475-5444
www.chriscleaners.com • bsil@chriscleaners.com
$: Dry cleaning starts at $200

Chris French Cleaners is a fabulous downtown dry cleaner that does precise, delicate work and knows how to take care of wedding-gown fabrics.

Jeeves of Bulgaria

39 East 65th Street • New York, NY 10021
212-570-9130
www.jeeves.co.uk
$: Dry cleaning is $350 and up, depending on gown style

This high-end dry cleaner has an excellent reputation for taking good care of designer and couture clothing.

Madame Paulette

1255 Second Avenue · New York, NY 10021
212-838-6827
$: Dry cleaning starts at $250

Madame Paulette has done couture bridal cleaning and preservation since 1959 and is recommended by a slew of designers, including Vera Wang and Badgley Mischka. For $1 each, the shop will even remove any buttons from your gown to prevent them from being damaged, then sew them back on after cleaning. They are super-meticulous with fabric, and use black light to find hidden stains. They even make stain-removal emergency kits you can bring with you on your wedding day.

CONNECTICUT

Orange Restoration

454 Old Cellar Road · Orange, CT 06477
1-800-950-6482
www.gownrestoration.com · wedngown@optonline.net
$: Silk, $249 and up; non-silk, $199 and up

If the heirloom gown you want to wear is discolored or has developed sugar stains (sugar can react with fabric, causing dark yellow stains), chances are Sally Lorenson Conant can restore its color close to the original. She can also dismantle headpieces to restore their coloring. (Most veiling doesn't hold up to cleaning, but antique headpieces can be cleaned and reused.) Conant's technique is recommended by Martha Stewart, Yumi Katsura, and *Modern Bride,* among others. She can work her magic overnight, but it's best to come to her early in your planning process. There can be some fabric shrinkage in color restoration, not all stains can be removed, and some fabrics loose their sheen after going through restoration. Ask about her free pressing deal.

A number of other tristate area cleaners offer the same color restoration process as Orange Restoration:

NEW YORK CITY

Hallak Cleaners

1232 Second Avenue • New York, NY 10021
212-832-0750
www.hallackcleaners.com
$: Wedding gowns start at $350

This dry cleaner has an amazing reputation for its work on wedding gowns. They use many techniques to protect delicate fabrics and can even arrange to pick up and deliver your gown.

Meurice Garment Care

800-240-3377
www.meuricegarmentcare.com

LONG ISLAND

Meurice Garment Care

800-240-3377
www.meuricegarmentcare.com

NEW JERSEY

Hallak Cleaners

172 Johnson Avenue • Hackensack, NJ 07601
201-343-7333
www.hallackcleaners.com
$: Wedding gowns start at $350

See under New York City.

VARIOUS LOCATIONS

Wedding Gown Specialists

www.weddinggownspecialist.com

Check out this website for a list of reputable gown restorers around the country.

Heirloom Gown Restoration and Restyling

NEW YORK CITY

Carolyn Niezgoda

2376 84th Street • Brooklyn, NY 11214
718-946-6652
www.carolynniez.com
$: Basic restoration and redesign for heirloom gowns starts at $1,000;
redesign of modern gowns starts at about $500

Carolyn Niezgoda will work within your budget to make an heirloom gown look as fresh and current as possible. If you want to honor a gown's spirit but don't want to completely restore it, Niezgoda can make the gown fit your style. She can take it apart and make it look wonderful and new, removing sleeves or changing the neckline or waistline to make your mother's or grandmother's gown your own. Neizgoda also cleans, restores, and restyles. She does headpieces, as well, though not tiaras. By appointment only.

NEW JERSEY

Creations Plus

16 Sears Place • Montclair, NJ 07042
973-783-6880
$: Averages $1,200 to $1,500, depending on the work to be done

Creations Plus alters, restores, and remodels antique and heirloom wedding gowns. How gown restoration is approached depends on what the client wants. Some brides want to wear their heirloom dress just as their mom did, but others want to use the gown's fabric to make an entirely new design. In the case of a severely damaged gown, they salvage what they can and can sometimes match fabric or lace to repair holes or tears. Restoration takes six to eight weeks, depending on the style of the gown, but the shop prefers three to six months. They also design dresses for the bride, mothers of the bride and groom, flower girls, and bridesmaids.

Marguerite Morgan Studio

P.O. Box 1575 · 6 Highland Cross · Rutherford, NJ 07070
201-939-7222
$: $300 and up, depending on the work to be done

Marguerite Morgan is simply a delight. She has a passion for antiques and has been in the textile business for over 20 years. She redesigns and restores wedding gowns, generally trying to keep the basic design intact. However, if a bride wants her vintage gown's design altered, she'll change a neckline, take in the skirt, drop a waistline, or otherwise modify the gown. She also does gown resizing. She likes to have three to six months to work on a gown.

CONNECTICUT

Carolyn Miller Vintage Dress Alterations

135 Long Meadow Hill · Brookfield, CT 06804
203-775-9065
$: Average restoration is $500

Carolyn Miller does heirloom-gown restyling as well as restoration. She is often called upon to make antique gowns fit modern brides. Her clients are mostly women who want to wear their mother's or grandmother's gown, but she's also made christening outfits and pillows out of wedding gowns. She can also preserve gowns by cleaning them and storing them in acid-free boxes. She likes to be contacted a year before a wedding but can do jobs in as little as two months.

BRIDESMAID DRESSES

Bridesmaid dresses are the stuff of legend and nightmares. Everyone knows, often firsthand, stories about disastrous and embarrassing outfits brides have picked out for their attendants, and the scary pictures from the wedding can provide years of hilarity whenever the wedding album gets pulled out. Here is a list of places that make good, chic bridesmaid dresses in a wide variety of styles that can accommodate any wedding.

Some tips for brides who are picking dresses:

● Consider going with a single color for the dresses, but allow your bridesmaids to wear a variety of styles. This way they can get dresses that flatter their figures. Some of the designers in the list specialize in providing a wide array of styles that can be made up in one fabric choice.

● Think about picking out bridesmaid dresses that have classic, rather then trendy, styles. Not only will your bridesmaids be grateful, your wedding pictures will look much less dated over the years. (A whole generation of women is trying to live down dresses with "bubble skirts" from the late '80s.)

● Don't worry if you have a pregnant bridesmaid. Many designers are prepared for anything and have started designing wonderful maternity bridesmaid dresses.

● Start shopping for dresses early and be sure to talk to your attendants about what they want and what would make them comfortable.

Ann Taylor

www.anntaylor.com
Dozens of locations across the country.
$: Prices vary per season; dresses can start at $50

If you want your maids to avoid being too "bridesmaidy" but still want them to have a uniform look, consider Ann Taylor. Their dresses and separates can be a bit conservative, but they are affordable, easy to find, and can be the perfect solution for brides looking to outfit their maids in something they can wear again. Ann Taylor is also a great resource for brides with far-flung bridesmaids. They can order online or visit any of the hundreds of stores across the United States.

Aria Bridesmaid Dresses

213-629-3085 or 800-658-8885
www.ariadress.com • inquiry@ariadress.com
Bridesmaid dresses from $175; Flower-girl dresses from $139

Aria Bridesmaid Dresses is a small Los Angeles design house that does elegant, sophisticated work in all-natural silk shantung, silk taffeta, and silk satin. Go to their website to see their wide range of designs and colors. They make dresses, separates and some accessories (bags and wraps). They are a wonderful resource and are eager to provide advice about the fit of their dresses, and the best choices to flatter figures. They even have a "Try-On Program" for out of state customers, where you can request that a favorite design be sent to you for up-close inspection. Dresses are usually ready 8 to10 weeks after your complete order has been placed.

Here Comes the Bridesmaid

238 West 14th St. · New York, NY 10011
212-647-9686
www.bridesmaids.com
and
218 Lakeville Road · Lake Success, NY 11020
516-466-2432
$: Dresses start around $170, but prices vary according to designer

Here Comes the Bridesmaid is a great one-stop shop for brides who are looking for a wide selection of bridesmaid and flower-girl dresses from an assortment of designers. The store stocks dresses by Nicole Miller, Siri, Watters & Watters, Jim Hjelm, Lazaro and more. They also carry some accessories. By appointment only.

Nicole Miller

780 Madison Avenue · New York, NY 10021
212-288-9779
and
134 Prince Street · New York, NY 10012
212-343-1362

NEW JERSEY:
The Mall at Short Hills
1200 Morris Tpk., Ste. D141 · Short Hills, NJ 07078
973-218-0911
www.nicolemiller.com
$: Prices start at about $255, but vary according to season

Nicole Miller is famous for her cocktail dresses, and her talent for stylish, comfortable, lively fashions carries over into her bridesmaid dresses. Her work is contemporary, colorful, easy to wear, and she makes sweaters, shawls, and bags to go with her bridal lines. If you're looking for something that isn't ultra-formal but which is still elegant, look no further. She works in a wide range of fabrics, patterns, and colors and styles dresses to fit all kinds of shapes.

Simple Silhouettes

542 Broadway, No. 2 · New York, NY 10012
212-219-2223 · Fax: 212-219-1488
www.simpledress.com · inquiry@simpledress.com
$: Knee length starts at $255; full length starts at $275

Designer Christina Dalle Pezze fell into the bridesmaid business by accident, designing elegant dresses for a friend's bridesmaids, and discovering the need for simple and wearable bridesmaid dresses. She works hard to keep her designs updated but classic, so that they have long lives and don't languish in closets. A benefit that Simple Silhouette offers is variety. Brides can come in and pick a color or palette of colors and then encourage her bridesmaids to select dresses or separates based on their own personal styles and what makes them comfortable. Customers can also shop through the website, which shows all of the designs, but it is recommended that someone visit the showroom to really get a sense of the styles. Simple Silhouettes also offers a small line of accessories including handbags, wraps, and some jewelry. They prefer for orders to be placed four months before the wedding.

Thread Design

26 West 17th Street, 3rd Floor
212-414-8844 · Fax: 212-414-9169
www.threaddesign.com · info@threaddesign.com
$: Prices starts at $250

Thread Design offers beautiful, classy dresses that bridesmaids would be hard-pressed to complain about. Beth Blake began designing dresses when her sister's bridesmaids needed dresses. Her creation can still be found on the Thread Design dress roster: "Style 901," a kicky spaghetti strap number. Their styles are clean and elegant with a wide variety of fabrics and colors, prints and solids, and they do spring and autumn collections. Thread also makes flower-girl dresses, bags, and wraps (that make wonderful presents), and in an especially savvy move, designs maternity bridesmaid dresses. Blake says it came out of necessity—every bride has a pregnant bridesmaid—and these dresses are fabulous. Thread Design is by appointment only, and they ask that brides give them 8 to 10 weeks to make the dresses.

Vanessa Fox

157 East 71St Street · **New York, NY 10021**
212-744-6960
www.vanessafox.com
$: Bridesmaid dresses start at $275

Vanessa Fox, a former fashion editor, started designing bridesmaid dresses when she saw how few good choices there were out there for her friends' weddings. Her dresses are traditional with a little twist, reminiscent of Jackie Kennedy's sexy but restrained style. She offers hundreds of colors for brides to choose from and adds details with her preppy signature element: grosgrain ribbon. Fox asks to have at least 12 weeks to prepare the dresses, which are made in standard sizes from each bridesmaid's measurements. Fox does not do alterations.

Vera Wang Maids

980 Madison Avenue · **New York, NY**
212-628-9898
www.verawang.com
$: Pieces start at $230 for dresses and $130 for separates
Flower-girl dresses start at: $230

You can't go wrong with Vera Wang's exquisite designs. Just as she achieved a reputation for excellence in wedding gowns, Wang is creating superior designs for bridesmaids, maids of honor, and flower girls. She works to keep her dresses sophisticated and timeless—no gasping with horror years later when wedding photos get trotted out. Wang's dresses come in a wide variety of rich colors and fabrics, including taffeta, matte jersey, and duchess satin.

Shoes

Many bridal salons carry a full line of shoes, but that's no reason you shouldn't go looking on your own as well, especially if you're looking for something a little different from the classic white satin wedding shoe.

When you buy your wedding shoes, remember that you're going to be wearing them for eight to twelve hours, so if you're not used to wearing super-high stilettos, this might not be the ideal time to start. Shoemakers advise that a two- to two-and-a-half-inch heel is ideal for people who are looking for some height but want to remain comfortable. Another comfort tip: look for shoes with a slightly wider heel (again, this nixes the stilettos). They are more comfortable for you to rest on for a long day.

Bergdorf Goodman

754 Fifth Avenue · New York, NY 10019
212-753-7300

The Bergdorf Goodman bridal shop can help you find the perfect wedding shoes (even if you didn't buy your gown from them), but don't deny yourself a trip through one of the most splendid shoe departments in town, especially if you're willing to look beyond white satin. Bergdorf's carries styles by Manolo Blahnik, Jimmy Choo, Christian Louboutin, Chanel, Oscar de la Renta, and more.

BridalShoes.com

1-800-575-7837
Fax: 516-569-4733

BridalShoes.com is a great Internet resource—especially if you're having trouble finding wedding shoes that come in wide widths. They have a large selection of shoes, organized on their website by heel height and in some cases by designer or style (they carry a lot of Kenneth Cole wedding shoes and a line of clear plastic "Cinderella" shoes) and it is very easy to order and do returns or exchanges. They also carry children's sizes in dyeable and "Cinderella" styles.

Christian Louboutin

941 Madison Avenue · New York, NY 10021
212-396-1884
$: Shoes start at $350

Christian Louboutin's shoes are like little works of art. He produces fabulous classic styles that often betray a sexy twist. For brides looking to stray from white, his satin shoes can be ordered in other colors including an elegant pearl gray. He also works in a variety of fabrics like crushed velvet. Even if you go with his fantastic white shoes, you can't help but be a little daring: all of Louboutin's shoes have his trademark red soles.

DiscountWeddingShoes.com

C/O Dyeable Shoes Online, Inc.
867 San Remo Drive · Weston, FL 33326
888-465-7330
dyeking@aol.com · www.discountweddingshoes.com
$: Shoes start at $30

A division of Dyeable Shoes Online (www.dyeableshoesonline.com), Discount Wedding Shoes carries Benjamin Walk "Touch Ups," in both dyeable and non-dyeable varieties and even stocks some Lucite shoes. They also carry a wide range of widths and some large-size shoes. DiscountWeddingShoes.com is also a great resource if you're looking for reasonably priced girl's shoes; they have dyeables and Lucite shoes in child sizes (kid's dyeables start at about $22).

Fenaroli

501 7th Avenue, Suite 416 · New York, NY 10018
212-764-5924
www.fenarolinewyork.com · www.fenaroli.com
$: Shoes start at $180

Fenaroli's shoes are lovely and elegant, and are all designed for maximum comfort. Styles for brides come in dyeable satin and have leather lining and soles, which lets them conform to the shape of your foot. Their selection includes a huge range of styles—everything from strappy sandals to boots—and heel heights. They also carry a wide range of dyeable bridesmaid shoes.

Jeffrey

449 West 14th Street · New York, NY 10014
212-206-1272

It often looks like this high-end department store was designed by a shoe-fetishist. There is no wedding department per se, but you might find something perfect in the dazzling displays featuring shoes by Manolo Blahnik, Prada, Fendi, Gucci, and more.

Kenneth Cole

95 Fifth Avenue · New York, NY 10003
212-675-2550
and
Grand Central Station (42nd Street and Vanderbilt) · New York, NY 10017
212-949-8079
www.kennethcole.com · Toll Free: 800-KEN-COLE
$: Bridal shoes start around $120

Kenneth Cole makes nonfussy, comfortable shoes for everyday wear, and also does a small bridal line in white and ivory satin. His shoes run the gamut from pumps to slingbacks and have a range of heel heights. You can purchase shoes from the stores or online, through the Kenneth Cole website.

Manolo Blahnik

31 West 54th Street · New York, NY 10019
212-582-3007
$: Shoes start at $450

Say no more. Manolo Blahnik's incredibly sexy and astronomically expensive shoes are on many brides' wish lists. His exquisite shoes come in a range of styles, colors, and heel heights and are supposed to be some of the most comfortable fancy shoes you can find. There is a bridal line, but you should think beyond the big day and check out Blahnik's classic collection for gorgeous shoes in metallic colors as well.

My Glass Slipper

423 King Street · Alexandria, VA 22314
703-838-8583 · Fax: 703-838-8926
www.myglassslipper.com · Toll free: 866-WED-SHOE
$: Sale shoes can start as low as $15; non-couture shoes start at about $40

If you know what you want, My Glass Slipper is a terrific online resource. Their easy-to-use website has shoes organized into "Couture Footwear" and "Shoes Under $100" categories. In addition they have a constant "Sale Shoes" section where you can find all kinds of treasures by great designers at a big discount. Some of the designers My Glass Slipper carries are: Kenneth Cole, Cynthia Rowley, Badgley Mischka, Fenaroli, Vera Wang, Richard Tyler, and Watters & Watters. The site also sells dyeable purses (couture and non-couture) and some jewelry, and provides a helpful FAQ section for shoe-seekers. If you're interested in their sales, you can sign up to get email notices that will let you know what's going to be discounted before it gets officially listed on the site.

Payless Shoe Source

1-800-426-1141
www.paylessshoesource.com
$: White dyeable shoes start around $30;
sandals start at $10

Some brides don't want to spend a fortune on white shoes that no one will see under their gown, and which they won't want to wear again anyway. For these women, there's always Payless, where you can find a range of standard dyeable white shoes (pumps, sandals, slingbacks) that are so reasonable you won't feel weird buying them, even if you only wear them once. You can order shoes online or use their website and toll-free number to find a store near you.

Peter Fox

105 Thompson Street · New York, NY 10012
212-431-7426
www.peterfox.com
$: Shoes start at around $230

Peter Fox's classic white satin shoes represent an array of wedding archetypes. He makes everything from Cinderella slippers to chic slingbacks and ornate boots with embroidery. Julia Roberts wore a couple of different sets of Peter Fox shoes in *Runaway Bride*, and Kate Winslet wore a daring pair of red boots in *Titanic*. After your wedding, Peter Fox can dye your shoes for you for a small fee.

Saks Fifth Avenue

NEW YORK CITY:
611 Fifth Avenue · New York, NY 10022

LONG ISLAND:
1300 Franklin Avenue · Garden City, NY 11530
516-248-9000
and
1 Hampton Road · Southampton, NY 11968
631-283-3500
and
Walt Whitman Mall
230 Walt Whitman Drive · Huntington, NY 11746
516-350-1100

CONNECTICUT:
205 Greenwich Avenue · Greenwich, CT 06830
203-862-5300
and
Town Center Mall
140 Atlantic Street · Stamford, CT 06901
203-323-3100

NEW JERSEY:
Riverside Square · 380 Hackensack Avenue
Hackensack, NJ 07601
201-646-1800
and
Mall at Short Hills
1200 Morris Turnpike · Short Hills, NJ 07078
973-376-7000

The shoe department at Saks is a shopper's dream, and they have a wide selection of designers and styles to pick from. You'll find shoes by Jimmy Choo, Kate Spade, Ferragamo, Stuart Weitzman, Isaac, Badgley Mischka, and more on their well-stocked floor.

Sigerson Morrison

28 Prince Street · New York, NY 10012
212-219-3893
$: Shoes start around $300

Visit this super-stylish Nolita store, if only to get inspiration. Sigerson Morrison makes exquisite shoes in a wide range of colors and styles that can fit almost any taste. You won't find the traditional white satin pumps here, though they do often have white leather shoes and sandals in their spring collections. Check out their metallic colors as well.

Stuart Weitzman

625 Madison Avenue · New York, NY 10022
www.stuartweitzman.com
$: Bridal shoes: $240 · Other styles: $168

Weitzman makes elegant, wearable shoes in a wide variety of styles—everything from pumps to sandals in a range of "wedding-safe" colors: white, silver, and gold, some with rhinestone detailing. Some of his shoes have bags to match.

Vamps

74 Second Avenue • New York, NY 10003
212-734-3967

Pay a visit to Vamps for great shoes at reasonable prices. They have a wide selection of everything from pumps to strappy sandals. Send your bridesmaids here, too, for good deals on good shoes.

Vanessa Noel

158 East 64th Street • New York, NY 10021
www.vanessanoel.com
$: Shoes start at $190 and go up to $465

Vanessa Noel makes great dyeable shoes in white silk crepe or satin for brides (and in other fabrics and colors for regular wear). Her styles are contemporary and comfortable—one of her design philosophies is that her shoes be wearable, not strictly costume pieces. Ideally, Noel feels, brides wouldn't hide their white shoes away after the wedding. She hopes that they'll dye them and wear them in their "regular" lives.

Shoe Dyeing

Shoe Service Plus

15 West 55th Street • New York, NY 10019
212-262-4823
$: Shoe dyeing starts at $40

A terrific place to go to get shoes dyed is Shoe Service Plus. Their work takes three to four days.

Bands and DJs

The entertainment at your reception will set the mood for the entire party. Along with the setting and decorations, the music is the memory your guests will take home with them, long after the taste of the chicken Kiev starts to fade.

Match your music to the theme and style of your wedding. If it's going to be a laid-back event and you want to kick up your heels, book a DJ or a rock band. If it's white-tie and you're dreaming of Fred Astaire–style dancing, hire an 18-piece orchestra. If you're having an intimate affair culminating in high tea, go for a classical trio. Whatever your taste, you'll find a match in our listings. Keep in mind that some bands will be booked extremely far in advance, especially big-name groups such as the Lester Lanin Orchestra. It may be wise to book your entertainment as soon as you decide on your ceremony and reception locations and the date. Booking up to a year (or more) in advance is not uncommon, especially in the tristate area.

Questions to ask before you buy

● How many hours will the band or DJ play?

● Will the band or DJ take requests?

● How many breaks will the band or DJ take? How long will the breaks be? Will recorded music be playing during breaks?

● If you're working with a large company that represents multiple groups, will the band you choose be the exact one that plays at your wedding? If this is important to you, be sure it's in your contract.

● Ask about the band or DJ's attire. What will they be wearing? You want to make sure the level of formality matches that of your reception. Most music professionals will wear tuxedos.

In-the-know tips

● Remember to feed the band. It's bad manners (and not very nice, to boot) to deny your musicians a bite to eat! They'll probably need to take at least one break, and a happy, rested, well-fed band is a better band.

● Tip your musicians or DJ. You can discreetly hand an envelope to the bandleader or emcee. Your 15- to 20-percent tip can be split up between band members by the leader.

● Be sure to sign a contract with your band or musicians or DJ, even if it's only a one-man operation.

A note about rates

Most of the prices in this chapter cover four hours of continuous reception music. Some groups listed play primarily at wedding ceremonies and during cocktail hours; the information will explain this. Overtime, travel expenses, extra band members, and variables such as season, night of the week, and any extra services will alter the price. The fees listed here will give you an idea of price variations between groups. Of course, fees are always subject to change.

NEW YORK CITY

Alex Donner Entertainment

429 East 52nd Street, Suite 34D · New York, NY 10022
212-752-2920 · Fax: 212-832-9780
www.alexdonner.com · info@alexdonner.com
$: Rates start at $3,600 for four hours

Alex Donner is the quintessential New York City bandleader. His musicians will dazzle your guests with sophisticated cabaret music, old standards, dance music, rock, and jazz. He can even provide specialty bands, classical groups, solo performers, society music, and DJ entertainers. He has played weddings all over the world in many kinds of venues and has a repertoire of over 3,000 songs, which allows him to customize the music to fit any taste. If you want to hear him, Donner often plays in Manhattan (he'll be a regular at the Café Carlyle starting in September 2002), or you can listen to samples from his albums (or even purchase them) on his website.

The Bob Hardwick Sound

138 East 61st Street · New York, NY 10021
212-838-7521 · Fax: 212-838-7611
$: Rates start at $5,000 for a small group

Bob Hardwick has been called a musical "top wizard," and his group remains one of the most requested big bands around. He's entertained Prince Charles and Presidents Carter, Reagan, and Bush, and even accompanied Aretha Franklin at the wedding of Al Gore's daughter, Karenna. His 15-piece orchestra—complete with four singers—will delight reception guests. He can also supply a small string orchestra to play at the ceremony.

Brooklyn Conservatory of Music

58 Seventh Avenue · Brooklyn, NY 11217
718-622-3300
www.brooklynconservatory.com
$: $100 per musician per hour, plus additional fees

Feel like contributing to a worthy institution? This service aids you in finding classical musicians for your wedding. They can provide flutists, string trios, jazz quartets, Latin bands, and more—and 20 percent of the musicians' fees go to the conservatory.

Duchin Entertainment

305 Madison Avenue · New York, NY 10165
800-433-5064
www.duchinentertainment.com
$: $5,500 for four hours (not including Peter Duchin as bandleader)

For more than three decades, Peter Duchin has been considered one of America's pre-eminent dance-band leaders. His orchestra debuted in 1962 at the St. Regis Hotel, and since then the big band has performed at all sorts of upscale events, including White House state dinners and inaugural balls, museum openings, debutante dances—and many, many weddings. Duchin himself plays at more than 100 events a year, while bands with his name play at many more. All Duchin groups have a large musical repertoire that embraces every style of popular music, from jazz to show tunes, swing, and rock and roll.

Gerard Carelli Orchestra

Grand Central Station · P.O. Box 1954 · New York, NY 10163
212-989-4042 or 800-427-4647 · Fax: 914-242-7305
www.1800gcsings.com
$: Call for rates

Gerard Carelli is a trombone player and former Rainbow Room bandleader who has played with greats such as Ray Charles, Vic Damone, Rosemary Clooney, Frank Sinatra, and Mel Torme. His smooth vocal style has led him to be hailed as a combination of Tommy Dorsey and Frank Sinatra. The orchestra's style ranges from swing to soul to classic rock, Motown, and R&B. Carelli's musicians are full-time professionals and will take great care of your guests. Needless to say, Carelli is extremely sought after, so book early. (Go to Carelli's website to hear the band's music.)

Hank Lane Music

65 West 55th Street · New York, NY 10023
212-767-0600
and
165 Rosyln Road · Rosyln Heights, NY 11577
516-626-8300
www.hanklane.com · info@hanklane.com
$: Call for rates

When you deal with Hank Lane Music, you can get it all. The company represents multiple bands, including the Hank Lane Orchestras, while its sister company, More Than Music, books DJs and provides high-tech lighting systems. Each band can perform music in all genres: jazz, big band, doo-wop, classical, Motown, soul, pop, rock, reggae, Latin, ballroom, and disco. They've put together everything from jazz trios and 20-piece big bands to contemporary disco and R&B groups and classical ensembles. They've been top rated by *Town & Country* magazine and have performed at events from Montreal to Monte Carlo, including the marriages of Billy Baldwin and Chynna Phillips, Kenneth Cole and Maria Cuomo, and Donald Trump and Marla Maples.

Jason Craig Entertainment

1650 Broadway · New York, NY 10019
212-397-0808
and
1123 Route 23 South · Wayne, NJ 07470
973-694-1515
www.jasoncraig.com · info@jasoncraig.com
$: Rates for the Jason Craig Orchestra range from $3,500
to $6,500 for four hours; other groups vary

Jason Craig Entertainment encompasses 10 bands. The Jason Craig Orchestra comes complete with both male and female vocalists and claims to test your stamina on the dance floor; they certainly encourage one and all to get moving to the music. The band's songlist includes popular tunes from all genres, from the thirties through today. They're in demand with those in the know, including New Jersey Governor Christine Todd Whitman (the Jason Craig Orchestra played at her inaugural ball) and comedian-actor Jay Mohr (they performed at his wedding).

Jerry Kravat Entertainment

404 Park Avenue South · New York, NY 10016
212-686-2200 · Fax: 212-689-9140
www.jerrykravat.com
$: Call for rates

Jerry Kravat manages all sorts of heavy-hitting musicians in addition to leading his own orchestra. His stable includes the Manhattan Rhythm Machine, Ray Cohen & the New York Dream Band, the Jerry Kravat Big Band, Jerry Kravat's New York Orchestra, the New York Jazz Trio, the Kole Quartet, and the Cantabile Trio (they play classical music and jazz). Kravat also represents stars such as Eartha Kitt and Barbara Cook (though they may be a little bit beyond your price range). The company offers DJ service as well. Music ranges from swing to bebop to disco—virtually anything you desire. Kravat's website allows you to listen to samples to get a feel for the range of musical styles his groups offer.

The Ken Gross Orchestras

209-20 18th Avenue · Bayside, NY 11360
800-688-4480 · 212-961-0210
kengrossorchestras@juno.com
$: Rates start at $6,000 for an eight-piece orchestra for four hours

When a Ken Gross Orchestra plays at your wedding, the fun and dancing never stop. From the first toast to the last dance, the musicians and vocalists are dedicated to making sure your wedding guests won't want to sit down. Ken personally works with each couple so that the playlist reflects their wishes. A Juilliard grad, Ken hires only the finest and most versatile musicians. For example, a typical eight-piece Ken Gross Orchestra consists of a female vocalist and seven musicians, five of whom are also lead singers. This results in a beautiful variety of voices and rich backup harmonies without sacrificing full rhythm and horn sections. They can masterfully perform a broad spectrum of music, including swing, Top 40, classic rock, R&B, Motown, standards, Broadway, jazz, classical, and more than 20 ethnic styles.

Kevin B. Westley T.M.R.F.

64-15 229 Street · Bayside, NY 11364
718-631-2528
IrishDJKevin@msn.com
$: Rates start at $150 per hour

Kevin Westley bills himself as "The Irish DJ." His musical library includes over 6,000 songs, half of them Irish and half popular music spanning from the era of Cole Porter to the present. Westley is even certified to teach Irish Ceili dancing (think

"Riverdance"). He can also provide Irish musicians to play pipes, the harp, or other instruments. So if you want your guests to kick off their slippers and become lords and ladies of the dance, call Westley and bring the luck of the Irish to your wedding.

The Lester Lanin Orchestras

250 West 57th Street • New York, NY 10107
212-265-5208 • Fax: 212-262-1247
$: Call for rates

Lester Lanin is the society bandleader. He's hugely famous and pals around regularly with all sorts of celebrities. He's entertained for everyone from Queen Elizabeth (she changed the date of her birthday celebration just so Lanin could lead the orchestra) to Ross Perot. He performed at Prince Charles and Lady Diana's wedding as well as at Christie Brinkley and Billy Joel's wedding. In fact, he's performed at hundreds of weddings over the past 30 years and is known as the high-society bandleader with a heart: He never cancels a scheduled event, even if a celebrity requests the same night. You can choose to go all out and hire the entire orchestra, or you can stay simple, with anything from one pianist to a string quartet.

Maura & Co.

212-722-3141 • Fax: 212-722-0647
mmolloy@attglobal.net
$: Rates start at $300 per musician per hour, with a two-hour minimum

If you're looking to lend an elegant, classical air to your wedding, Maura & Co. may be perfect for you. Maura Malloy provides classical instrumentals and vocals for the ceremony and beyond. Groups are usually trios—flute (flute, cello, and harp) or harp (harp, cello, violin) are the most popular. Besides offering trios and string quartets, Malloy specializes in Irish music.

Mix 'n' Match Music

31-20 12th Street • Astoria, NY 11106
718-278-5331 • Fax: 718-278-6960
$: Rates for a duo start at $600 for four hours; trios start at $900 for four hours; quartets start at $1,200 for four hours

Mix 'n' Match books groups to play everything from jazz to salsa, flamenco, and popular standards. Music coordinator Carol Sudhalter manages a mind-boggling combination of instruments and an immense repertoire. In fact, the only things she doesn't have are DJs and Top 40 music. If you're looking for a string quartet, jazz trio, salsa band, woodwind quartet, flute-and-guitar duo, or swing band, give Sudhalter a call. Her own group, the Astoria Big Band, specializes in jazz. All fees are negotiable.

The Michael Carney Orchestra

175 Fifth Avenue · New York, NY 10010
212-353-5301
MCM1540@aol.com
$: Rates start at $10,000 to $12,000 for a weekend night

This 8- to 10-piece orchestra will perform anywhere within an hour of New York City. They perform all the classics in five musical styles: fast swing, medium swing, bossa nova, samba, and rock (from the fifties to the nineties). If you're looking for a group that will take you from the cocktail hour through the last dance, give the Michael Carney Orchestra a call.

Park Swing Orchestra

150 West 28th Street, Suite 902E · New York, NY 10001
212-229-1642
billkinslow@mindspring.com · www.parkswingorc.com
$: A seven-piece group starts at $5,000 for four hours

The Park Swing Orchestra has been playing for 15 years, providing a blend of swing, classic big band, and popular standards from the likes of Cole Porter, George Gershwin, and Duke Ellington, as well as throwing in a dash of rock and R&B. They're a great band for dancing, but the company can also supply string quartets, trios, and duos with repertoire from the classics to modern tunes. The largest the group gets is 17 pieces. Go to their website to download a music sample.

The Persuasions

Headline Talent · 1650 Broadway, Suite 508 · New York, NY 10019
212-581-6900 · Fax: 212-581-6906
headlinetalent@aol.com · www.thepersuasions.com
$: Fees start at $2,500, plus airfare and hotel

This a cappella quintet is famed for "cool-as-a-breeze harmonizing," specializing in soul, gospel, and R&B—everything from "Papa Was a Rolling Stone" to Nat King Cole. They started out in the sixties singing on street corners in Brooklyn, and have since performed with the likes of Frank Zappa, Stevie Wonder, Bette Midler, the Grateful Dead, and Paul Simon. The group is a great alternative to typical piano cocktail-hour music. Since one group member lives in Arizona and must fly up for tristate weddings, their fees are a bit steep, but they're well worth it.

Russell Daisey Big Band

3111 Broadway · New York, NY 10027
212-663-7598 · 917-662-1421
$: Quartet rates start at $1,900 to $2,500 for four to five hours;
eight-piece band rates start at $3,750 for four to five hours

Russell Daisey's group can perform as a big band or as a trio or quartet for medium-size weddings. Daisey himself also performs as a solo pianist and singer. His big band is a classic swing band and is in high demand, having performed at the Ocean Club in Palm Beach, Florida, for the millennium and even for Hillary Clinton at New York City's Grand Hyatt. During Mayor David Dinkins's tenure, the band performed every other week at Gracie Mansion. The band can play pop music and other popular 20th-century styles.

Starlight Orchestras

180 West 80th Street · New York, NY 10024
212-595-0999
$: $8,000 to $20,000

Starlight Orchestras, one of the most popular New York society bands, can offer your wedding everything from classical ensembles to a full orchestra—with the added romance and glamour of beautiful female bandleaders. Starlight orchestras can provide a huge range of music and musical styles, and have been known to accompany Barbra Streisand, Whitney Houston, and Tito Puente. They've played private parties for Jon Bon Jovi and for the wedding of Michael Douglas and Catherine Zeta-Jones. They have wonderful singers, fabulous musicians, and enough charm to get your whole party dancing.

The Stingers

35 Fieldmere Street · New Rochelle, NY 10804
914-633-1700
www.stingersband.com
$: Rates range from $5,000 to $10,000 for a
5- to 13-piece band for four hours

If you really want your guests to cut the rug, turn to the Motown, R&B, and blues of the Stingers. This is one energetic, toe-tapping, get-your-great-aunt-to-dance R&B group. They have a stamp of approval from Quincy Jones, the music maestro himself, whom they have played for, as well as Jimmy Buffet, Martha Stewart, Bruce Willis, and Donald Trump. Visit their website to download song clips and see a sample songlist.

Tropical Music

P.O. Box 3880 · New York, NY 10160
212-288-1133
and
P.O. Box 302 · Wilton, CT 06897
203-359-1133
www.cmproductions.com
$: Call for rates

Looking to bring a cool Caribbean breeze to your wedding? Tropical Music special-izes in calypso, reggae, and steel drums. The eight-member group is called the Caribbean Cruisers and includes both American and Caribbean musicians. They can also play swing, Motown, blues, and other non-Caribbean music. They'll wear tuxe-dos or tropical shirts, depending on the theme and formality of your wedding. The group has played around the world, from the Royal Palace in Marrakech, Morocco, to Tavern on the Green. When making initial inquiry, ask for Arthur.

LONG ISLAND

Bill Harrington Orchestra

130 Shore Road · Port Washington, NY 11050
516-627-0388
Harringtonmusic@aol.com
$: Rates for the 14-piece band start at $550 to $600
per musician for four hours

The Bill Harrington Orchestra can put together groups ranging from 6 to 14 pieces and plays all sorts of music, from standards and big band to R&B, Motown, and everything in between. They run the gamut from "Jump, Jive & Wail" to Viennese waltzes, with the music remaining tasteful and lively throughout. They've done all sorts of high-profile weddings, including Tricia Nixon's White House wedding, Jane Seymour's wedding, and John McEnroe's wedding to Tatum O'Neal; they have played at four presidential inaugural balls, including Kennedy's, Nixon's, and Bush's; and they are a big favorite of Martha Stewart, appearing throughout her book *Weddings*.

Don Michael's Swing and Contemporary Orchestra

Valley Stream, NY
866-890-5381 • 516-314-2428
info@donmichaels.com • www.donmichaels.com
$: Rates average $3,500 for four hours

Don Michael's Swing Orchestra plays everything from big band to disco. The 10-piece (and up) group has male and female vocalists and provides standards, Latin, Dixieland, ballroom, and rock—in short, tunes from the forties to the 21st century. Michael himself has been a working musician since 1942, when he joined a big band at age 15. If you're looking for an old-fashioned swing band, check him out.

Hart to Hart Productions

25 West Jefryn Boulevard • Deer Park, NY 11729
800-541-HART • 631-595-2288 • Fax: 631-595-1785
www.harttohart.com • requestinfo@harttohart.com
$: Call for rates

Hart to Hart's high-energy party packages provide the best of all worlds: a DJ with innumerable records at his (or her) fingertips; an emcee to keep your reception lively and even act as on-site director; and live musicians (like a solo saxophone or a jazz trio) to play at your ceremony and to complement the recorded music at your reception. Hart to Hart can also provide lighting, and they even have dancers if you think your guests will need a little extra motivation.

Jim Turner

P.O. Box 352 • Sag Habor, NY 11963
631-725-5626
www.jimturnermusic.com • jt@jimturnermusic.com
$: Rates start at $2,200 for four musicians for four hours;
five musicians start at $2,600 for four hours

Jim Turner has shared the stage with Paul McCartney, B. B. King, and Phoebe Snow, playing a repertoire of rock, blues, reggae, jazz, folk, Celtic music, and more. His playlist includes over 1,500 songs. Turner, a veritable institution in the Hamptons and beyond, can play solo or with his 4- to 8-piece band. He is well known for performing everything from elegant non-intrusive background music to music that is a treat for your ears, your spirit, and your dancing feet.

King's Brass

510 Spruce Lane · East Meadow, NY 11554
516-485-4717 · 516-485-0066
kingsbrass@aol.com · www.kingsbrass.com
$: Rates start at $450 for two musicians for two hours in one location

Feel the need for some fanfare? King's Brass will provide ceremonial trumpets and musicians dressed in 16th-century costumes (you can also request tuxedos or top hats and tails). The musicians can play renaissance, baroque, and classical music. Harpists, pianists, violinists, bagpipers, and vocalists can be brought in to flesh out the brass ensemble for the cocktail hour.

The Stan Wiest Orchestra

Stan Wiest Music
271 Bread and Cheese Hollow Road · Fort Salonga, NY 11768
631-754-0594
www.stanwiest.com
$: Average of $4,300 for the Stan Wiest Orchestra 6-piece band

With over 17 bands and orchestras working for him, Stan Wiest can get you the perfect music for your wedding, and, because he's a member of the Association of Bridal Consultants, Wiest really understands the intricacies of wedding performances. The list of musicians he can get for you is enormous, since he handles everything from ballroom dance bands to steel drums, mariachi groups, bagpipers, bluegrass bands, classical groups, Greek bouzouki music, sitars, German Oktoberfest, and even DJs. Go to his website and take a look at the 112 music pages he has set up. He's great to work with and an amazing wedding resource.

Variety Music

Offices in Nassau and Suffolk counties
516-922-2299 · Fax: 516-922-7398
www.varietydj.com
$: $700 and up

Variety Music DJs offer all sorts of popular music, from the forties through the present. They'll bring whatever songs you ask them to and will also take requests from your guests. Their fun and personable DJs encourage lots of audience participation. They can additionally provide live singers, keyboardists, videography, lighting, and invitations.

WESTCHESTER

Big Apple Music and Entertainment

2005 Palmer Avenue • Larchmont, NY 10538
914-833-0001 • Fax: 914-833-9635
$: Call for rates

With this DJ company, you can have anything from a low-key affair to an all-out, high-energy bash. They don't just play music—their emcees lead your party. They have an extensive music collection ranging from the twenties to the present, along with 18 years of DJ experience. The staff wears formal attire (usually tuxedos) to match the formality of your wedding. Big Apple can also supply lighting.

The N.Y. Big Band

Joe Battaglia • 316 Millwood Road • Chappaqua, NY 10514
914-241-1387 • 800-307-3179
www.nybigband.com
$: $2,500 and up

Joe Battaglia and the N.Y. Big Band will have your guests dancing with their wonderful music and terrific personalities. They play everything: big band music, Latin, swing, tunes from the 1930s to the 1990s—even Polish and Italian music. They don't play much rock music, but the big band (6 to 17 pieces and vocalists) will get your entire crowd dancing. The band often plays in New York City, and if you can get to one of their gigs, you can get their CDs.

The Smith Street Society Jazz Band

Muskrat Productions • 1635 Winfield Avenue • Mamaroneck, NY 10543
800-441-3144 • 914-592-3144 • Fax: 914-698-0529
www.muskratproductions.com • muskrat@bestweb.net
$: $400 per musician for four hours

The Smith Street Society Jazz Band is one of the groups Muskrat Productions offers: The company also represents groups specializing in everything from Dixieland to classical chamber music, society dance music, and classic rock. The Smith Street Society Jazz Band itself plays good-time music from the twenties and the swing era through rock-and-roll music from the fifties. The group has performed at Avery Fisher Hall, Lincoln Center, and the Newport Jazz Festival, along with scores of private parties and weddings. If you're interested in different music for your cocktail hour, check out Muskrat's groups Las Antillas Strolling Mariachi Band, the Caribbean-inspired Calypso Carnival, classical duos and quartets, and European entertainment including an Italian group, a French concertina, a Russian balalaika ensemble, and Moroccan musicians.

NEW JERSEY

Bob Smith's Lamplighters

56 Federal City Road · Trenton, NJ 08638
609-883-7986 · Fax: 609-637-0292
$: Rates start at $3,500 for four hours, ending before midnight
(beyond midnight is overtime)

Looking to put those swing-dancing classes to good use? The Lamplighters are a 15-piece big band with male and/or female vocalists. They play music by such swing greats as Glenn Miller, Benny Goodman, Tommy Dorsey, and Artie Shaw, and can also play Broadway show tunes, Dixieland, polkas, waltzes, and other traditional dance music. Bob Smith does a great job of reproducing the original swing sound. One thing he stays away from is rock, so don't expect to hear any Rolling Stones from the Lamplighters. Hiring this band will give even Grandma a chance to cut the rug! (If you want only the Dixie band, the Dixiecrats, ask for prices and availability.)

Events Plus

622 Route 10 · Whippany, NJ 07981
973-503-1700 · Fax: 973-503-9848
www.events-plus.com · eventsplus@aol.com
$: DJ rates start at $650 for four hours

Looking to boogie down on your wedding day? Events Plus supplies straight-ahead DJs to get your party going. They can also provide a karaoke machine and recording booth if you want to take home some hilarious souvenirs of your reception.

Gramercy Arts Trio

Gramercy Arts Ensemble · 111 Shelbern Drive · Lincroft, NJ 07738
732-536-8531 or 732-918-8092
www.gramercyarts.com
$: Rates for ceremony music start at $600 for three musicians

This trio and ensemble play everything from classical music to Broadway standards and popular dance tunes. The basic instruments are flute, violin, and cello, but they will work with vocalists and other musicians. They can play classical selections at your ceremony, then play throughout the reception. The Gramercy Arts Trio will travel throughout the tristate area. Group is fully insured and amplified.

Hester Street Troupe

14 Princeton Road • Cranford, NJ 07016
908-276-5245 • 570-646-4272 (summertime)
www.hesterstreettroupe.com • hstroupe@aol.com
$: Weekend rates start at $1,200 for three hours,
$300 for each additional hour

The Hester Street Troupe plays both klezmer and secular music. They're a three-person group, with one musician on saxophone and clarinet, one on drums, and one on keyboards. All do vocals. They even have a political stamp of approval: they've played for former U.S. Senator Al D'Amato. The Hester Street Troupe will travel within the tristate area and beyond. Three of their albums are for sale on their website.

Peter Evans Orchestra

Leonard Bornstein Entertainments • 44 Main Street • Millburn, NJ 07041
973-467-3060 • Fax: 973-467-5015
www.lb-music.com
$: Rates start at $4,500 for five musicians for four hours

Peter Evans Orchestra offers elegant ballroom entertainment but won't sacrifice a party-all-night, fun-filled atmosphere for staid sophistication. The musicians can perform everything from ethnic tunes to popular standards, from rock-and-roll to special requests. Evans's bands make a special effort not to be too loud so that guests can talk while others are dancing. They can also play classical music during the ceremony and cocktail hours. In addition, each band is supplemented by a DJ at no extra cost.

Total Entertainment

77-99 West Sheffield Avenue • Englewood, NJ 07631
201-894-0055
www.totalentertainment.com
$: The "Totally Live" wedding package starts at $10,000
and includes a DJ and emcee along with a live band

Can't decide whether you want a DJ or a band? Total Entertainment provides both.

They can provide a DJ to play the tunes, an emcee to lead the party, and a live horn and percussion section with vocalists to add some spice to the recorded music. The musicians can play mellow music during the ceremony and cocktail hour, then break out into more funky stuff along with the DJ when the reception gets going. Total Entertainment has 12 bands, ranging from trios to 25 pieces.

CONNECTICUT

Bach to Broadway

Westport, CT
203-454-2561
$: Rates vary depending on length of booking and number of musicians

Bach to Broadway provides elegant background and dance music for weddings. Meryl Kaplan manages a number of bands that play all types of music, including classical, show tunes and popular standards, jazz, and even Israeli/Jewish selections. Her Cafe Carlyle combo plays a wonderful repertoire of Cole Porter, Gershwin, Rogers and Hart, and Latin tunes. The number and type of musicians may vary depending on the event, but a flutist, pianist, harpist, guitarists, and more are available. Kaplan can also book sophisticated DJs for your event.

Eric Walters Orchestra

c/o David Schroeder
5 Lexington Avenue, Suite 4 • Greenwich, CT 06830
203-863-9015
www.bigeric.com • eric@bigeric.com
$: Rates start at $5,000 for four hours

While this sounds like two different bands, it's actually two sides of the same group. One rocks, and one's a bit classier. Although the number of band members can vary depending on the event, 7 to 10 musicians is average and includes a horn section along with female and male vocalists. Both bands play everything—standards, R&B, Motown, rock-and-roll, and swing. Eric Walters can also provide DJ services as well as classical music for your ceremony and cocktail hour—a solo piano or harp, a piano and flute/violin duet, or a string or brass quartet. Visit their website to download sample tunes.

Janet Marlow Jazz Quartet

P.O. Box 945 · Litchfield, CT 06759
860-567-9217
www.janetmarlow.com · jmarlow@snet.net
$: Call for rates

Janet Marlow plays the 10-string guitar and takes care of the vocals while her husband plays jazz violin and the five-string fretless bass; they also have a keyboardist. They specialize in all styles of jazz and are also skilled classical musicians. At weddings, they often play classical tunes for the ceremony, move into the cocktail hour with some bossa nova and light jazz, and then pull out the jazz stops for the reception. They can bring in additional musicians (up to seven) upon request.

The Pat Dorn Orchestra

900 Chapel Street · New Haven, CT 06510
203-865-0360
$: An 18-piece band with a vocalist starts at $5,500 to $6,500 for five hours

One of Pat Dorn's claims to fame is that his orchestra has played at the inaugural balls for four U.S. presidents—including President Clinton's last inaugural, during which Dorn performed with the First Lady of Soul, Aretha Franklin. He's been performing for 45 years and has also played with Tony Bennett, Johnny Mathis, and Ella Fitzgerald. He designs his orchestra's playlist individually for each wedding. He'll play all sorts of music but specializes in big band, Latin, and ballroom. The band can play with 3 to 18 pieces.

Sally (Ranti) Perreten

18 Sunset Road · Old Saybrook, CT 06475
860-388-1170
$: For Ranti playing solo, the first hour is $250 (this includes harp setup and transport); traveling expenses are extra if Ranti must travel over 25 miles

Sally Ranti is a harpist who can supply elegant music with a twist for your ceremony or cocktail hour. She can supply solo harp instrumentation in both classical and Celtic styles, as well as bring in a flutist for a classical duet. She can also put together a Celtic harp ensemble (which includes either two harps or a harp and a pennywhistle). She can supply discreet amplification for outdoor events or large parties. Ranti has a one-hour minimum playing time.

Photography and Videography

Your photographs are a lasting memento of your wedding: You'll treasure them for the rest of your life. As such, you should take special care when choosing a photographer. After all, if the cake is a mess, that's one thing (people will eat it anyway), but if you don't love your photographs, you'll never be able to have them reshot. This chapter includes photographers who are esteemed by both their peers and their clients. Still, each person has his or her own taste and style, so be discriminating.

Photography rates

The prices listed here are the photographers' base fees for wedding work. When you find a photographer you like, he or she will probably tailor a package to your needs and desires, and the price may be significantly different.

Rates usually cover film, the photographer's time, perhaps the help of an assistant, and usually a set of proofs. However, the proofs sometimes are marked "Proof," which will make them unusable in an album—you would just choose which prints you wanted made from them. Some photographers also include an album or even two in their base fee; some even require brides and grooms to choose one of their albums. Others offer less-expensive services and will charge you for an album only if you decide you want them to put one together for you (you might opt to buy and assemble your own once you have your prints). Still other photographers include the negatives in their base price (or perhaps just the color negatives) or allow you to buy them for an extra fee. Purchasing your negatives means that you can get reprints made any time by any commercial photo developer, rather than paying your photographer up to $40 each for enlargements. Be sure to ask specific questions, and be sure to get everything in writing.

In-the-know tips

● Almost all photographers will travel to out-of-town weddings for an additional fee. Some will even travel overseas to shoot a wedding.

● If she has one, check out the photographer's website before scheduling an appointment. You may discover that you have different ideas or philosophies about photography; save both of you some time by looking elsewhere.

● Make sure the photographer you've chosen—and not an associate—will be the one who actually shoots your wedding.

● Some photography studios also provide videography services. This may be an uncomplicated solution if you want your wedding documented in still film and on video. Or, you may choose to hire someone who specializes in videography only, in addition to your photographer.

● Be sure your chosen photographer's aesthetic style matches yours. Do you want to avoid your vows being interrupted by the pop of a photographer's flash? Do you prefer candid shots to formal, posed ones? Do you love black-and-white photographs but want some color shots, too? Do you want any special effects, such as soft focus or silhouetting? Be sure to discuss these things before signing a contract.

● Make sure you get along personally with your photographer. This person is going to be spending a hectic day with you, and you want him or her to be a calming presence, not an annoying one. If you love the photographer's photos but don't get good vibes from him, consider booking someone else.

● Be sure to get references. If other couples loved the photographer and his or her wedding photographs, you can rest assured. If a photographer won't provide references, don't hesitate to choose another one.

● Your written contract should include:

✓ The number of hours the photographer will work on your wedding day

✓ How many rolls of film will be shot

✓ The percentage of color and black-and-white photos to be shot

✓ The number of proofs you'll receive, along with the format (and whether or not they'll be stamped "Proof")

✓ Overtime rate (usually charged by the hour)

✓ Cancellation and refund policy

✓ Emergency photographer substitution plan

✓ When formal shots (portraits) will be taken (e.g., after the ceremony but before the reception)

NEW YORK CITY

Alan Klein Photography

381 Broadway, 3rd Floor · New York, NY 10013
212-334-8099 · Fax: 212-334-3125
aklein@alanklein.com · www.alanklein.com
$: Rates start at $3,100 for 7 hours of shooting, up to 25 rolls of film,
and online proofs posted on a private website.

Alan Klein says that his approach to photographing weddings emphasizes action, beauty, and joy. His fine sense of humor and eye for detail ensure that his photos are artistic while still capturing the authentic emotions of the wedding day: Take a peek at Klein's website for a look. He consults with couples on details like albums for a range of fees. Clients keep their negatives.

Andrea Sperling

102 East 22nd Street · New York, NY 10010
212-674-5314
www.andreasperling.com
$: Rates start at $5,000

Andrea Sperling is excellent at the informal shot. She captures the mood and feel of each wedding by using a storytelling approach. Sperling prefers to work with black-and-white film but will shoot in a mixture of color and black-and-white if you prefer. She photographed the photos in *Greenmarket*, a photo essay on farmer's markets, and also provided photos for the books *Emily Post's Weddings*, *A Wedding for All Seasons*, and *Centerpieces*. If you choose Sperling, book her early; she only shoots 10 to 15 weddings a year.

Bill Fredericks Studio

214 West 29th Street · New York, NY 10001
800-379-6884
info@billfredericks.com · www.bfstudio.com
$: Rates start between $3,650 and $5,950

You'll have your pick of four photographers at Bill Fredericks Studio: Fredericks himself, Gabriel Pintado, Sam LaHoz, and Barbara Corella. Each has his or her own style, but the overall Fredericks feel is photojournalistic. Their photos capture spontaneous moments throughout the wedding, from the bride's preparation to the bouquet toss. Their shots are not usually posed, and the photographers possess the sort of humor that makes wedding photographs come to life. Look at the Fredericks website for examples. Fees include color and black-and-white prints and an album.

Cappy Hotchkiss

41 Wyckoff Street, Garden Apt. · Brooklyn, NY 11201
718-596-6609
cappyh@earthlink.net · www.cappyhotchkiss.com
$: Rates start at $4,000

Cappy Hotchkiss specializes in modern, nontraditional wedding photography that's so deceptively simple (while remaining attentive to detail) that it's like the visual equivalent of Japanese haiku. Her photos are quiet yet pack a distinctive emotional punch. They are framed so well that they seem more like art than wedding pictures. Her black-and-white shots are crisp and elegant, while her color photos are saturated with rich hues. See her website for examples of her stylish photos. Hotchkiss's work has appeared in publications including *New York Wedding*, *Modern Bride*, *Elegant Bride*, and *The Knot Wedding Pages*. Her base fee does not include an album.

Carolina Salguero

168 Beard Street · Brooklyn, NY 11231
718-852-0821 or 917-414-0565 · Fax: 718-852-0821
carolinas@earthlink.net · www.knottheusual.com
$: Rates start at $2,800

Carolina Salguero is an award-winning photojournalist who is also an unobtrusive wedding photographer skilled at shooting intimate candids. She works in both color and black-and-white and will take posed portraits if the client requests them. She has a wonderful eye for "moments," shooting one bride walking outside with her mother from grass level, and her party photos are exuberant. See her website for an image portfolio. Negatives are included in Salguero's fee.

Carolina Kroon

212-691-2621
ckroon@bway.net · www.carolinakroonphotography.com
$: Rates starts at $1,800, plus expenses

Carolina Kroon takes a straightforward and lively photojournalistic approach to the weddings she shoots. She catches lots of spontaneous moments, full of movement, and has a lot of fun with candid shots. Kroon also can do portraits, so if you want mostly photojournalistic style images with a few formal pictures, she can certainly accommodate all of your needs. Kroon doesn't do packages or albums, and her fees are based on a starting rate plus film expenses (she charges $40 per roll of film shot). In addition to weddings, Kroon also does events and fine art work.

Celeste Crosby

99 Jane Street, Apt. 3F · New York, NY 10014
212-675-9388
celeste@celestecrosby.com · www.celestecrosby.com
$: Rates start at $3,950

Celeste Crosby's photographs are bright and happy, with a definite sense of humor—one of her "before the wedding" photos features a bride checking her makeup through her eyeglasses. Her black-and-white and color pictures are nontraditional but classic. Her clients keep both proofs and negatives. Crosby does not provide prints or albums.

Fred Marcus Photography Studio

245 West 72nd Street · New York, NY 10023
212-873-5588 · Fax: 212-873-8200
andymarcus@fredmarcus.com · www.fredmarcus.com
$: Call for rates

Fred Marcus founded this photo studio, now run by his son Andrew, over 50 years ago. With a roster of celebrity clients, including Donald Trump, Mary Tyler Moore, Princess Yasmin Aga Khan, and Billy Baldwin and Chynna Phillips, the studio has ample experience dealing with grand events. Their photos and videos have appeared on "Weddings of a Lifetime," and the Marcus video division was chosen to create "Disney's Fairy Tale Wedding" promotional video. Several photographers currently work for the studio, and while they each have their own style, the overall Marcus look is bright and emotional. The photos are creative but within the range of traditional wedding candids.

Fusion Video

244 Fifth Avenue · New York, NY 10001
212-684-4086 · Fax: 212-684-0649
$: A full-day video shoot starts at $2,500

Fusion Video specializes in special events and has a number of packages available. They can include music, stock footage, still photographs, or a variety of special digital effects in your video.

Gruber Photographers

315 West 57th Street · New York, NY 10019
212-262-9777
www.gruberphotographers.com
$: Rates for Terry Gruber start at $15,000 for events of up to 125 guests (this includes two assistants); rates for his associates range from $4,500 to $12,000

With eight photographers, it's impossible to describe each associate's style here, but the company's extensive website includes portfolios for all. Terry Gruber himself began as an assistant to Francesco Scavullo, and his photographs have appeared in *Martha Stewart Living*, *Bride's*, *Glamour*, and at the International Center of Photography. Gruber's photos have an appealing spontaneous quality and soft, rich color. He prides himself on catching intimate moments. He's the most revered wedding photographer in New York City, and his rates reflect this status. His fee includes assistants, film, and negatives; albums are extra.

Harold Hechler Associates

654 Madison Avenue • New York, NY 10021
212-472-6565
$: Photography rates start at $4,200; videography rates start at $2,800

Harold Hechler is the father of candid photography, and his wedding photographs (color and black-and-white) and videography have a lively, vibrant style. His low-key style yields artsy, charming photographs that truly capture the spirit of the wedding. Hechler does family portraits but works quickly and efficiently. His small staff does high-quality work with the care he would give to "my own son or daughter's wedding." His staff includes six other photographers, and the fee includes a complete wedding album.

Jinsey Dauk Photography

666 Greenwich Street • New York, NY 10014
212-243-0652
www.jinsey.com • info@jinsey.com
$: Rates are $4,000 to $6,000

Jinsey Dauk's photographs have been featured in *Martha Stewart Weddings* and *Bride's*. She loves black-and-white photographs, but she makes sure to shoot enough color film to capture the flowers, food, and other vivid wedding moments. Her pictures have nostalgic yet timeless flair, and she prides herself on being easygoing and unobtrusive, catching real-life, spontaneous moments rather than stiff, posed shots. She calls her style "romantic photojournalism." Dauk's rate includes all proofs, plus unlimited color and black-and-white film, a pre-wedding creative meeting, and a hand-bound custom album.

Joel Greenberg & Wendy Stewart

Fine Photography & Videography
274 Water Street • New York, NY 10038
212-285-0979 • www.wedphotos.com
$: Photography rates range from $3,850 to $4,500;
videography rates range from $1,500 to $3,000

This group encompasses the styles and abilities of five different photographers, plus two videographers. The photographers shoot high-quality traditional and photojournalistic photos, in both color and black-and-white, with a subtle touch. The color is rich, and the black-and-white shots are classic without being staid. You can keep your negatives (both color and black-and-white). Videos follow the same philosophy: unobtrusive and photojournalistic. Check out their inspiring website—a great wedding resource guide of photos of dresses, cakes, flowers, etc.

Karen Hill Photography

New York, NY · 212-414-5115
hill@karenhill.com · www.karenhill.com
$: Rates start at $7,000 for eight hours of shooting,
40 rolls of film, and an assistant

Karen Hill creates absolutely beautiful, fairy-tale wedding photographs. Her candids are full of life, and her posed photos never seem stiff. She has an eye that captures the important—yet often hidden—elements of a wedding: the bridesmaids' bouquets, a lit-up tent at night, the hem of a gown. Hill tries to narrate the wedding day through her photographs. Her albums are beautifully put together by hand. While Hill specializes in black-and-white photography, she can also work in color. Her work has been featured in Lois Brady's book *Love Lessons* and in magazines such as *Martha Stewart Weddings* (where she is a contributing photographer), *Town & Country*, *New York Wedding*, and *Wedding Bells New York*. Hill's fee includes her time and proofs; prints and albums are extra.

Linda Harris

276 Prospect Place · Brooklyn, NY 11238
718-638-5865
lindaharris@earthlink.net
$: Rates start at $2,300

Linda Harris does both wedding and editorial photography. Her work has appeared in *Family Circle* and other magazines. Her wedding photographs are nontraditional, and her clients tend to be creative people looking for something memorable and unusual. She prides herself on being a great observer, capturing spontaneous moments in photographs that are full of life. She takes mostly candid shots but also some formal—yet intimate—portraits. Harris believes in making her services affordable, and her fees include film and proofs; clients have the option of purchasing their negatives. She doesn't produce albums, but she can advise you on a format.

Maria Quiroga

41 East 28th Street · New York, NY 10016
212-532-5320
www.bigoxmedia.com
$: Rates start at $3,000

Maria Quiroga is a still photographer by training, and it shows in her artistic wedding videography. She is also a documentarian, so her style is focused, refined, and lively. Her fees are based on a 3-hour shoot and include travel (within an hour of New York City), editing, and videotapes. The final videos are 45 to 60 minutes long, and, for an additional fee, Quiroga can also produce interactive DVDs of your wedding. She will add music, but does not use voice-overs and the only graphic title will be the opening credits. Quiroga is selective about the clients she chooses to work with—she wants to make sure they share her artistic vision.

Mary Adele Photography

422 East 72nd Street, Suite 10B · New York, NY 10021
212-570-0600 · Fax: 212-570-5150
www.maryadele.com · madele@rcn.com
$: Rates start at $8,500; her associates' rates start at $3,500.
Videography starts at $2,850 for seven hours
of coverage, including a finished video.

Mary Adele's company includes five photographers as well as several videographers. She has been in the wedding business for almost 20 years, and video coverage by her group has been featured on "Weddings of a Lifetime" and A&E's "American Wedding." Adele's photography often reflects a light touch. For example, while strolling Manhattan streets on their wedding day, Brian and Stephanie Werther were photographed with a gaggle of construction workers congratulating them. Mary Adele Photography provides both color and black-and-white photos, with most being photojournalistic in approach—a mixture of completely candid and casual poses. Along with traditional albums and prints, Adele also offers an "online photo album": 50 or more photos placed on her website shortly after your wedding for the benefit of friends and relatives who couldn't make it.

Olivier Lalin

110 West 17th Street, 5th Floor · New York, NY 10011
212-252-3952 · 917-541-6384
weddinglight@hotmail.com · www.weddinglight.com
$: Rates start at $5,000

Based in France and New York, Olivier Lalin produces classically timeless black-and-white photos. He has a painterly eye and a beautiful sense of space and composition, which results in very "quiet" photographs with a lovely sense of detail. As a photojournalist, Lalin views weddings as events in time, stories—yours—being told.

Philippe Cheng

180 Varick Street, Studio 400 · New York, NY 10014
212-627-4262
pcheng@bway.net
$: Rates start at $9,000

Philippe Cheng focuses on the quiet, still moments of the wedding: the details of the bride's veil, a blissful post-ceremony embrace, a ring bearer's shenanigans. His photos have a painterly, narrative sense and have been featured in *Martha Stewart Weddings* and in his own book, *Forever and a Day.* He offers album services. He's an extremely popular photographer, so contact him well ahead of time.

Sarah Merians Photography & Company

104 Fifth Avenue · New York, NY 10003
212-633-0502
www.sarahmerians.com
$: Photography rates start at $3,300; videography rates start at $2,275

Sarah Merians has a large staff of photographers, whose work has been featured in *New York Magazine, Town & Country*, and *Martha Stewart Weddings.* They each have their own style, so every couple is invited to look through all their books to choose the right individual. Overall, these photographers have a great sense of humor and shoot both candid and posed pictures.

Scott Whittle

12 Whitwell Place · Brooklyn, NY 11215
212-479-0809
scottwhittle@scottwhittle.com · www.scottwhittle.com
$: Rates start at $3,200 for four hours and $5,000 for nine hours

Scott Whittle shoots weddings in a casual, intimate way. His photos often have a soft, sensitive touch, but he also manages to catch wedding guests and attendants in moments of great celebration. Whittle can shoot both candids and casually posed pictures; see his website for a portfolio. He charges a flat fee that isn't based on the number of rolls of film shot.

Teri Bloom Photography

300 Mercer Street • New York, NY 10003
212-475-2274
terinyc1@aol.com • www.teribloom.com
$: Rates average $3,500 without an album

Teri Bloom has over 18 years of experience, including photojournalistic and editorial work (for *Rolling Stone*, *Time*, and other publications) in addition to wedding photography. In fact, she's shot over 400 events in the last ten years. Bloom shoots in both black-and-white and color and likes to capture stolen moments between the bride and groom and images of the guests kicking up their heels. Bloom also offers albums and prints, and clients receive their negatives to keep.

LONG ISLAND

Bart Stevens

230 Daly Road • East Northport, NY 11731
631-499-6998 • Fax: 631-462-1853
bartsteven@aol.com • www.bartstevensphoto-video.com
$: Photography rates start at $3,000 for Stevens himself,
$2,000 for an associate; videography rates start at $1,500

Bart Stevens is more of a traditional studio, though clients have the choice of traditional or photojournalistic style. Traditional photography includes "glamour shots" of the bride, complete with soft focus. The studio's color photos are rich and jewel-like, and their photographers capture outdoor settings beautifully. They also do some clever, if staged, indoor shots.

Deborah Kalas Photography

22 Indian Hill Road • East Hampton, NY 11937
631-324-1862 • Fax: 631-329-9051
dkalas1@optonline.net • www.kalasstudios.com
$: Rates start at $3,500

Deborah Kalas's fine arts degree shows in her celebratory wedding photos. She does take some posed shots of the wedding party, but her style tends to be nontraditional and more spur-of-the-moment, capturing the romance between the newlyweds. She also takes sweet photos of children. Kalas shoots in both color and black-and-white. She does albums for an additional fee.

Liz and Joe Schmidt Photography

366 Hempstead Avenue • Malverne, NY 11565
516-887-7900
smile@lizjoephoto.com • www.lizjoephoto.com
$: Rates start at $3,500

Liz and Joe Schmidt do traditional and photojournalistic wedding photography. In fact, they can combine both styles to create the perfect package for you. However, if you choose traditional, posed photos, they'll remain unobtrusive by finishing the formal portrait shoot before the reception starts. They work in color and black-and-white and try to remain low-key even while taking shots of the ceremony. Look at their website for a gallery of images. Their fee varies based on whether albums and prints are included.

Park Ave. Studio

8 St. John's Street • Sayville, NY 11782
631-589-7735
email@parkavestudio.com • www.parkavestudio.com
$: Photography rates range from $1,295 to $3,000;
videography rates range from $1,295 to $2,295

If you're looking for traditional photography services on Long Island, Park Ave. Studio may be your best bet. Their photographs highlight details such as the sumptuous fabric of the bride's dress to emphasize the beauty of the wedding day. Photo services include the bride's wedding-day makeup, formal photos prior to cocktail hour, and an album that's guaranteed to be ready within four months after the wedding. Video services can include a finished video with music, special effects, baby photos of the bride and groom, and any other photos you'd like to include.

Ray O'Connor Photography

218 Laurel Road • East Northport, NY 11731
613-261-1908
rayphoto@aol.com • www.rayoconnorphotography.com
$: Rates start at $2,500; rates for videography start at $1,700

Ray O'Connor combines beautiful posed portraits of the wedding party with unobtrusive pictures of the bride and groom having a ball at their reception to create a wonderful document of your wedding. He has been in business for over 25 years, and his team of photographers shoots in both color and black-and-white. His fee includes several albums.

Roma Photographers

24 Main Street • Sayville, NY 11782
613-563-1414
romaphoto@aol.com • www.romaphoto.com
$: Rates start at $4,000

Alex Benvenuto shoots in a natural photojournalist style. He works in both color and black-and-white and has a knack for capturing the newlyweds in intimate moments.

WESTCHESTER

Derek Photographers Group

121 East 71st Street • New York, NY 10021
800-44-DEREK • 212-628-5100
newyorkcity@derekgroup.com

118 Craft Avenue • Bronxville, NY 10708
914-961-8600

2 Chase Road • Scarsdale, NY 10583
914-725-3030
scarsdale@derekgroup.com

234 Greenwich Avenue • Greenwich, CT 06830
203-661-9400
greenwich@derekgroup.com

www.derekgroup.com
$: Rates start at $2,695

Derek Photographers' primary location is Scarsdale, but so much of Derek Jackson's business is based in New York City that he maintains a Manhattan number. Jackson has been in business for 31 years, and he and his associates tailor their wedding photography to each couple's wants and needs. Their style veers toward the photojournalistic, capturing spontaneous moments as they occur rather than putting family members in strained poses. The studio also offers video services; call for prices.

NEW JERSEY

Images by Berit

29 Riverside Drive · Florham Park, NJ 07932
973-408-6566
berit@imagesbyberit.com · www.imagesbyberit.com
$: Rates start at $4,900

Berit Bizjak takes celebratory photographs in a basic photojournalistic style. Her pictures capture the happiest moments of a wedding. Bizjak gets to know her clients personally and tries to capture the essence of who they are as a couple, taking an extra amount of film with her to shoots. She loves weddings and has a ball photographing them. Her rate includes an assistant, full set of paper proofs, unlimited film, and website; albums are priced separately.

Jasper-Sky Wedding Photographer

138 Wayne Street · Jersey City, NJ 07302
800-357-8011
jasper.sky@verizon.net · www.jasper-sky.com
$: Call for rates

Stephanie Jasper and Paul Sky, a husband-and-wife team, work quickly and unobtrusively to create a fairy-tale photographic rendition of each wedding. Their work is featured in the book *Colin Cowie Weddings*, they shoot celebrity nuptials for *In Style*, and they're the only wedding photographers that the Bloomingdale's bridal registry recommends to clients. They shoot a mix of color and black-and-white, candid and formal. Their photographs have a wonderful sense of humor while remaining classically elegant, and their sense of detail is magnificent. Their fee includes the services of both photographers plus proofs.

Thomas Studios

720 Monroe Street · Hoboken, NJ 07030
800-316-2220
info@thomasstudios.com · www.thomasstudios.com
$: Rates start at $2,900

Ray Thomas is a straightforward photographer with a photojournalistic edge; he shoots posed color portraits and group shots, and uses black-and-white film for the reception pictures. He documents the whole day, aiming to tell your wedding story through the photos; he uses a number of special effects, like fish-eye lenses, while avoiding flash photography. His package includes the negatives and a 16-inch-by-20-inch engagement portrait with exposed mat for signing at the reception. He represents three album companies.

Video by Maurice

101 Lexington Avenue • Cresskill, NJ 07626
201-568-7038
vbmvideo@aol.com • www.videobymaurice.com
$: Rates start at $1,600

Three videographers, including owner Maurice Brown, shoot for Video by Maurice. All work is done digitally, and all the videographers are also in the film business, so they look at your wedding video as a film unto itself. They'll provide the works for you. Your wedding documentary can be finished as DVD.

CONNECTICUT

Derek Photographers Group

234 Greenwich Avenue • Greenwich, CT 06930
203-661-9400 or 800-44-DEREK
www.derekgroup.com

See Westchester listing.

Maring Photography

824C East Center Street • Wallingford, CT 06492
203-949-9370
maring@snet.net • www.maringphoto.com
$: Rates start at $6,000

Charles and Jennifer Maring, a married couple themselves, have a style that crosses all boundaries. They do posed and candid photos in black-and-white and color, as well as hand-tinted photos (all photos are printed in-house). In fact, they believe that wedding photography is about more than just portraits: it's also about the details of the day. As such, they beautifully capture the cake, bouquet, place settings, and more. Clients can view all proofs on a password-protected website, and an album is included in their fee. Wedding albums are also available on DVD. Getting married in Zanzibar? They will travel worldwide.

PHOTO RETOUCHING

Marilynn Hawkridge

63 West 20th Street · New York, NY 10011
212-206-1342
$: Prices vary

Marilynn Hawkridge can retouch and restore almost any photograph you bring her. She can make you look younger, give you more teeth, make your teeth whiter, even make you look thinner. She works hard to make sure that her work is natural and invisible. Hawkridge's airbrushing work starts at about $25 and her digital retouching starts at $50. Simple retouching only takes two or three days, but restoration can take two weeks.

WEDDING ARTIST

Anne Watkins

227 Riverside Drive · New York, NY 10025
212-866-0057
$: Rates start at $5,000 and depend on the size of the wedding.
Call for rates for individual portraits.

As a complement or alternative to traditional wedding photos, artist Anne Watkins provides an elegant and unusual service. She attends the wedding with an easel and watercolor set, carefully observes the event, and paints beautiful, ethereal, abstract images of what she sees: the bride getting dressed, an excited flower girl about to start the procession, the ceremony, the first dance, and incidental moments that might otherwise go unobserved. She has painted the weddings of Darcy Miller, editor of *Martha Stewart Weddings*, actor Kyle MacLachlan, and writer Susan Orlean. A typical wedding yields 8 to 12 paintings, and the couple can opt to have Watkins scan her work and bind it into an album. She says that people often give some of the originals to relatives as presents but with the album they'll always have a complete set. She also does portrait work and recently painted a bride at a fitting who then gave the picture to her groom as a wedding present.

Notes

Invitations and Calligraphy

You'll be confronted with all sorts of options when choosing your wedding invitations. You may select a traditional style from a catalog (in fact, many of the stationers in City Weddings offer a discounted rate on catalog invites) or opt for custom invitations, from the wildly eccentric to the ultimate in elegance. There a number of techniques used to create invitations (specifics are below), as well as a large number of international paper stocks available—including the currently popular rice paper embedded with real flowers. The most classic wedding invitations are made with 100-percent cotton paper stock, but don't be held back by tradition. With so many options to choose from, you can create just about any invitation you can imagine.

Decide well ahead of time how many invitations you'll need. As few as 25 additional invitations can cost up to $200.

The basics

A basic invitation set usually includes a ceremony invitation, a reception card, and an outer envelope. The set you choose may also contain an inner envelope and a response card, with or without its own envelope. Some stationers also include thank-you notes.

Printing techniques

There are a number of different techniques used to create formal and informal invitations. From most to least expensive, they include:

● Engraving: Creates a raised design, with an impression, or bruise, left on the back of the paper. A copper or steel plate is actually engraved with your invitation wording and design; the etchings are filled with ink and forced against the paper.

● Thermography: Also creates raised lettering, but without an impression left on the back of the paper. A resinous powder reacts to heat and raises the lettering and design. Thermography allows for a wide choice of ink colors.

● Letterpress: Invites are created using an old-fashioned printing press with movable squares of type that leave an impression on the paper. This works well if you want to use textured, handmade paper or simply wish to create a more distinctive, personalized invitation.

● Laser printing: Done on a computer. Well-done laser invitations can look as nice as thermographed or engraved ones (especially if they are printed on fine paper), although the lettering and design won't be raised.

Extras include:

● Calligraphy: Beautifully hand-lettered and/or hand-addressed invitations can look stunning. Machine-done calligraphy is a less-expensive and faster option.

● Embossing: An inkless raised impression. You can have your initials or return address embossed on the invitations or response-card envelopes. Or, buy your own hand embosser and do this yourself. (One caveat: You can't emboss on lined envelopes.)

● Lined envelopes: These feature an inner lining, sometimes in a different color, patterned, or metallic paper.

● Ribbons and bows: Can be attached to your invitations to add dimension and color.

● Confetti, flower petals, and other small decorations: Can be inserted loose into the invitation's outer envelope.

Invite assembly

Once you've decided which invitations to purchase, you'll be faced with the task of assembling them for mailing. Generally, enclosures such as the reception card, response card, and response envelope are tucked into a folded invitation (or placed on top of the invitation if it's not the folded variety). Remember to put a stamp on the response-card envelope. If you are sending formal invitations, all of this will go inside the inner envelope, which is "addressed" with the recipient's name only. The inner envelope remains unsealed (it is ungummed) and is placed into the outer envelope, with the front of the inner envelope facing the back of the outer. The outer envelope is usually hand addressed in calligraphy (or just very nice handwriting), using guests' full names and titles. When you're ready to send them out, have a fully assembled invite weighed at the post office to see how much postage each will need. Don't forget to request special "love" stamps.

When to order and send

Depending on the your stationer's requirements, you should generally order your invitations three or six months before the wedding (leave yourself a few weeks to address and assemble them, too). Ask to see a proof before the invites are printed to check for typos. Many stationers will do rush orders; some can provide invitations within 24 hours, but you'll have to pay a sometimes hefty extra fee. Send invites about six to eight weeks before the wedding to give guests time to write you in on their calendars and make travel arrangements.

How many sets to order

Order 10 or 12 more invitation sets than the number of addresses on your list (remember that couples or families can share an invitation) so you have extras for last-minute guest-list additions, as well as keepsakes. Also order 20 or 25 extra envelopes to compensate for inevitable addressing mistakes.

Additional note about calligraphy

Calligrapher Nan DeLuca has a few recommendations for couples preparing to order their invitations. Don't have your stationer assemble your unaddressed invitations for you. It wastes a lot of time for the calligrapher if she or he has to unstuff every set of invitations before addressing them. She also suggests that you pick a calligrapher and invitations at the same time. That way you can ask the calligrapher about your choices. Some paper doesn't take ink well and can blur or run. The calligrapher can advise you ahead of time of any potential pitfalls. Finally, if you're planning a spring or summer wedding, try to get a calligrapher on board very early (January or February) because they do get booked up fast.

NEW YORK CITY

Bernard Maisner Calligraphy
and Fine Stationery

212-477-6776
bmaisner@aol.com
$: Custom design starts at $30 per invitation;
calligraphy is $2 to $3 per line for addressing

Bernard Maisner is considered the best hand-letterer in the country. His work has appeared on books, the album covers of Whitney Houston and Mick Jagger, and in advertising campaigns. He also does custom calligraphy and hand-lettered wedding invitations. Invitation designs start at $350 for a mechanical, while addressing is priced based on the two most popular basic styles of calligraphy: semi-embellished Spencerian and embellished Spencerian. Standard is $2 a line, while florid embellished (Maisner's specialty) is $3 a line. It can get quite pricey, but if you're looking for beautiful artwork suitable for framing, Maisner's your man.

Blacker & Kooby Stationers

1204 Madison Avenue • New York, NY 10128
212-369-8308 • Fax: 212-860-7177
www.blackerandkooby.com
$: Starts at $2.50 per set (for very basic invitations)
and goes up to $100 per set

Blacker & Kooby offers everything from simple laser-printed invites to ultra-luxurious, gilt-edged engraved styles. This stationer has a huge selection of papers and ribbons from around the world—including British, Indian (embedded with real flowers), French, Italian, and Belgian paper stocks—and hundreds of invitation catalogs to choose from, as well as the ability to create custom creations. Blacker & Kooby has in-house calligraphy services and can hand-assemble your invites. If you're looking for super-elegant invitations, plan to order three to four months in advance (though rush service is available).

Calligraphy by Nanette DeLuca

77 Bleecker Street • New York, NY 10012
212-477-3732
Deluca212@aol.com • www.scribenyc.com
$: Envelope addressing starts at $3.75 per set

**(including inner and outer envelopes); price varies based on
ink color, paper stock, and addresses in excess of five lines**

Nanette DeLuca can work with printers to design beautifully customized invites. She specializes in copperplate lettering. If she's addressing envelopes for you, she can match the color of the invitation ink. Allow three weeks for completion.

Calligraphy Studios

**100 Reade Street · New York, NY 10013
212-964-6007 · Fax: 212-964-9170
callig100@aol.com
$: Minimum order of $500 for address calligraphy or custom invitations**

If you're looking for personal attention, look no further than Linda Stein's Calligraphy Studios. Clients such as Natasha Richardson and Quincy Jones come to Stein for the former sculptor's extraordinary calligraphy. She does invitations, place cards, and menus (she can do about 90 writing styles and works in a variety of languages, including Arabic, Chinese, Hebrew, and Polish); she also designs personal monograms and creates gorgeous custom invitations. Stein needs at least two weeks to do most jobs, although rush jobs are possible. She works by appointment only.

Celebrations, Ink

**425 East 58th Street, 19B · New York, NY 10022
212-813-1806 · Fax: 212-935-7215
$: Starts at $175 per 100 sets**

Celebrations, Ink works by appointment only. They offer both catalog invitations and hand-calligraphed invitations, place cards, rehearsal-dinner invites, napkins, as well as stationery, announcements, and gifts.

Continental Corporation Engravers

**31-00 47th Avenue · Long Island City, NY 11101
718-784-7711 or 800-285-5643 · Fax: 718-784-26983
info@continentalengravers.com · www.continentalengravers.com
$: Starts at $800 for 75 engraved sets**

Continental has been in business since 1890, creating engraved, customized invitations for customers throughout the tristate area. The stationer offers a choice of art papers from around the world and can provide embossing, foil stamping, invitations die-cut to specific shapes, engraved images, offset printing, matched ink colors, and hand assembly, including ribbons, tassels, and lined envelopes. All work is custom; you consult with designers to create unique invites.

Dempsey & Carroll

110 East 57th Street · New York, NY 10022
212-486-7526 or 800-444-4019 · Fax: 212-486-7523
www.dempseyandcarroll.com
$: Starts at $1,000 for 100 sets

Dempsey & Carroll is the traditional choice of presidents, royalty, ambassadors, and other famous and elegant folk. This stationer has been creating beautiful engraved wedding invitations for more than 120 years, stocking only 100 percent cotton paper embellished with the prestigious Dempsey & Carroll watermark. You must order at least four to six weeks in advance of when you plan to send out your invitations.

Ellen Weldon Design

273 Church Street · New York, NY 10013
212-925-4483 · Fax: 212-941-9862
ellen@weldondesign.com
$: Starts at $25 per set

Ellen Weldon creates wonderful invitations with unique papers made around the world, including rice papers and handmade papers, and her high-quality work is reflected in her high prices. She works with engravers, printers, hot-stampers, and silkscreeners to make customized designs, but she can also do hand calligraphy.

Gracious Home

1217 Third Avenue · New York, NY 10021
212-517-6300 · Fax: 212-249-1354
and
1992 Broadway · New York, NY 10023
212-231-7800 · Fax: 212-875-9976
info@gracioushome.com · www.gracioushome.com
$: In-stock prices range from $136 to $146 per 25 of the most basic sets

Do you like tough choices? Gracious Home has a collection of over 500 custom and in-stock stationery designs. You have a choice of thermographed or engraved invitations. You can also order thank-you notes. The store offers free delivery in Manhattan.

Kate's Paperie

561 Broadway • **New York, NY 10012**
212-941-9816 • **Fax: 212-941-9560**
and
8 West 13th Street • **New York, NY 10011**
212-633-0570 • **Fax: 212-366-5421**
and
1282 Third Avenue • **New York, NY 10021**
212-396-3670 • **Fax: 212-366-6532**
www.katespaperie.com
$: Ranges from $5 to $30 per set

Invitations from Kate's Paperie are individual works of art. The designers at Kate's can create exquisite customized designs, including details such as wax seals and lavish ribbons. All three of Kate's Manhattan stores have a superb selection of papers, from handmade rice paper to traditional card stock. You can choose from a number of printing options, including letterpress printing, embossing, and engraving. Kate's also offers wedding stationery from fine paper mills including Crane's and William Arthur. Call the store most convenient to you for an appointment.

Margaret DiPiazza Ink

442 Third Avenue • **New York, NY 10016**
212-889-3057 • **Fax: 212-725-7363**
www.dipiazzaink.com
$: Ranges from $2 to $50 per set; envelope addressing is $1 per line

Margaret DiPiazza offers a large variety of invitations and calligraphy by appointment only. You'll have a broad choice of paper and printing options (engraving, thermography, letterpress, etc.) and hand-lettered or typeset designs. DiPiazza can do calligraphy in a large number of styles, including copperplate and italic. She also works with floral-embedded papers and a variety of ribbons and wax-seal impressions. She does hand-painted designs and will address the envelopes in calligraphy to match the invitation style.

Papivore

223 Elizabeth Street • **New York, NY 10012**
212-334-4330 • **Fax: 212-334-4304**
www.papivore.com
$: Prices vary per set based on quantity.

This upscale Soho outfit offers all sorts of luxurious paper goods, as well as the Cavallini and Soolip lines of wedding invitations (both lines are handcrafted, using letterpress printing). Papivore also carries an amazing range of European papers in various colors and sizes and can arrange for letterpress printing on these.

Papyrus

Five stores in New York City, one in Garden City, six in New Jersey, and one each in Danbury and Farmington, Connecticut
212-717-0002
(see website for store addresses and phone numbers)
www.papyrusonline.com
$: Prices range from $135 to $1,300 for 100 invites

Papyrus has stores across the country that specialize in custom-printed invitations on unique paper. All sorts of printing options are available—engraving, thermography, flat printing, letterpress—as well as a variety of decorative elements to incorporate into your invitations.

Rae Michaels

521 Madison Avenue · New York, NY 10022
212-688-2256 · Fax: 212-688-2004
$: Starts at $700 for 100 sets

Rae Michaels has created custom wedding invitations for a celebrity-studded client list. She creates traditional as well as custom designs, using both handmade and imported paper, adorned with ribbons, bows, hand-painted flowers, and gold leaf. She can provide calligraphy services and also does letterpress, engraved work, and thermography. She is the coauthor of *Pen Passion: A Cylindrical Obsession*. Michaels works by appointment only.

Rebecca Moss

510 Madison Avenue · New York, NY 10022
800-INK-PENS · Fax: 212-832-7690
www.rebeccamoss.com
$: Call for prices

This upscale stationer offers society-worthy wedding invitations. Many celebrities and world leaders have ordered personal stationery and invitations through Rebecca Moss. Browse through four books of predesigned invitations, or choose a custom design that can be printed onto 100 percent cotton paper using engraving, thermography, or flat printing. Rebecca Moss also offers a line of accessories, including the stationer's signature writing instruments.

Soho Letter Press

69 Greene Street • New York, NY 10013
212-334-4356 • Fax: 212-334-4357
$: Prices start at $600 for 100 sets.

Soho Letter Press makes absolutely beautiful, reasonably priced wedding invitations. The company offers hand-printed letterpressing on almost any type of paper, from traditional 100 percent cotton to one-of-a-kind handmade styles. Jobs typically take three to six weeks. Soho Letter Press is by appointment only.

LONG ISLAND

Have You Heard?, Inc.

2544 Merrick Road • Bellmore, NY 11710
516-409-0283 • Fax: 516-409-0284
party@haveyouheardinc.com • www.haveyouheardinc.com
$: Starts at $350 per 100 sets

This Bellmore stationer is family owned and operated and offers all sorts of wedding goodies, from invitations and imprinted ribbons to wedding-party gifts and wedding and shower favors. Choose from many lines of catalog invitations including C'est Papier, Elite, Krepe-Kraft, Nu-Art, and Encore. The stationers will work with you to find the invite to match your wedding style or theme. They provide calligraphy services and can even create invitations using original photographs.

Invitation House

118 Forest Drive • Jericho, NY 11753
516-681-0664
$: Starts at $1.25 per set

If you're looking for invitations made with unusual materials, visit Invitation House. The company works with rice paper, silk moiré, and suede, among other unique textiles, and adorns their invites with ribbons and silk roses. Choose from a variety of catalogs at a 25 percent discount; if you don't find what you're looking for, the stationers will work with you on a custom design. Thermography and copperplate engraving are among the available printing options.

Marcia Kahan

46 Rose Lane • East Rockaway, NY 11518
516-374-1167 • Fax: 516-374-7168
marciakahan@aol.com • www.marciakahan.com
$: Ranges from $65 per 100 simple sets to more than
$1,500 per 100 elaborate sets

Marcia Kahan is an international stationer, with clients in the United States and Europe. She can do calligraphy in Hebrew and also works in many other foreign languages. Kahan represents about 90 stationery companies, offering their predesigned invites at discount prices; she also has her own line of stationery and can create original artwork. If you see an invitation elsewhere that you especially like, bring a copy to Kahan and she'll duplicate it at a lower price. She will do hand or laser calligraphy on envelopes and invitations.

Notes by Jan

635 Lakeview Avenue • Rockville Center, NY 11570
516-536-9519 • Fax: 630-982-2948
jan@optonline.net • www.notesbyjan.com
$: Starts at $6 per set

Owner Jan Weisblum makes one-of-a-kind invitations. Her vivid, hand-colored invitations include such motifs as flowers, lovebirds, or Hebrew lettering. She incorporates all sorts of nontraditional materials, such as glitter, fabric, even feathers and rhinestones, and uses only high-quality paper in heavy card stock. She can even personalize each invite to address the invitee. Weisblum requires no minimum order, so she's a great source for super-personalized invites for an intimate wedding.

WESTCHESTER

AB Creative Designs, Etc.

16 High Acres Drive • Thornwood, NY 10594
914-747-0007 • Fax: 914-747-0001
abcreativedesigns@netzero.net
$: Starts at just under $4 per set

This Thornwood stationer offers any invitation style your heart desires, from the formal to the fantastic. AB Creative Designs carries a number of stationery lines, including Inscribe, Nu-Art, Carlson Craft, Krepe-Kraft, and Birchcraft. Owner Adriane Bonfiglio requires no minimum order and can deliver within a week in most cases, so if you're planning an intimate wedding or had a whirlwind engagement, this may be the stationer for you. AB Creative Designs offers computer addressing, shower and bridal-party gifts, as well as many kinds of wedding favors.

The Paper Depot

17 Deer Run • Rye Brook, NY 10573
914-939-6055 • Fax: 914-934-2333
$: Starts at $5 per set

Owner Michelle Weiner has been creating custom invitations for 15 years. She has a number of invitation catalogs on hand, with all styles offered at a 20 percent discount, or she can work with brides and grooms to create an original invitation at a reasonable price. She also does computer calligraphy for envelope addressing. Weiner sees clients at her home studio by appointment only.

Sincerely Staci

94 Deerfield Lane North • Pleasantville, NY 10570
914-769-6902 • Fax: 914-769-2368
$: Starts at $5 per set

Owner Staci Rahamin offers both predesigned and custom invitations. She offers engraving and thermography and can emboss your envelopes with your return address or monogram. She can hire calligraphers to address your envelopes by hand. Her catalog invites come at a 20 percent discount.

New Jersey

By Royal Request

1220 Route 46 West • Parsippany, NJ 07054
973-334-4434 • Fax: 973-334-4699
$: Starts at $200 per 100 sets

This Parsippany stationer offers an extensive collection of invitation books to choose from, all at a 20 percent discount. Invitations are produced using flat printing, engraving, thermography, and letterpress techniques. Hand or machine calligraphy is also available. Owner Judy Polansky pays extraordinary attention to special requests, such as artwork.

Invitation Hotline

68 Hawkins Road · Manalapan, NJ 07726
800-800-4355 · Fax: 732-972-4875
info@invitationhotline.com · www.invitationhotline.com
$: Starts at $60 per 100 sets

This Manalapan stationer provides designer invitations from over 90 books, all at a discount. Invites are ready about two weeks after your order is placed (which you may do online 24 hours a day), so there's no rush to order them months ahead of time. Owner Marcy Slachman was a consultant for the book *Bridal Bargains*. She also has a degree in fine arts, so she knows her stuff. She works by appointment only, but orders may be made later with a book and item number. The business does calligraphy and favors, too.

Invitations Et Cetera

129 South Livingston Avenue · Livingston, NJ 07039
973-992-3020 or 888-222-RSVP · Fax: 973-992-5237
$: Starts at $300 per 100 sets

Invitations Et Cetera sells traditional invitation lines from over 175 books as well as custom invitations using silk flowers, ribbons, and drawings. Their own selection can be printed in-house and ready to mail in 24 hours (for small quantities), so if you're in a rush to tie the knot, head here. They offer hand and machine calligraphy, as well as accessories such as place cards.

Papier Maché

1258 Teaneck Road · Teaneck, NJ 07666
201-816-0726 · Fax: 201-816-0196
$: Prices start at $250 for 100 sets

This is the spot if you're looking for a great variety of custom work, including hand lettering and monograms. Papier Maché has everything from 100 percent cotton papers suitable for copperplate engraving or embossing to delicate, handmade papers inlaid with flower petals or seeds. They can also design monogrammed or otherwise personalized gifts for showers or attendants.

Personalized Papers by Arlene

One Highview Court • Montville, NJ 07045
973-299-1772 • Fax: 973-263-0797
littlear@hotmail.com
$: Ranges from $75 per 100 thermographed sets
to $1,000 per 100 engraved sets

Personalized Papers is the perfect place to shop if you have a hard time making up your mind! The stationer stocks a large number of books filled with designer invitation styles at a discount, and you can actually take several books home to peruse at your leisure. If you want true full service, owner Arlene Koenigsberg will even come to your home to help you select a design.

Presence

637 Wyckoff Avenue • Wyckoff, NJ 07481
201-848-0023 • Fax: 201-848-0024
$: Starts at $85 per 100 sets

The staff at Presence prides itself on personal service—they're quick to suggest unique touches such as hand-tied ribbons, and they'll even hand-deliver invitations to your door. Invites are printed and addressed on site with a computerized calligraphy system, and the store stocks a large number of high-quality papers, so rush orders are possible. Presence also carries a number of invitation catalogs, with prices ranging from moderate to expensive.

CONNECTICUT

Gail Brill Design

866-481-2056 • Fax: 866-481-2057
gail@gailbrilldesign.com • www.gailbrilldesign.com
$: Starts at $7 per offset set; letterpress invitations are $12 per set;
engraved invitations are $17 per set.
Calligraphed addressing ranges from $1.25 to $2 per line.

A contributor to *Martha Stewart Living* and *Weddings*, Gail Brill certainly knows her stuff. She was featured on NBC's *"Today Throws a Wedding 2002."* Her custom invitations are first done in hand calligraphy and are then engraved, letterpress printed, or offset printed. Brill also creates customized table cards, place cards, menu cards, wedding programs, and favor tags. She advises couples to contact her six to eight months before the wedding.

Joan Segal Stationery

28 Kaysal Court • Armonk, NY 10504
914-273-5650 • Fax: 914-273-6312
jsegalstat@msn.com
$: Prices start around $100 for 100 of the most basic invitations

Joan Segal has a fantastic selection of stationery and invitation materials and is happy to work with you to make all the printed matter for your wedding perfect. She can get you handmade papers, Cranes invitations, Cranes boxed stationery, and all kinds of beautiful, unusual papers. Segal can also arrange for any kind of printing you want, from engraving to thermography, and can even do computerized lettering and calligraphy. Segal recommends that couples come in six months before the event to start studying her books of invitations, but she can work on shorter notice as well.

Personalized Print by Marcie G.

18 Meadow Lane • Norwich, CT 06360
860-MARCIEG • Fax: 860-859-9103
marcieg2@aol.com • www.marcieg.invitations.com
$: Computerized invitations start at $1.85
per six-by-nine-inch set; smaller invitations are less

This former English teacher will work within any budget to create your dream wedding invitation. Her very creative approach allows you to select the art, color, and wording for your invite by coming in for a personal appointment or simply by looking at her website. If you select your style online, she'll mail or fax you a proof for approval. Marcie G. is the perfect stationer for the couple who wants a more informal approach: her computerized invitations are available immediately, she can incorporate your sense of humor, and she can even scan your own photos to use as art.

Florists

A wedding's style is often guided by the flowers and floral arrangements. After all, your bridal bouquet will appear many times in your wedding photos, and table centerpieces help set the mood for the party. The total cost of your wedding flowers depends on the kinds of blooms you choose to use, how many arrangements you have, how lush you want those arrangements to be, and what design details (e.g., candles, ribbons, vases, or other containers) are incorporated. Sit down with your chosen florist and discuss how much you can spend before you start selecting flowers: You may decide that Dutch rose bouquets and Dutch rose centerpieces won't fit your budget. Your florist should be able to suggest alternatives you can afford. Perhaps you can have the rose bouquets but choose table centerpieces that use different flowers in the same color scheme—or maybe a less expensive type of rose.

We've listed the cost of each florist's bridal and bridesmaid bouquets, as well as centerpieces for 10- to 12-person tables. However, some florists work by planning the entire floral design for each wedding and so have given us their prices in terms of overall cost. Of course, all prices listed are estimates, and costs will vary depending on the time of year, the flowers used, and the bouquet and centerpiece styles.

As with all other wedding vendors, be sure to get your agreement with your florist in writing. Confirm what types of flowers are to be used (as well as what alternates are acceptable), how many bouquets/boutonnieres/centerpieces you will get, when and where personal bouquets will be delivered, and how far in advance the florist needs access to your reception site.

Typical wedding flowers

- Bridal bouquet and optional throw-away bouquet (for tossing)

- Bouquets for bride's attendants (the maid of honor's bouquet is sometimes slightly different than the bridesmaids')

- Bouquet or basket of petals for flower girl

- Optional headpiece for flower girl

- Corsages or nosegays for mother of the bride, mother of the groom, and any other special family members or honored female guests

- Groom's boutonniere (traditionally a sprig pulled from the bride's bouquet)

- Boutonnieres for the best man, groomsmen, ushers, father of the groom, father of the bride, ring bearer (optional), and any other special family members or honored male guests

- Decorations for the church or ceremony site, including (but not limited to) pew decorations, aisle runners, a chuppah (Jewish wedding canopy), and altar or stage decorations

- Decorations for the reception, including arrangements for the head table and guest tables, arrangements for the buffet and/or cake table; and additional arrangements for windowsills, entryways, place-card table, and any other spot needing some decoration

Kinds of bouquets

HAND-TIED

This is currently the most popular bouquet for both brides and attendants. It's an elegant, sophisticated look, with a dense grouping of flowers tied firmly with ribbon (often French wire ribbon, which is wired at the edges so it can be tied in beautiful, sculpted bows).

NOSEGAY

The nosegay was a Victorian floral staple. It's a small, tight, perfectly round gathering of blooms, the stems of which are tied together with ribbon. Usually nosegays consist of only one type of flower or of just one color.

CASCADE

This bouquet style was popular in the fifties and again in the eighties but has recently fallen out of favor for being a bit too much of a handful. It incorporates a large bunch of flowers cascading down from a holder. Quite often, this classic style incorporates lilies and roses.

POMANDER

This type of bouquet is usually used only by flower girls. It's a tight ball of blooms dangling from a ribbon.

Floral tips

- Reserve your florist at least three to six months before the wedding.

- Most caterers and event planners can recommend a reputable florist.

- Most flower varieties are available year-round these days, thanks to increasingly more efficient delivery systems. If you're dying for out-of-season flowers, don't hesitate to ask your florist. Chances are he or she can accommodate your wishes. Remember, however, that you may pay more for delicate or exotic blooms.

- Many florists also rent tents, do lighting design, or can create other decorations for your wedding. Ask them for details.

- Smaller florists (who do fewer weddings) may be able to give your celebration more personal attention.

- Most florists are willing to travel, so if you fall in love with a Manhattan florist but are getting hitched on Long Island, chances are it's not a problem.

- Be sure to ask your florist how much time will be needed to set up at the ceremony and reception sites. Then make sure he'll have access when he needs it.

- If you want to be extra economical, check out New York City's flower market in the West 20s. It opens very early on weekday mornings—get there at 9 A.M. and you'll have slim pickings. Most florists are located on Sixth Avenue between 26th and 30th streets, with some located on 28th and 29th. Many of these shops have "Wholesale Only" signs in their windows, but many sell to individuals as well.

New York City

Ariston Florist

69 Fifth Avenue · New York, NY 10003
212-929-4226 or 800-422-2747 · Fax: 212-242-5479
www.aristonflorist.com
$: Bridal bouquets, $150 and up; bridesmaid bouquets, $60 and up;
centerpieces, $75 and up

No event is too big or too small for Ariston Florist. This lower Fifth Avenue florist has twice been given the Circle of Excellence Award by Teleflora and specializes in Dutch, spring, and exotic flowers. Ariston creates traditional centerpieces and bouquets, frequently including orchids. There are a number of different chuppah designs to choose from as well.

Atlas Floral Decorators

46-12 70th Street · Woodside, NY 11377
718-457-4900
and
The Plaza Hotel · 2 Central Park South · New York, NY 10019
212-753-3260
ATLAS11377@aol.com
Bridal bouquets start at $200; bridesmaid bouquets start at $100;
low centerpieces start at $200; high centerpieces start at $300

Atlas Floral Decorators has been a New York–area mainstay for weddings and special events for many years. Larry and Elliot Atlas love to work with couples and will remove all worry from the flower-planing process. Atlas Floral Decorators works in a wide range of styles, from traditional to contemporary, so you can feel confident when working with them that they will do everything they can to make your wedding beautiful. By appointment only.

David Beahm Designs

522 West 33rd Street · New York, NY 10001
212-279-1344 · Fax: 212-279-1346
cs@dbdny.com · www.dbdny.com
$: Call for prices

While David Beahm's work as the floral designer for the wedding of Michael Douglas to Catherine Zeta Jones and his other socialite clients has earned him a

reputation as a darling of the Park Avenue set, he insists he can work on any wedding on any budget on any scale. He can do anything from a small house wedding to a full-blown Newport, Rhode Island extravaganza, draping five tents in 15,000 yards of fabric. David Beahm Designs can work in any style and no matter what, won't produce a "cookie-cutter wedding" for you. They never cook up the same designs twice, and will do anything to make their clients happy no matter what the budget. Beahm is also a bouquet specialist. He uses an old, and little used, style of hand-wiring the bridal flowers together so that each blossom stands out on its own, instead of forming the more familiar clump. Charming, approachable, and easy to work with, David Beahm Designs is a pleasure.

Belle Fleur

11 East 22nd Street • New York, NY 10010
212-254-8703 • Fax: 212-254-8704
www.bellefleur.com
$: Bridal bouquets, $190 to $275; bridesmaid bouquets, $90 to $150;
centerpieces, $125 and up

Marilyn Waga and Meredith Waga Perez, a mother-daughter team, create sophisticated arrangements for weddings in New York and New Jersey. Belle Fleur does flower arranging in a broad range of styles, from a European traditional aesthetic to a contempoary "Zen-inspired" look. They make chuppahs as well.

Bloom

16 West 21st Street • New York, NY 10010
212-620-5666
and
541 Lexington Avenue • New York, NY 10022
212-832-8094
www.bloomflowers.com
$: Bridal bouquets are $175 and up; bridesmaid bouquets are $75 and up;
centerpieces are $175 and up

Walk into Bloom's stores and you will immediately feel inspired and transported by the beautiful design and amazing flowers that surround you. Bloom does wonderful wedding work and their signature aesthetic—simple, lush, tone-on-tone floral designs—inspires their arrangements. While their arrangements are often monochromatic, they include many inventive additions like fruit (miniature apples, cranberries, and strawberries) to add texture. Bloom is very careful about working within the existing architecture of the space so that every element is harmonious and gorgeous. Bloom also does fantastic hand-tied bouquets. The store is always expanding and you can even hold weddings and events in the Chelsea shop's ballroom space.

Blue Ivy

762 Tenth Avenue · New York, NY 10019
212-977-8858
www.blueivyinc.com
$: Bridal bouquets, $200 and up; bridesmaid bouquets,
$75 and up; centerpieces, $100 and up

This upscale shop caters to weddings as well as to New York's finest hotels (the Plaza, the Ritz-Carlton). They like to use traditional flowers, including lilies, roses, and orchids. Many of their blooms are imported directly from Holland. Blue Ivy brides tend to choose nosegays in pastel shades. This florist works by appointment only.

Blue Meadow Flowers

336 East 13th Street · New York, NY 10003
212-979-8618
$: Bridal bouquets, $150 and up; bridesmaid bouquets, $100 and up;
centerpieces, $100 and up

If you're looking for something funky, head to this East Village flower shop. They combine a traditional look with offbeat flair, creating unique, extremely original floral arrangements. Bouquets are tightly arranged yet packed with an extravagant number of flowers. Blue Meadow's florists pride themselves on what they call "neo-Victorian" style.

Castle & Pierpont

353 West 39th Street, #301 · New York, NY 10018
212-570-1284
www.castlepierpont.com
$: Bridal bouquets are $250 and up; bridesmaid bouquets are
$150 and up; centerpieces are $200 and up

To Castle & Pierpont, each wedding is unique. Their styles are chic, contemporary, and elegant. Their designers work especially hard to understand the wedding's style and streamline their work to complement the bride's dress. They are known for the care they take with couples and their willingness to work hard to create wonderful styles.

Christina Pfeufer Distinctive Floral Designs

143 West 29th Street · New York, NY 10001
212-695-6680
$: Bridal bouquets start at $175; bridesmaid bouquets start at $95;
centerpieces start at $150

Christina Pfeufer is a florist wanted by those in the know. Popular among Broadway celebrities, she also does the flowers at the New York Botanical Garden. She prides herself on really getting to know each bride. Recently she's been doing lots of nosegays in shades of white, including lily of the valley, stephanotis, and orchids. Pfeufer works by appointment only.

Elan Flowers

148 Duane Street · New York, NY 10013
212-240-9033
www.elanflowers.com
$: Bridal bouquets average $150; bridesmaid bouquets average $100;
centerpieces average $150

Elan's style is European classic. Arrangements are lush with all sorts of textural elements, including berries, fruits, and vegetables, depending on what the bride and groom desire. Bridal bouquets tend to be round and full, sometimes made with only one type of flower, and are always custom-designed to the bride's taste. Centerpieces are often arranged in elegant glass vases, but there are many other options, including moss-covered wire containers, frosted glass, brushed metal, and terra-cotta containers.

Elizabeth Ryan

411 East Ninth Street · New York, NY 10003
212-995-0474
www.erflowers.com
$: Bridal bouquets, $100 and up; bridesmaid bouquets, $75 and up;
centerpieces, $150 and up

The funky East Village neighborhood that's home to Elizabeth Ryan's flower shop belies the elegance of the blooms found inside. Ryan often incorporates fruits and vegetables into her lush, hip bouquets. Quinces, poppy and iris pods, artichokes, miniature persimmons, pears, grapes, and pomegranates all appear in her arrangements, and Ryan's rose selection is especially beautiful. Her eclectic style has attracted many clients from the music and film industries, and she's even celebrity wedding planner Colin Cowie's florist of choice—a gold star indeed! Beyond flowers, she does full-service lighting and event design.

Flowers by David Browne

399 Bleecker Street · New York, NY 10014
212-352-1224
$: Bridal bouquets start at $250; bridesmaid bouquets start at $175;
centerpieces start at $350

David Browne incorporates the unusual into his elaborate floral arrangements: Ostrich eggs, bee hives, fruits and vegetables, tree bark, and butterflies have made appearances. He likes texture so much that *Time Out New York* has said that "given the choice, Browne would pick branches and twigs over leaves." He also uses amazing, unique flowers in his lush arrangements, which are popular with celebrities like Helmut Lang, Diane Sawyer, and Lou Reed. If you're looking for something extremely original, call Browne: He may be expensive, but his designs are worth it.

Henry's Florist

8103 Fifth Avenue · Brooklyn, NY 11209
718-238-3838
www.henrysflorist.com
$: Bridal bouquets, $50 and up; bridesmaid bouquets, $40 and up;
centerpieces, $25 and up

Henry's Florist is a traditional, economical choice in Brooklyn. They import flowers from around the globe and can create whatever you want. Henry's is located across the street from Kleinfeld, so brides can head to Bay Ridge to take care of two wedding tasks in one trip. Henry's doesn't have a signature style, so be prepared to describe your preferences (and bring pictures).

Hybrid Michael Georges Flowers

5 Tutor City Place · New York, NY 10017
212-883-0304 · Fax: 212-883-0405
www.michaelgeorgecustomfloral.com
$: The minimum price for a wedding is $10,000

Upscale florist Michael Georges is one of Martha Stewart's darlings. His flowers are often on the cover of her magazines, and he even did the wedding of Martha's daughter, Alexis. Georges's signature style is graphic and minimalist. However, his arrangements are extremely customized. If you're searching for a high-fashion look, Georges is your man; his clients include Calvin Klein, Giorgio Armani, Valentino, and the late Gianni Versace. He works with each bride's personal style to create floral arrangements to match the wedding theme. Georges is pricey, so before calling be sure you're willing to spend, spend, spend on your wedding flowers.

Jennifer Houser Flowers, Ltd.

20 Park Avenue, Apt. 12C • New York, NY 10016
212-532-8676 / 631-537-5532 (Hamptons)
jhfleurs@optonline.net
$: Bridal bouquets start at $225; bridesmaid bouquets start at $150;
centerpieces start at $125

Put yourself in Jennifer Houser's hands and most of your wedding worries will vanish. Noted for her simple, elegant, romantic styling, and originality, Houser will bring the perfect mood to your ceremony and reception, and while her specialty is flowers, she can also arrange for calligraphy, table linens, cake, DJs, even accommodations. After 12 years in the business, Houser really knows how to listen to her clients and is amazing at figuring out how to focus their budgets and make a strong, tasteful impact within any budget. Jennifer Houser Flowers keeps two studios, one in Manhattan, the other in the Hamptons, where she does a lot of work. Her hand-tied bouquets come crisp and cold in water so that they'll be fresh and beautiful for the event. Houser works by appointment only, but you can call her on short notice and she'll put together something fabulous. To get a taste of Houser's creative, whimsical, classy style, visit her shop Candy & Flowers in Sag Harbor.

Karen Bussen

336 West 37th Street • New York, NY 10018
212-643-6880 • Fax: 212-643-6882
kabuss@aol.com
$: Starts at $5,000

Karen Bussen is a wedding designer. She does flower work, and while some clients do hire her just for her arrangements, most come to her to design the atmosphere for their weddings. From lighting and visual effects to invitations and party favors, Bussen gives each event a unique and comfortable ambiance that matches the personalities and imaginations of the bride and groom, and conveys their feelings about the occasion. All of her work is customized and she has done everything from writing poetry on a wedding cake to creating a gentleman's cigar lounge—complete with leather couches, a humidor, and oriental rugs—under a tent for a wedding in Connecticut. Call Bussen if you want someone to read your mind and execute your fondest wishes.

Magnolia Flowers & Events

434 Hudson Street
Phone 212-243-7302 • Fax: 212-243-7196
www.magnolia-nyc.com
$: Bridal bouquets start at $125; bridesmaid bouquets start at $65;
centerpieces start at $150

Magnolia Flowers does beautiful wedding work and prides itself on working in any-size venue, any kind of budget. They love to sit down with a couple and really get into what they want. While their work has appeared in *Martha Stewart Living, Elegant Bride, InStyle Weddings,* and on the "Today" show, you shouldn't feel intimidated. Magnolia is so relaxed and friendly and interested in making you happy that you won't have to worry about a thing. By appointment only.

Matthew David Events

246 West 18th Street • New York, NY 10011
212-627-2086
info@matthewdavidevents.com • www.matthewdavidevents.com
$: Call for prices

Matthew David Events creates stunning "environments for entertaining" that are at once dramatic and intimate. Visit the website to see images of astonishing floral sculptures, amazing color schemes, and romantic settings. Matthew David Hopkins has a degree in architecture and you can see his training in his elegant, inventive work that explores and enhances any space into a dream world. Matthew David Events will do parties of any size "from 10 to 10,000," and no matter what size your event is, you will have flowers that are truly original and breathtaking. By appointment only.

Marlo's Flowers

428A East 75th Street • New York, NY 10021
212-628-2246 • Fax: 212-628-5776
marloflowers@earthlink.net
$: Bridal bouquets, $200 and up; bridesmaid bouquets,
$75 and up; centerpieces, $200 and up

Marlo's specializes in elegant, deeply colored blooms with lots of fragrance. Owner Marlo Phillips admits to being "obsessed with flowers." She keeps a whole slew of antiques, props, and other objects on hand to use as unusual containers for centerpieces. A typical Marlo arrangement is dense: several dozen French roses in a glass bowl with no leaves, no baby's-breath, just fragrance-rich blooms. She also does boutonnieres for the groom and groomsmen.

Perriwater, Ltd.

960 First Avenue · New York, NY 10022
212-759-9313
$: Bridal bouquets, $150 and up; bridesmaid bouquets, $95 and up;
centerpieces, $100 and up

Classic white and ivory bouquets will never go out of style at Perriwater, and the shop has been creating more and more hand-tied bouquets. Perriwater uses entwined branches and soft-colored narcissus, hyacinths, and tulips in monochromatic groupings. They also make braided satin bouquet handles to protect the bride's gown. Whether you have a huge budget or a small one, quality is extremely important at Perriwater. They'll work to create beautiful arrangements in any price range.

Preston Bailey

147 West 25th Street, 11th Floor · New York, NY 10010
212-691-6777
$: Call for rates

Preston Bailey is on the high end of Manhattan florists. However, his work is so exquisite that if you have an unlimited budget, you will want to consider his lush designs. Bailey works with flowers, props, and all the physical elements of the wedding space to create exquisite environments. He did Liza Minnelli's wedding, but don't be intimidated: he works in a wide variety of spaces and themes. He adds satin and organza to his chuppahs for a luxurious look. Consultations are by appointment only.

Prudence Designs

228 West 18th Street · New York, NY 10011
212-691-1356
www.prudencedesigns.net
$: Bridal bouquets start at $150; bridesmaid bouquets start at $100;
centerpieces start at $200

This upscale florist specializes in funky French country bouquets and arrangements. They create tight all-one-flower arrangements placed in interesting containers, such as coconut shells and moss-covered terra-cotta urns. They've worked for designer Cynthia Rowley and photographer William Wegman, and they also did the flowers for actress Illeana Douglas's wedding. Prudence Designs also does full-service event planning.

Renny, Design for Entertaining

505 Park Avenue 212-288-7000 · New York, NY 10022
www.rennydesign.com
$: Bridal bouquets, $325 and up; bridesmaid bouquets, $175 and up;
centerpieces, $175 and up

Renny has been creating the most beautiful weddings in New York for the last 25 years. His arrangements are fresh and new, designed by Renny himself to suit each bride's fantasy. Renny goes beyond the flowers in creating an entire romantic atmosphere that enhances any location. Expect to pay for the best.

Salou

105 West 72nd Street · New York, NY 10023
212-595-9604
salou@bellatlantic.net · www.salou.citysearch.com
$: Bridal bouquets start at $125; bridesmaid bouquets start at $100;
centerpieces start at about $125

Salou, named "the Picasso of flower arranging" by the *Zagat Guide*, is a secret garden behind an unobtrusive door on West 72nd Street. Don't look for a storefront, just walk in, go down the stairs and into an enormous basement greenhouse and workshop. Salou's arrangements are exquisite, elegant designs in a range of styles. For weddings, they prefer to visit the space even before the initial consultation with the wedding couple, so they can imagine what kinds of designs go best with the room. They are a wonderful group to work with because they are so concerned with the overall atmosphere of the wedding and are so careful about helping with your choices.

Seasons, A Floral Design Studio

888 Eighth Avenue · New York, NY 10019
212-369-4000
$: Bridal bouquets, $150 and up; bridesmaid bouquets, $100 and up;
centerpieces, $150 and up

Seasons specializes in English garden-style floral arrangements. Bridal bouquets are often hand tied with French wire ribbons, and the lush nosegays—overfilled with roses, lilies, peonies, lily of the valley, and sweet peas—are spectacular. They also do contemporary and architectural designs.

Spruce

75 Greenwich Avenue • New York, NY 10014
212-414-0588
www.spruceup.com
$: Bridal bouquets, $150 and up; bridesmaid bouquets, $75 and up;
centerpieces, $150 and up

Spruce's arrangements are classic, clean, and fresh. They favor a New England garden style, using Dutch blooms such as parrot tulips, sweet peas, and garden roses. For bridal and bridesmaid bouquets, they use all shades of ivory and white or else an array of vividly hued flowers. Hand-tied nosegays are their most popular bouquet style.

Surroundings Florist

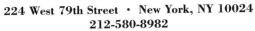

224 West 79th Street • New York, NY 10024
212-580-8982
www.surroundingsflowers.com
$: Bridal bouquets start at $125; bridesmaid bouquets start at $85;
centerpieces start at $100

Surroundings has been an Upper West Side institution for over 25 years and is famous for its attentive and careful customer service. When you go to them for weddings, you'll get lots of personal attention and good advice. They rely on their wonderful relationships with the best flower markets in Europe and the tristate area to secure the freshest and most beautiful flowers. If you visit the Surroundings website, you can see samples of their work and their wonderful signature styles, which have been featured in *Architectural Digest*, *In Style*, *House Beautiful*, *Gourmet*, and many other publications. They love working on weddings and are also a terrific resource for all kinds of floral presents.

Takashimaya

693 Fifth Avenue • New York, NY 10022
212-350-0113
$: Bridal bouquets, $175 and up; bridesmaid bouquets, $125 and up;
centerpieces, $250 and up

If you're working with a large budget and crave European style, this upscale florist may be perfect for you. They create French-style, hand-tied bouquets and arrangements that are actually worked in the designer's hand, not in the container. They are often texture-rich, tight mixtures of flowers, foliage, berries, and twigs: they have a twist on the traditional nosegay—flowers wrapped in leaves. Takashimaya does the floral arrangements for many small, unique weddings and caters to thirtysomething brides who crave—and can afford—contemporary, simple elegance.

Wildflowers

101 New Dorp Plaza · **Staten Island, NY 10306**
718-979-6561 · **Fax: 718-979-2338**
**$: Bridal bouquets, $150 and up; bridesmaid bouquets, $75 and up;
centerpieces, $50 and up**

Wildflowers owner Sean Psomas creates breathtaking bouquets complete with lush blooms and delicate ribbons. He sent me an exquisite bouquet for my last WOR bridal show: If God is in the details, these flowers were heaven sent. His shop provides flowers for some of New York's biggest names, and Psomas can also plan and style your entire wedding—everything from table settings and linens to arranging for the baker and caterer.

LONG ISLAND

Flowers by Brian

44 Jericho Turnpike · **Mineola, NY 11501**
516-873-7900
fbb4@aol.com · **www.flowersbybrian.com**
**$: Bridal bouquets start at $175; bridesmaid bouquets, $65 and up;
centerpieces, $60 to $350**

Although their style can range from Victorian to English garden and grand style, Flowers by Brian works with the bride and groom to create a customized look. Brian favors lush arrangements and specializes in centerpieces designed around brass candelabra but can also create many other types of arrangements, from a few blossoms floating in a lily bowl to more ornate pieces that require a stand. If you're looking for an interesting chuppah design, Flowers by Brian offers a variety of options—including square, round, and tree designs—all enhanced with fabric draping and such floral trim as grapevine, ivy, and exotic flowers. Brian works by appointment only.

Jill Chaffin Flowers

P.O. Box 35 · **Seacliff, NY 11579**
516-671-8973
jillchaffin@aol.com
$: A complete wedding ranges from $2,000 to $10,000

Small, independent florist Jill Chaffin specializes in weddings and parties on Long Island and in New York City. She's willing to work within any budget and with brides of all ages. Most of her recent brides want to carry vivid, jewel-toned bouquets and favor small, round arrangements of one or two types of flowers (such as roses or hydrangeas). Chaffin says her work is "inspired by my communication with nature," so her arrangements tend toward the natural. By appointment only.

Hren Country Florist

530 Montauk Highway • East Hampton, NY 11937
631-324-0640
lori@hrensnursery.com
$: Bridal bouquets, $75 and up; bridesmaid bouquets, $50 and up;
centerpieces, $75 and up

Hren focuses on a natural, English-garden style, with simple bouquets of wildflowers, all types of roses, peonies, lilacs, freesia, and hydrangeas. The florists use a lot of whitewashed pottery and a wide range of clay and ceramic containers to achieve an elegant country look. They only work on Long Island and are by appointment only.

Simply Elegant

532 Cedar Swamp Road • Glen Head, NY 11545
516-759-1300 • Fax: 516-759-1394
info@flowersanddreams.com • www.flowersanddreams.com
$: Bridal bouquets, $125 and up; bridesmaid bouquets, $50 and up;
centerpieces, $50 and up

If you're looking for traditional flower arrangements featuring oodles of roses at reasonable prices, Simply Elegant may be the florist for you. They create traditional, spiky centerpieces and flower arrangements and also utilize all sorts of candles, from votives to pedestal holders.

WESTCHESTER

Diana Gould Ltd.

12 Frontage Street · Elmsford, NY 10523
914-347-7134 or 800-959-6887 · Fax: 914-347-7408
www.dianagouldltd.com
$: Bridal bouquets start at $150; bridesmaid bouquets start at $75;
complete weddings start at $4,000

Diana Gould's floral empire encompasses a 20,000-square-foot arboreal wonderland. She has an extensive walk-in flower fridge stocked with blooms from across the world. Gould's so well-known on the flower front that *National Geographic* included her in a piece about international blooms. Her look tends to be very natural and colorful, but Gould and her team always incorporate the bride's style. They also do lighting design, manufacture their own table linens, and can use fabric to transform the ambience of a room. (Consult with them, too, for invitations, place cards, and other accessories.) Gould works by appointment only and accepts clients in the tristate area.

Greenwich Orchids

Yellow Monkey Village · 792 Route 35 · Cross River, NY 10518
914-763-4600
$: Tall flower arrangements, $250 and up; centerpieces start at $100

See listing under Connecticut.

Petals by Alice

Bridal bouquets start at $175; bridesmaid bouquets start at $55;
centerpieces average $100

Alice Norwick has run Petals by Alice, a special-event floral-design studio for over ten years, and she has done beautiful designs for weddings and parties throughout the tristate area. Her designs are classic and elegant, and her charming site decorations—she has given a statue a bouquet to hold and filled a wheelbarrow with blossoms—are terrific. Petals by Alice, a member of the Association of Bridal Consultants, works by appointment only.

NEW JERSEY

Florals of Waterford at Waterford Gardens

74 East Allendale Road • Saddle River, NJ 07458
201-327-0337
www.floralsofwaterford.com
$: Bridal bouquets average $225; bridesmaid bouquets average $100;
centerpieces start at $100

Celebrities like Tommy Hilfiger, Missy Elliott, Whoopi Goldberg, and Lynn Redgrave all flock to this Saddle River florist. Florals of Waterford works with a huge range of blooms, including amarylis, water lilies, dahlias, roses, calla lilies, pansies, hydrangeas, lilies of the valley, and tulips, and they even grow many of their seasonal flowers in their own greenhouse. They also incorporate fruits, vegetables, and berries for a fresh, simple look. They believe in mixing it up a little, using several different styles of centerpieces.

The Garden Shop

246 Bellevue Avenue • Upper Montclair, NJ 07043
973-746-8455
$: Bridal bouquets, $100 and up; bridesmaid bouquets, $75 and up;
centerpieces, $75 and up

Garden Shop brides prefer full, hand-picked, fresh-from-the-garden bouquets. Bouquets are hand-tied with lemon leaves and include an assortment of roses, calla lilies, sweet peas, and tulips. Centerpieces and arrangements are often so full and lush that they appear about to burst. Choose any containers you like: moss-covered pots, urns, glass bubble bowls, and big birch baskets covered with moss are all available. The designers are especially proud of their large floral topiaries made with birch stems.

Wine & Roses

710 River Road • New Milford, NJ 07646
201-262-9463 • Fax: 201-262-7519
wineroses@aol.com • www.wineroses.com
$: Bridal bouquets, $125 and up; bridesmaid bouquets, $65 and up;
centerpieces vary depending on flowers selected

Traditional bouquets are always in fashion at Wine & Roses. The current trend of hand-tied arrangements lets this florist spotlight their eponymous roses in various hues. They also feature Casablanca lilies, dendrobium orchids, and lisianthus. Wine & Roses believes in personal attention and only accepts 50 to 75 weddings a year. Their designers are especially interested in the style of the bride's gown and will create flower arrangements to match. You do have to plan ahead with this florist—they take bookings one year in advance.

CONNECTICUT

Bonfleur

149 Cherry Street · New Canaan, CT 06840
800-695-0514 / 203-966-3180
www.bonfleur.com
$: Bridal bouquets, $150 and up; bridesmaid bouquets, $85 and up;
centerpieces, $150 and up

Bonfleur's arrangements have European-garden flair. Arrangements and bouquets alike focus on freshness and variety. Bonfleur doesn't stop at traditional glass vases, but also uses moss-toned English garden containers. They have up to 50 varieties of specialty cut flowers available almost every day.

Daybreak Flowers

500 Main Street · Westport, CT 06880
203-227-1218 · Fax: 203-227-0299
$: Call for prices

Daybreak Flowers puts the needs of the bride and groom first, working with their budget to create wedding flowers that fit their theme. Bridal bouquets range from single blooms tied with ribbon to large, full bouquets. Daybreak usually makes traditional flower choices, using roses, freesia, stephanotis, calla lilies, sweet peas, and peonies, and also incorporates unusual ones such as ivy.

Greenwich Orchids

106 Mason Street · Greenwich, CT 06830
203-661-5053 or 203-661-5544 · Fax: 203-661-8149
and
Yellow Monkey Village
792 Route 35 · Cross River, NY 10518
914-763-4600
$: Tall flower arrangements, $250 and up;
centerpieces start at $100

Greenwich Orchids is more than just a florist. They will work with you to design the overall look of your wedding. They'll arrange for everything from the table linens, lighting design, and tent decor to the rental of potted plants and trees and, of course, amazing flower arrangements full of blooms from their huge inventory of homegrown orchids. They even have a range of special containers on hand to create a personalized look. Greenwich uses more than just orchids, though; they have a large demand for dahlias, hydrangeas, and full-blown English garden roses, all mixed with berries, fruits, pods, and other unusual elements. Wedding consultations with Greenwich Orchids are by appointment only.

Ivy Lane Florist

One Elm Street · New Canaan, CT 06840
203-966-8989
ivylanenewcanaan@aol.com · ivylanenewcanaan.com
$: Bridal bouquets, $150 and up; bridesmaid bouquets, $75 and up;
centerpieces, $50 and up

Roses are the flower of choice at Ivy Lane Florist. They excel in putting together traditional nosegays filled with roses. Their bouquets can be small or large, and they work with densely packed bunches of one color and type of flower as well as mixed blossoms. The hand-tied bouquets are finished with French wire ribbon or incorporate hand-braided ribbon up and down the stems. The same feeling goes into centerpieces, which tend to incorporate lots of heavy-headed roses for an English garden look.

McArdle's Florist

48 Arch Street · Greenwich, CT 06830
203-661-5600
Mcardle@javanet.com
$: Bridal bouquets start at $125; bridesmaid bouquets, $60 and up; centerpieces average $60

The folks at McArdle-MacMillen think wedding flowers are a matter of the bride and groom's taste. Instead of sticking with a specific style, these designers can copy any look, so if you've seen something wonderful in a magazine or book, bring it in and they'll reproduce it. They order flowers from all over the world, including Holland, California, Florida, and South America. They also incorporate mirrors and candles into their designs.

Nobu Florist of Stamford

135 Main Street · Stamford, CT 06901
203-324-4370
www.nobuflorist.com
$: Bridal bouquets, $125 and up; bridesmaid bouquets, $75 and up; centerpieces, $45 and up

The floral designers at Nobu believe each wedding is different and deserves its own style. When brides arrive for a consultation, they're encouraged to look through books filled with pictures from other weddings Nobu has done, as well as a plethora of bridal magazines. Don't be afraid to get exotic: Nobu orders flowers from Holland, California, and Hawaii and also gets orchids directly from Thailand.

Taylor's Floral Arts and Gifts

12 Post Road West · Westport, CT 06880
203-227-9534
www.taylorsfloral.com
$: Bridal bouquets, $150 and up; bridesmaid bouquets, $75 and up; centerpieces, $50 to $300

Looking for flowers with a presidential seal of approval? Taylor's did the blooms for a recent Connecticut presidential luncheon. While their style tends toward the traditional, with large, spray-type centerpieces and bouquets of red roses or champagne-toned blooms, they can also do big tropical designs. With four designers on staff, you're sure to find one who suits your style.

Notes

Cakes

The traditional cutting of the cake can be a key moment of your wedding reception. You probably already have visions of flower-covered layer cakes dancing in your head, but take a moment to consider the cakes at weddings you've attended. Did you actually taste them?

After cocktails, various hors d'oeuvres, a scrumptious seated or buffet meal, and often a dessert buffet, it's no wonder that wedding guests often just pick at the wedding cake. Think about ways to get around this. One beautiful Hawaiian wedding I attended featured a delicious luncheon and then teatime cake and coffee at another location. By the time the guests arrived, all their attention was focused on the beautiful cake and their stomachs were ready to appreciate a sweet dessert. Another option is small wedding cakes for each table—or even wedding cupcakes. Skip the dessert buffet and serve everyone their cake at the same time, perhaps cutting a small version of the cake just for the bride and groom's table. Everyone will dig in with relish.

Some wedding cakes look better than they taste. Do you want a beautifully decorated cake or a yummy-tasting one? The bakeries below are all top-of-the-line and their cakes are gorgeous and tasty, but if you go elsewhere, remember that for your guests, taste is as important as looks.

Wedding cakes range from traditional styles to amazing one-of-a-kind artistic visions. Whatever you're looking for, you'll definitely find it in the tristate area. A large number of caterers can supply wedding cakes along with the other wedding food, enabling you to cross "cake baker" off your list right at the start. But if you'd like an extra-special cake, we've listed the best bakeries around.

One note: Some bakers charge a delivery fee. Ask before you set your final budget.

NEW YORK CITY

Alba Italian Pastry Shoppe

7001 Eighteenth Avenue · Brooklyn, NY 11204
718-232-2122 · Fax: 718-234-1218
www.albapastry.com
$: Starts at $200 for 100 people

The Alba family has owned this Brooklyn-based Italian bakery for more than 70 years. With a roster of celebrity clients, including Mario Cuomo, Donald Trump, and the late Frank Sinatra, they have the track record to ensure high-quality wedding creations. Their cakes are all custom made, and the bakery is famed for sugar flowers and amazing marzipan finishes. They can also incorporate fresh flowers. Alba offers 10 different cake fillings, including ricotta cheese and coffee liqueur, and will ship cakes all over the country, including to Hawaii and Alaska (if you decide on a destination wedding).

Cheryl Kleinman Cakes

448 Atlantic Avenue · Brooklyn, NY 11217
718-237-2271 · Fax: 718-488-7813
$: Starts at $8 per person

Cheryl Kleinman is famous for her delicate, Wedgwood china–inspired cakes. Her creations range from classic to romantic, from streamlined modern to elaborate Victorian. If you're looking for a truly romantic piece de resistance, work with her. Kleinman offers all sorts of flavor options, including framboise liqueur, buttercream, and jam filling, apricot pound cake, hazelnut and almond torte cake, and a chocolate cake that's so rich it's almost devil's food. She works with couples to match the cake to the spirit, drama, season, and colors of their wedding, and has created sweet confections for all sorts of celebrities, including model Eva Herzigova, singer Bette Midler, and the Clintons. You must book at least six weeks in advance.

Colette's Cakes

681 Washington Street · New York, NY 10014
212-366-6530 · Fax: 212-366-6003
cakecolet@aol.com · www.colettescakes.com
$: Starts at $10 per person

Colette Peters has ample experience as a baker—and she's even written four books on the subject. Her cakes are all custom creations, with hand-sugared flowers and specially designed cake toppers. To see her colorful, whimsical designs—including cakes that look like gift-wrapped presents, cakes with birch-bark decorations and butterfly motifs, and cakes decorated with stunning frosting sunflowers—see her website. Peters works by appointment only.

Confetti Cakes

212-877-9580
elisa@confetticakes.com • www.confetticakes.com
$: $10 to $20 per person

Elisa Strauss, the genius behind Confetti Cakes, prides herself on her sculpting abilities. After studying art at Vassar and the Art Institute of Chicago, Strauss perfected her baking skills at the Institute of Culinary Education, and she applies all of her skills in her work. She can concoct exquisite wedding cakes with beautiful hand-painted designs but she can also work magic, producing wonders like a perfect replica of a Manolo Blahnik shoe (and box) or the Bugatti sports car she made for Ralph Lauren. She likes couples to come to their appointments armed with things that inspire them: pictures, objects, flowers, lace from a dress, even color schemes. While she has gotten "emergency" calls for cakes on very short notice, Strauss prefers to start working with couples four to six months before the wedding. By appointment only.

Creative Cakes

400 East 74th Street • New York, NY 10021
Phone/fax: 212-794-9811
$: Starts at $600 for 100 people

If you're looking for a funky, lighthearted wedding cake, Creative Cakes is the bakery for you. Spurning tradition for imagination, this bakery can create your fantasy cake. Don't come here for flowery layered cakes—the bakers at Creative Cakes prefer fun to froufrou. They've made everything from a golfing cake (complete with miniature alligator) to a taxicab cake, and even one featuring a bride and groom in a 1963 Corvette with tin cans dragging behind. You got engaged at the top of the Empire State Building? Creative Cakes can build you an Empire Cake, no problem.

The Cupcake Cafe

522 Ninth Avenue • New York, NY 10018
212-464-1530 • Fax: 212-465-1069
$: Starts at $6 per person

If you're looking for lavish, rich buttercream flowers to decorate a cake that tastes absolutely scrumptious, look no further than the Cupcake Cafe. This gem of a bakery may be located in Hell's Kitchen, but its baked goods are simply heavenly. The bakers work by appointment only, and you must call four to six weeks in advance. No two cakes are ever the same, and the bakery will do any flavor, style, color, or flower type you want. Delicious!

Gail Watson Custom Wedding Cakes

335 West 38th Street • New York, NY 10018
212-967-9167 • Fax: 212-967-3856
www.gailwatsoncake.com
$: Starts at $6 per person

Gail Watson creates amazing cakes to fit almost any budget—they come in two cost levels. Freshness is key for Watson, who makes everything from scratch and offers 17 cake flavors and 17 fillings. Her traditional-style creations are replete with sugar seashells and both sugar and real flowers. She makes edible bridal favors as well as kosher cakes. Watson's cakes have been featured in *Victoria*, *Martha Stewart Living*, and *Bride's*. Check out her website for a look at her sophisticated, classic designs. In a do-it-yourself mood? Watson also sells decorating kits.

Mother Mousse

3767 Victory Boulevard • Staten Island, NY 10314
718-983-8366 • Fax: 718-698-5282
www.mamamousse.com
$: Starts at $350 for 100 people

Mother Mousse is a quality alternative to more expensive New York City bakeries. Order a custom-made cake or choose from basic or whipped-cream varieties. The bakers will create whatever you want—they can copy from pictures and put mousse or fruit inside the cake. They have made whimsical gift-box cakes (tied with icing ribbons), castles, carousels, and sandcastles. Specialties include chocolate and cappuccino mousse cakes and coconut-lemon or lemon-mousse confections. You can also order custom figurine wedding cookies (starting at $1.50 each) to give as favors.

Ron Ben-Israel

42 Greene Street • New York, NY 10013
212-625-3369 • Fax: 212-625-1867
www.weddingcakes.com
$: $10 to $15 per person

A Martha Stewart discovery, Ron Ben-Israel is your man for amazing one-of-a-kind cakes. Ben-Israel works in his own style—a cross between modern and classic, traditional and whimsical. Everything on his fanciful cakes is edible, from the ultra-delicate sugar flowers and the sugary figurine toppers to the columns between tiers. His sugar flowers are unbelievably realistic. Ben-Israel offers more than 12 combinations of mousse filling and buttercream frosting to match the season (light for summer, rich for winter), and he'll even work with the dress designer, florist, and location to fully reflect the personality of the couple and the spirit of the wedding. For groom's cakes, he can be quite wild: once he re-created the groom's tattoo. Because he has appeared on "Oprah" and in *The New York Times* and has worked for Donald Trump and Leona Helmsley, Ben-Israel is in great demand and must be booked six months to a year in advance. He works by appointment only. To see examples of his sugary concoctions in advance, check out his extensive website.

Sylvia Weinstock Cakes

273 Church Street · New York, NY 10013
212-925-6698 · Fax: 212-925-5021
sylviaweinstockcakes.com
$: Starts at $10 per person

Famed for sugar flowers that look exactly like the real thing—with perfect buds, petals, and leaves in garden-fresh colors—this Manhattan cake whiz boasts a sizable roster of celebrity clients: Liam Neeson, Mariah Carey, and Rupert Murdoch have all ordered from her. Sylvia Weinstock is on the high end of cake design, and her price reflects the demand for her work, but she's worth it. She creates only custom cakes and uses the finest fresh ingredients. Her bakers are considered "cake engineers."

Toba Garrett

212-234-3635
Institute of Culinary Education
212-847-0700 x249
tobagarrett@prodigy.net · www.tobagarrett.com
$: Prices start at about $10 per serving

Toba Garrett, an instructor at the Institute of Culinary Education, creates exquisite, classy wedding cakes that will be the glory of any wedding reception. The author of *Creative Cookies*—with a forthcoming book on cake decoration—Garrett practices what she teaches about pastry design and decoration. With a background in fine arts, she constructs sophisticated wedding cakes with beautiful classical styling and precise pipework in the ornamentation. She doesn't do theme cakes; instead, she concentrates on building cakes with wonderful architecture and striking details. Garrett likes to start planning wedding cakes at least three months in advance and she works by appointment only. Her cakes are stunning.

Wedding Cake Online by Food Attitude

235 East 25th Street • New York, NY 10010
212-686-4644
www.weddingcakeonline.com
$: Prices start at $5 per person

If you want a delicious cake, but don't want cake selection to be wildly time-consuming, visit Wedding Cake Online, a subsidiary of Food Attitude (one of the largest French pastry suppliers in New York City). They offer two general styles of cakes, which you can see on their website and in the showroom: Love Story and Honeymoon. Within each genre, couples can customize their cake, picking flavors, icing colors, decorations, etc. When you visit Wedding Cake Online for your appointment, they will give you a tasting, getting you to sample their cakes and specialty fillings (triple-chocolate mousse and caramel mousse are among the favorites), and they are even prepared to help you pick flavors by playing rating "games" with you. If you're still indecisive, you can take samples home for other people to taste. Wedding Cake Online is by appointment only, and if you're getting married during busy seasons (spring and fall), you should make an appointment at least four months in advance. To ensure quality control, Wedding Cake Online will only make 20 cakes per weekend—and they do get booked.

Zucchero Cakes

29-03 West 15th Street • Brooklyn, NY 11224
718-946-7575
www.zuccherointernational.com
$: Starting price is $12.50 per person for basic cake;
sculpted cake starts at $15 per person

Raffaela Russo di Martino makes incredible wedding cakes that you have to see to believe. She started working in Italy over 15 years ago and now owns her own shop in Coney Island. She can make anything from a traditional tiered cake covered with flowers to replicas of the Cyclone roller coaster, the Empire State Building, and she even did a *City Wedding* one—where the book cover was embedded in a wedding cake. Zucchero Cakes can make anything you can think of, so let your imagination go wild. Their cakes taste wonderful, and you should explore the most-requested flavors listed on their website. Among the favorites are Angel's Kiss (lemon pound cake filled with white-chocolate mousse and raspberry jam flavored with Grand Marnier), Chocolate Passion (chocolate cake, chocolate mousse, Kahlua), and Pistachio Delight (vanilla pound cake, pistachio mousse flavored with Calvados). By appointment only.

LONG ISLAND

Culinary Architect Catering

28 Chestnut Street • Greenvale, NY 11548
516-484-7431 • 212-410-5474
info@culinaryarchitect.com • www.culinaryarchitect.com
$: Starts at $6.50 per person

If you're having a Long Island wedding and are looking for an original, creative cake, look no further than Culinary Architect Catering. This Port Washington operation can make almost anything. For one couple, who met at a bowling alley, the bakery created an amazing bowling-alley cake, complete with moving pins. If you're craving a springtime bouquet to top your cake, they also work with all sorts of fresh flowers as well as incredibly lifelike, edible royal-icing flowers. Culinary Architect offers a range of flavors and fillings, from traditional carrot cakes to lemon-filled, summery cakes. And if the bride loves chocolate but the groom can do without it, ask for the half chocolate, half yellow cake to keep everyone smiling.

NEW JERSEY

Back Street Bakers

530 Broad Street • Glen Rock, NJ 07452
201-652-7259
$: Call for prices

Brides and grooms looking for scrupulous service should consider Back Street. A few months before the big day, the couple gets a private tasting of the 15 fillings (mostly mousses) that the bakery offers. They even leave with their own sample cake! Back Street does custom cakes, pastries, cookies, and petit fours. If the cake designed for your wedding becomes especially popular with other customers, they'll even name it after you. The bakers pride themselves on fresh ingredients and are also known for their decadent chocolate groom's cake.

The Chester Bakery

19 West Main Street • Chester, NJ 07930
908-879-5350
$: Call for prices

If you're looking for an extremely unusual wedding cake (or an interesting groom's cake), consider The Chester Bakery. The specialty of the house is portraits painted directly onto the cakes with marzipan. One employee even had her husband's motorcycle painted on the top of their wedding cake. These friendly and helpful bakers also make traditional tiered wedding cakes with a variety of fillings, from fruit to chocolate mousse and rum custard.

Rosemary's Cakes

299 Rutland Avenue • Teaneck, NJ 07666
201-833-2417 • Fax: 201-833-8227
$: A ten-inch basket-of-roses cake, which can feed
40 to 50 people, is $325 plus delivery

Is the frosting your favorite part of the cake? If so, Rosemary Littman is just the ticket. A butter-cream specialist, Littman makes everything from traditional tiered floral cakes to smooth, porcelain-finish fondant creations. She creates edible art. Her works have included a 3-foot-tall Statue of Liberty (whose torch held a mini bride and groom), an all-cake champagne bottle in an ice bucket, replete with clear Jell-o ice cubes, and a two-and-a-half-foot-high sculpture of a bride and groom in complete wedding attire. Littman delivers cakes all over the tristate area.

Gift Registries

Some brides and grooms feel that registering for wedding gifts is mercenary, but in truth it's gracious to let your guests in on what you want and need. You'll want to register at your store or stores of choice a month or two before prewedding parties begin—that usually means showers, which, by definition, are gift-giving occasions. However, if you'll be having a formal engagement party you may want to register quite early on in your planning process (engagement gifts are optional, but guests may opt to bring something).

You may decide to register at one big department store, or perhaps you'll supplement your traditional choices like china, silver, and crystal with stylish housewares and other products from a specialty shop or online registry. Wherever you choose to register, make sure you give the consultant who works with you a shipping address (usually the bride's). And remember to send thank-you notes!

ABC Carpet and Home

800-888-7847 or 212-473-3000
www.abchome.com (no online registry)

This luxurious New York City home shop offers upscale china, crystal, silverware, linens, furniture, electronics, unique knickknacks, and much more.

Amazon

www.amazon.com

This online superstore sells everything from books to housewares. They have an easy-to-use online registry.

Baccarat Crystal

800-777-0100 or 212-826-4100

This Manhattan crystal emporium has top-notch pieces for all sorts of entertaining needs.

Bed Bath & Beyond

800-GO-BEYOND
www.bedbbathandbeyond.com

Stores in New York City, Long Island, New Jersey, and Connecticut carry everything you need to set up house from bedding to hardware, kitchen appliances, and so on. Registry is available online as well as in the stores.

Bergdorf Goodman

212-753-7300

This exquisite New York City department store offers a pricey, traditional registry.

Bloomingdale's

800-888-2WED
www.bloomingdales.com

Bloomingdale's is the classic bridal registry. You can visit their flagship New York City store or one of their many locations, or register online.

Crate & Barrel

800-967-6696
www.crateandbarrel.com

Crate & Barrel has a catalog, a website, and computer-connected stores across the country offering classic and contemporary housewares. You can also register for Crate & Barrel gifts through Weddingchannel.com.

Felissimo

212-247-5656
Fax: 212-956-0081 or 212-956-3955
www.felissimo.com (no online registry)

This Manhattan boutique carries all sorts of eclectic home items and offers both in-store and by-fax registering.

Home Depot

800-430-3376
www.homedepot.com (no online registry)

Home Depot has over 900 stores across the country, including locations in New York City, Long Island, New Jersey, and Connecticut. Get a jump start on your home improvements with their registry services.

JCPenney

800-JCPGIFT

www.jcpenney.com

This department store has a traditional bridal registry and locations throughout the tristate area. You can also register via catalog or online.

The Knot

www.theknot.com

This online wedding registry includes stylish home goods, sporting gear, and travel certificates.

Land's End

800-345-3696

This outdoor-goods catalog also has a home-goods bridal registry. Just call and request their special "Coming Home" catalog. Your guests can purchase via catalog, as well.

L. L. Bean

800-341-4341
Fax: 207-878-8418

L. L. Bean offers a catalog registry filled with outdoor and adventure gear and clothing. Call for a special gift registry kit.

Lord & Taylor

212-391-3344
www.mayco.com (no online registry, but they have an online store locator)

Lord & Taylor has a traditional department-store bridal registry, with locations in New York City, Long Island, and New Jersey.

Macy's

800-456-2297
www.macysbridal.com

Macy's offers a traditional department store registry with locations throughout the tristate area. You must call to make an appointment with a consultant to register in the store, or you can register online.

Metropolitan Museum of Art Shops

800-468-7386
www.metmuseum.org/store/index.asp
(no online registry)

Register for unusual art objects and books at stores located in New York City, Long Island, and New Jersey.

Moss

146 Greene Street · New York, NY 10012
866-888-6677 · 212-204-7100
store@mossonline.com · www.mossonline.com

Moss is an amazing store filled with gorgeous design items, china, furniture, cookware, flatware, and more. There's no online registry.

Museum of Modern Art Design Store

800-793-3167
www.momastore.org (no online registry)

Register in the New York City store for modern design, housewares, and art objects.

Neiman Marcus

888-888-4757 · 214-741-6911
www.neimanmarcus.com

Neiman Marcus offers an upscale department-store registry. You can register in person by appointment, or online. Guests can also purchase gifts over the phone. The Neiman Marcus registry is also part of Della Weddings.

Paragon Sporting Goods

212-255-8036

www.paragonsports.com (no online registry)

This huge Manhattan sporting-goods emporium offers everything from cross-country skis to bows and arrows. It's a must for the sporty bride and groom.

Smith & Hawken

212-925-0687

www.smith-hawken.com (no online registry)

Smith & Hawken's New York City store has a bridal registry featuring gardening and household items. You must register in person.

Target

1-888-304-4000

www.target.com

Target's Club Wedd registry lets you register for anything Target offers, from home goods to electronics. You can look at products online, but you must register in person. Target has stores all over the tristate area.

Tiffany & Co.

800-843-3269

www.tiffany.com (no online registry)

Register for Tiffany's signature silverware, crystal, and china at shops in New York City, Long Island, and New Jersey.

WeddingChannel.com

www.weddingchannel.com

This online registry lets you create gift lists at a number of shops and department stores, including Crate & Barrel, Gump's, Neiman Marcus, REI, and Williams-Sonoma.

Williams-Sonoma

800-541-2233
www.williams-sonoma.com

To-be-weds can register in a store or online, at the Williams-Sonoma site or through WeddingChannel.com. There are locations throughout New York City, New York state, New Jersey, and Connecticut.

Windsor Gift Shop

800-631-9393

This Chatham, New Jersey, shop specializes in discounted crystal, china, flatware, and decorative accessories for the home.

The Yellow Door

718-998-7382 or 732-531-1110

This is a great shop for sterling-silver items, jewelry, crystal, and more—all at great prices. There are shops in Brooklyn and in Deal, New Jersey.

Men's Formalwear

Although he doesn't have to wear a tuxedo to the big event, it's traditional for the groom—along with his best man, groomsmen, ushers, and often male family members—to sport the penguin suit or another type of formalwear. What to wear may initially seem confusing—there are a number of different types of jackets and suits, but there are guidelines: the time of day and formality level of the wedding dictate the type of formalwear worn. Look below to see what's appropriate for your wedding.

The proper formalwear

Daytime, SemiFormal

The men in the wedding party can go with nice suits and (preferably silk) ties.

Daytime, Formal

Grooms and groomsmen can wear British-inspired morning coats or gray strollers.

Daytime, UltraFormal

This type of wedding calls for a morning coat with gray striped trousers. This dapper look is pulled together with a vest and ascot. You can even go all out with a cane, spats, and a top hat.

Evening, SemiFormal

This type of wedding calls for a tuxedo. Wear one with a cummerbund or vest and bow tie; they can be patterned or colored if you like. In the summer, you can choose a white dinner jacket with black tuxedo trousers. If you'd rather not go with a tux, you can also wear a nice, dark suit.

Evening, Formal

Men in the wedding party generally wear black tie, which means a black tuxedo with a black bow tie and cummerbund or vest.

Evening, UltraFormal

Wear white tie, which means a black tuxedo jacket or tailcoat with a white pique shirt (this is a type of textured cotton fabric), white pique bow tie, and white waistcoat. Finish the look with patent-leather dress shoes and nice cuff links and shirt studs.

Formal accessories

Vests or Waistcoats

Brits often wear bright, personalized vests with their tuxedos. Bow ties, regular ties, or ascots finish this look.

Cummerbund and Bow Tie Sets
This is the most common choice to wear with a tuxedo.

Cuff Links and Shirt Studs
(instead of buttons)

Most tuxedo shops also carry cuff links to attach formal French cuffs at the wrist.

In-the-know tips

- If you're renting, decide on the formalwear style for the groomsmen at least three months before the wedding and let all the men know.

- Head to your shop of choice a month to three months before the wedding to get measured and to reserve the tuxes.

- Have everyone go in person to be sized. Don't trust measurements you take on your own or you may end up wearing high-waters to the big event.

- Some bridal shops also rent tuxedos. Have your fiancée ask when she's looking at gowns.

- Many formalwear-rental stores will offer the groom's tuxedo for free or at a discount with a minimum number of rental orders. Always ask.

NEW YORK CITY

A. T. Harris Formalwear

11 East 44th Street • New York, NY 10017
212-682-6325 • Fax: 212-682-6148
$: Rental of basic tux ranges from $145 to $195; rental of tails and cutaways starts at $175; retail price of tux starts at $450

The salespeople at A. T. Harris bill themselves as outfitters of formal attire to ten U.S. presidents. They rent and sell designs from Lord West, Perry Ellis, Ralph Lauren, and more and have all sorts of styles—from dinner jackets to cutaways and strollers—plus a fine collection of shoes and formal accessories such as top hats, walking sticks, kidskin gloves, and silk ascots. With ten or more rentals, one rental tux is free, or a 10 percent discount is credited to each rental. A. T. Harris can turn around orders in one day, but they prefer notification one month in advance to fit wedding parties.

Baldwin Formals

52 West 56th Street • New York, NY 10019
212-245-8190 • Fax: 212-956-5831
marshal@nyctuxedos.com • www.nyctuxedos.com
$: Rental prices start at $110

Baldwin Formals offers rental formalwear and accessories by Perry Ellis, Chaps by Ralph Lauren, Oscar De La Renta, Fezza, Bill Blass, Lord West, After Six, and more.

A New York City formalwear staple since 1946, this shop stocks all merchandise in-house and offers on-site tailoring, same-day service, and free delivery and pickup in Midtown. Baldwin's expertise lies in classic white tie and morning attire, and they even have top hats in stock. All men's sizes are available, from boys' 3 to men's 64, as well as portly, extra long, athletic, husky, and extra short sizes.

Eisenberg & Eisenberg

16 West 17th Street • New York, NY 10011
212-627-1290
fineduds@aol.com • www.eisenbergandeisenberg.com
$: Rentals start at $85; tuxes retail for $239 and up

This old-fashioned tuxedo-rental shop carries many upscale designers, including Perry Ellis, Ralph Lauren, Principe, Chiavari, Geoffrey Beene, Jeffrey Banks, and Karl Lagerfeld. They offer same-day service if your order is placed by 3 P.M. With every seven rentals one is free, so bring all your groomsmen here, too.

Gentleman's Resale

322 East 81st Street • New York, NY 10028
212-734-2739
$: Tuxedos start around $110 for jacket and pants

This consignment shop offers preowned, upscale men's clothing, including designer suits and, on occasion, tuxes. Items not sold within 30 days are discounted 20 percent—items not sold in 60 days are discounted even more.

Giorgio Armani

760 Madison Avenue • New York, NY 10021
212-988-9191
www.giorgioarmani.com
$: Call for prices

These are the tuxes movie stars wear to the Oscars. If you're looking for a classic tux with a designer label attached, go to Armani. (Of course, you can always get the look on the cheap by renting an Armani from Zeller Tuxedos.)

Helmut Lang

80 Greene Street • New York, NY 10012
212-925-7214
www.helmutlang.com
$: Tuxes retail for $1,790

You'll find upscale formalwear for the extremely fashion-conscious groom at Helmut Lang. High-fashion tuxes are available in a number of styles, including peak- and shawl-lapel coats in wool. All alterations are done in the store.

INA Men

262 Mott Street • New York, NY 10012
212-334-2210
$: Prices vary depending on availability

This upscale, designer consignment shop in Nolita stocks suits and other formalwear items. Since it's a resale shop, the styles and designers available vary. The shop sets prices based on what consigners ask for: If an item hasn't sold within one month, the price drops 20 percent. After two months, it drops 50 percent. So if you're dead set on sporting Richard Tyler or Prada at your wedding but can't afford retail, stop into INA every few weeks—you just may score big.

Jack and Company Formalwear

128 East 86th Street • New York, NY 10028
212-722-4609
$: Rentals range from $116 to $136; tuxes retail for $279 to $600

Jack and Company has sold and rented formalwear since 1925, and their salesmen are experts in knowing what's appropriate for any occasion. The shop carries a wide selection of tuxedos and formal accessories from designers including Oscar de la Renta, Chaps by Ralph Lauren, Pierre Cardin, Lord West, Perry Ellis, Fumagalli, Geoffrey Beene, and more. Home delivery and pickup is available in Manhattan, and you get a free rental for the seventh tux. Same-day service is available at no extra charge.

Marty's Men's Fashions

31-16 Steinway Street · Astoria, NY 11103
718-726-1356
$: Tuxes retail for $80 and up

Marty's sells tuxes as well as shirts and bow ties. Their tuxes are all new, though their incredibly low prices may have you stumped. You'll find no brand names here, but there is a wide selection of unknown labels. The tuxes are made of polyester, not wool, but they still look good.

RK Bridal

318 West 39th Street · New York, NY 10018
800-929-9512
www.rkbridal.com
$: Rentals start at $60; shoe rentals start at $20; tuxes retail for $295 and up

In addition to bridal gowns, RK Bridal offers over 80 tuxedo styles, from Ralph Lauren, Perry Ellis, After Six, and more. Their retail tuxes are manufactured by a wholesaler who also makes designer tuxedos; they don't have the designer label, but the suits are exactly the same. RK also has a great selection of formal shirts, cuff links, bow ties, and cummerbunds and carries sizes from boys' 4 to men's husky 60. If six members of the wedding party rent tuxedos here, the groom's tux is free.

Rothman's

200 Park Avenue South · New York, NY 10003
212-777-7400
info@rothmansny.com · www.rothmansny.com
$: Tuxes retail for $350 and up; formal shirts start at $75

Rothman's Union Square offers 18,000 square feet of formalwear and accessories. The store carries some of the finest designer tuxedos, including top picks from Joseph Abboud, Canali, DKNY, Hugo Boss, Hickey-Freeman, Lauren by Ralph Lauren, Jack Victor, Corneliani, and more. There are tailors on the premises, and although they prefer several weeks' advance warning on wedding parties, same-day alterations are possible in emergency situations. Rothman's can offer discounts to wedding parties; call for details.

Today's Man

625 Sixth Avenue · New York, NY 10009
212-924-0200

529 Fifth Avenue · New York, NY 10017
212-557-3111

$: Tuxes retail for $230 and up; you can also purchase separates,
with jackets starting at $159, trousers at $69

Today's Man is a less-expensive alternative for retail tuxedos in New York City. The shops mostly carry 100 percent wool suits and tuxes by well-known designers in addition to their own formalwear label. You can purchase separates or complete tuxedos. Tailoring is available for an extra charge. Today's Man carries regular, short, long, and extra-long trousers in sizes 30 to 46 and offers accessories including pleated formal shirts, cummerbunds, vests, bow ties, and even formal socks.

Zeller Tuxedos

MANHATTAN
1010 Third Avenue 212-688-0100 • 421 Seventh Avenue 212-290-0217
459 Lexington Avenue 212-286-9786 • 201 East 23rd Street 212-532-7320
and
BROOKLYN
947 Kings Highway 718-627-7400 • 8201 Fifth Avenue 718-238-7628
Kings Plaza Mall 718-253-6453 • 5407 Flatlands Avenue 718-531-2984
and
BRONX
2127 Williamsbridge Road 718-828-1202
and
QUEENS
116-08 Queens Boulevard–Forest Hills 718-268-4448
www.zellertuxedo.com
$: Rentals range from $125 to $165; retail starts at $450

This tuxedo powerhouse carries styles from Giorgio Armani, Valentino, Joseph Abboud, Perry Ellis, Oscar de la Renta, Chaps by Ralph Lauren, Christian Dior, Pierre Cardin, and more. They have the largest selection of European and American designers for rent in Manhattan and feature on-site fitting and tailoring, same-day service, a free shop-at-home service, delivery and pickup for a fee, as well as a 10 percent discount for parties of seven or more (or one free rental).

LONG ISLAND

Antique Costume and Prop Rental

709 Main Street • Port Jefferson, NY 11777
516-331-2261 • Fax: 516-331-9692
$: Rentals range from $100 to $150

If you plan on a storybook or theme wedding, a trip to Antique Costume and Prop Rental is a must. They carry thousands of costumes for the bride and groom (and even guests). The shop is housed in a Victorian mansion and is one of the largest outfitters for historic weddings in the country, carrying clothing from every time period from medieval to modern.

Foresto

309 Willis Avenue • Mineola, NY 11501
800-843-8894 or 516-746-1410 • Fax: 516-747-8192
$: Rentals range from $105 to $125; tuxes retail for $395 to $1,200

Founded in 1940, Foresto is still family run and carries tuxedo styles from Chaps by Ralph Lauren, Oscar de la Renta, Lord West, Hickey-Freeman, After Six, Perry Ellis, and more. All their inventory is on-site for immediate selection, and tailoring is performed on the premises as well. Foresto also carries a full line of accessories and jewelry for rent and sale.

Rothman's Southampton

2 Jobs Lane • Southampton, NY 11968
613-283-3151

See New York City listing.

Victor Talbots

47 Glen Cove Road • Greenvale, NY 11548
516-625-1787 • Fax: 516-625-1730
info@victortalbots.com • www.victortalbots.com
$: Rentals range from $85 to $150; tuxes retail from $595 to $6,000

You'll find both rental and retail tuxedos at Victor Talbots (which was featured in the film *Meet the Parents*). Founded over a decade ago, this shop carries designs by

Brioni, Ralph Lauren Purple Label, Oxford, Hugo Boss, and more. Talbots does special alterations on rentals to achieve a perfect fit and has an on-site tailoring facility. If you buy a tux here, you'll get a lifetime alteration guarantee. You can also take advantage of their free tailoring maintenance program. The groom receives a complimentary tux rental with rentals by seven or more wedding-party members. Be sure to contact Talbots at least 60 days before the wedding.

Zeller Tuxedo

29 Northern Boulevard · Greenvale, NY 11548
516-621-5840
and
467A Old Country Road · Westbury, NY 11590
516-338-7679
and
3285 Sunrise Highway · Wantaugh, NY 11793
516-679-0654
www.zellertuxedo.com

See New York City listing.

WESTCHESTER

After Hours

The Westchester
914-289-0931 · 800-6SMALLS
www.tuxonthenet.com

See New Jersey listing.

Rothman's Scarsdale

1 Boniface Circle · Scarsdale, NY 10583
914-713-0300

See New York City listing.

New Jersey

After Hours

22 New Jersey locations;   •   13 New York City locations;
4 Conneticut locations
Go to www.afterhours.com to find nearest store   •   www.tuxonthenet.com
$: Rentals range from $50 to $100; tuxes retail from $199 to $499

This multistate tuxedo retailer has been in business for over 65 years and carries over 110 tuxedo styles (from Givenchy, Gianni, Perry Ellis, and more) in sizes from 3 to 72, including portly and husky. They have over 240 stores in 20 states and can even service your wedding party at several different locations—if the groom is in Connecticut and the groomsmen are in Pennsylvania, it's no problem. Everyone can go to the After Hours nearest him and end up with a matching tux. With five paid rentals, the sixth is free.

Barry's Tuxedos Rentals & Sales

315 Monroe Street   •   Passaic, NJ 07055
973-777-1022 or 800-648-0116   •   Fax: 973-777-0359
barrystux@aol.com   •   www.barrystuxedos.com
$: Rentals range from $50 to $150; tuxes retail from $92 to $1,200

In a showroom that spans two city blocks, Barry's offers 20,000 tuxes from a slew of designers, including Joseph Abboud, Talia, Geoffrey Beene, Calvin Klein, Perry Ellis, and Ralph Lauren and has 10 tailors on the premises, available 12 hours a day. The shop even does dry cleaning. They offer complimentary home fittings as well as free delivery and pickup. The groom gets a free rental with four or more groomsman rentals.

David's Formal Wear

14 Mountain Avenue   •   Springfield, NJ 07081
973-379-7595 or 888-264-3504
tuxedos@davidsformalwear.com   •   www.davidsformalwear.com
www.tuxedodirect.com
$: Rentals range from $85 to $150; tuxes retail from $350 to $800

David's has an excellent selection of rental and retail tuxedos, including styles by Chaps by Ralph Lauren, Perry Ellis, Lord West, Pierre Cardin, Oscar de la Renta, and more. They also carry accessories such as formal shoes and 100 types of silk vests and cummerbund/bow-tie sets. If you'd like personalized service, David's will come to your home to help the entire wedding party select their formalwear. You should book at least two months before your wedding date, but if you're in a rush, David's can handle last-minute orders up to a week before the wedding—even same-day service.

Starlight Tuxedo

606 Bloomfield Avenue · Bloomfield, NJ 07003
973-743-7566
www.starlighttuxedo.com
$: Rentals range from $70 to $150; wool tuxes retail from $265 to $1,000; polyester tuxes retail for $135

Starlight has been in business for nearly 50 years and has an enormous selection of tuxedos in stock (including Raffinati, Perry Ellis, and more), as well as accessories and formal shoes. The groom's tux is free with five or more groomsman rentals.

Today's Man

240 Route 10 · East Hanover, NJ 07936
973-884-7400
and
835 Lancer Drive · Moorestown, NJ 08057
856-235-5656
and
776 Route 17 · Paramus, NJ 07652
201-670-7117
and
85 Willowbrook Blvd. · Wayne, NJ 07470
973-812-8000
and
1200 U.S. Highway 9 · Woodbridge, NJ 07095
732-602-0440

See New York City listing.

Zeller Tuxedo

Menlo Park Mall
732-548-6363
and
The Mall at Short Hills
973-564-9009
www.zellertuxedo.com

See New York City listing.

CONNECTICUT

After Hours

Buckland Hills Mall
860-648-9779
and
Stamford Town Center
203-325-4210
and
Trumbull Shopping Park
203-372-3475

800-6SMALLS
www.tuxonthenet.com

See New Jersey listing.

Bogey's Tuxedos

71 Newtown Road · Commerce Plaza · Danbury, CT 06810
203-794-0072 · Toll free: 800-779-4004

95 Willenbrock Road · Willenbrock Park · Oxford, CT 06478
203-262-6140 · Toll free: 800-779-4004
www.bogeystux.com
$: Rentals range from $69 to $110; tuxes retail from $225 to $675;
all preworn tuxes are $149 (including tie, shirt, and cummerbund)

This Connecticut tux retailer and rental shop carries styles from the classic designers: Calvin Klein, After Six, Perry Ellis, Oscar de la Renta, Ralph Lauren, and more. The shop also sells shoes, shirts, and accessories (including vests, ties, and jewelry). If you want to buy a tux without spending a bundle, consider their preworn designer tuxes.

Notes

Wedding Day Details

So your planning is almost done—you just need to complete a few more details. This chapter includes a few of my favorite spots for wedding day beauty, fabulous favors, and ceremony and reception props and rentals. These names are tried and true and will give you a leg up on perfect finishing touches for your wedding.

HAIR & MAKEUP

On your big day, the sheer excitement of the moment will most likely bring a rosy glow to your cheeks and a smile to your lips. But to ensure a flawless look, you may want to turn to the professionals. The salon you usually use most likely offers wedding hairstyling and may be able to suggest a reputable makeup artist. Otherwise, here are my picks.

NEW YORK CITY

Kimara Ahnert Makeup and Skincare Studio

1113 Madison Ave · New York, NY 10028
212-452-4252 or 800-452-9802
www.kimara.com
$: Within NYC: $300 for the bride; with Kimara Ahnert: $500 for the bride.
Outside NYC: 3 person minimum starts at $600,
$150 for each additional person; with Kimara Ahnert: $950 with
a 3-person minimum and $225 for each additional person.
Trial Application in the studio: $75; with Kimara Ahnert: $125.
One-hour Makeup Lesson and Application: $125; with Kimara Ahnert: $200.

Kimara Ahnert has been doing wedding makeup for many years and knows how to work with brides to customize their looks so that they are comfortable, beautiful, and feel like themselves. Her lavish studio is cozy, luxurious, and professional. You can see why Catherine Zeta-Jones hired Ahnert to do her wedding makeup. The studio offers all kinds of options for wedding parties. You can get lessons in-house so you can apply your make up yourself. Artists can also go to your New York City wedding or travel to far-flung locations. Kimara Ahnert herself is even available for weddings. The studio also does eyebrow and eyelash shaping and tinting and another pre-wedding service that has become very popular is their fabulous self-tanning applications (the color makes everyone look healthy and evens out skin tones). Ahnert has even packed her website with tons of information, including Wedding Day Beauty Tips (apparently frosted lipstick doesn't photograph so well). Ahnert recommends you book at least six months in advance. By appointment only.

Laura Geller Make-Up Studios

1044 Lexington Avenue · New York, NY 10021
212-570-5477 or 800-625-3874
www.laurageller.com
$: Bride's makeup starts at $250

The queen of makeup in the New York area, Laura Geller caters to television and film stars as well as brides. Her competent staff travels to most locations and they'll do your hair, too. Appointments are essential—she's heavily booked during the wedding season.

Madina Milano

151 Spring St · New York, NY 10012
646-613-0838
www.madina.it
$: In-store makeup lesson and application $150
Prices vary for wedding applications but are usually around $200 for the bride.

This comfortable Soho store will provide you with everything from a makeup lesson to actual wedding day applications. Madina Milano, an Italian makeup designer with a degree in art and a background in theater, has a fantastic line of products in hundreds of colors. If you prefer to do it yourself, you can get a lesson and application in the store that you'll be able to recreate before the wedding. You can also hire one of the Madina Milano freelance artists to come to your wedding. Prices for on-site wedding applications vary, but usually cost about $200 for the bride and $70 for each additional person.

Marina Vance Bridal Makeup and Hair Salon

927 Madison Ave · New York, NY 10021
(212) 570-6500 · Fax: (212) 570-1296
www.marinavance.com
$: Prices vary depending on how far in advance you book, how large your party is, and whether you go to the salon or have them come to you.

Marina Vance has done makeup for fashion shows and television, and specializes in bridal work. Take a look at their website to see their remarkable collection of "before and after" pictures of brides. Often, they can put together a package for the bride, bridesmaids, and the mothers of the bride and groom. For an extra fee, Marina Vance stylists will make "house calls" and do hair and makeup at home. By appointment only.

Minardi Salon

29 East 61st Street · New York, NY 10021
212-308-1711
$: Prices start at $95 in the salon; house calls are $250 per hour

Minardi Salon specializes in chic, wearable, contemporary hairstyles—just remember to book well in advance during wedding season. If you want a stylist to travel to your ceremony site, you must come in for a consultation first, then set up the traveling details.

Stephen Knoll Salon

625 Madison Avenue · New York, NY 10022
212-421-0100
www.stephenknoll.com
$: You must come in for a consultation first; prices vary depending on the 'do

This top Manhattan salon caters not only to celebrities but to brides, as well. Book well in advance.

Tonya Noland

347-528-6990 or 888-443-0342
$: Bride's makeup starts at $150, plus $40 for an advance consultation;
$100 each for bridesmaids; $100 for the mother of the bride

Makeup artist Tonya Noland's work appears regularly in magazines like *Glamour*, *Oprah*, and *Fitness*. She knows all the tricks of the beauty trade and is fast and calm, having worked under pressure from the fashion world's best photographers. She can also provide hairdressers upon request.

LONG ISLAND

BP Cosmetics

19 Adele Road · Cedarhurst, NY 11516
516-239-9061
$: Bride's makeup starts at $150; bridesmaids start at $100 each

Owner Bobbi Perlowin will travel anywhere in the tristate area. She did the makeup for my producer's wedding, and it was gorgeous!

Favors & Gifts

There are a myriad of boutiques and stores throughout the tristate area that carry wonderful attendant gifts and wedding favors, but I've compiled a few of my favorites here. You may just find something great at your corner store, but if you're looking for additional inspiration, try these hot spots.

NEW YORK CITY

B&H Photo

420 Ninth Avenue · New York, NY 10001
800.606.6969 · 212.444.6615
www.bhphoto.com

This photography superstore will have everything you need to shoot your wedding at great prices. Not only do they sell still cameras, video cameras, and audio equipment, they have great deals and a wide selection of one-time use cameras (for your guests to play with), batteries, digital videotapes, and film.

Candy Direct

5694 Mission Center Road #378 · San Diego, CA 92108
www.candydirect.com · Information: info@candydirect.com
Orders: orders@candydirect.com
619-326-7215

This website offers great deals on bulk candy, hard-to-find candies, and candy favors and novelties. Check out their "candy bouquets" as fun presents for younger attendants. They also have great deals on enormous quantities of Jordan almonds.

Discount Photo Supplies

www.discount-photo.com

Order all kinds of photo equipment from one-time-use cameras to Polaroid film.

Economy Candy

108 Rivington Street · New York, NY 10002
212-254-1832 · 800-352-4544 · Fax: 212-254-2606
www.economycandy.com

Visit this Lower East Side emporium of delights; order by phone or off the website. Economy Candy has been in business since 1937 and sells almost every kind of candy you can imagine, in bulk or small quantities: fireballs, marzipan fruit, and nostalgia items like Tootsie Rolls and candy corn. They also sell Jordan almonds (a popular wedding favor rumored to symbolize everything from luck to good fortune and fertility) in lots of colors, including gold and silver, and they always stock "conversation hearts," which are pretty scarce except around Valentine's Day.

Judy Paulen Designs

130 West 57th Street · Suite 5A · New York, NY 10019
800-952-2645
and
2 North Dean Street · Englewood, NJ 07631
201-871-1335
$: Prices vary

Choose from bags filled with candy, wine with personalized labels, monogrammed Tic Tacs, and more. By appointment only.

The Knot

1-877-THE-KNOT (1-877-843-5668)
www.theknot.com

The Knot, an online wedding planning and information site, established in 1996, has a reputation for being the most comprehensive Internet wedding resource. The site features: a wedding-gown catalog, searchable by style and designer,; articles; hugely popular "community" features (bulletin boards and chat rooms); vendor listings (sorted by cities); an online registry (in partnerships with Fortunoff and Linens n' Things); and a store. The online store offers all kinds of wedding supplies, favors and attendants' gifts. Some items like chocolate bars, napkins, one-time-use cameras, and matchbooks can even be personalized for your wedding.

Martha Stewart

Customer Service: 1-800-345-7795
www.marthastewart.com/weddings

You may as well check out Martha Stewart's site, after all, she did put wedding planning on the map. This well-designed site is full of wedding information, interesting ideas, useful advice, and of course, gives you a chance to buy things or register. The Martha Stewart wedding registry is well organized and nicely set up (there's even a section called "petkeeping" so if you're not comfortable registering for yourself, at least your dog can get wedding presents).

Natureperfect

1-888-328-8821
www.natureperfect.com

If you're looking to do something a little different for wedding favors, consider Nature Perfect's suggestions. They offer a range of botanical favors. Most of their wedding items are live lucky bamboo plants that you can use first as centerpieces and then break up as parting favors for your guests.

Oriental Trading Company

www.oriental.com
1-800-875-8480

Order all kinds of inexpensive party supplies and favors online from the Oriental Trading Company. They sell everything from candy to bubbles, confetti, and votive candles, and they have latex and Mylar balloons in stock. They are a great resource for kitschy shower decorations and theme items.

Pearl River Mart

277 Canal Street
New York, NY
212-431-4770
Canal Street Branch is moving to:
477 Broadway, New York, NY 10013
and
Grand Street Branch:
200 Grand Street
New York, NY
212-966-1010 · Toll free: 800-878-2446
www.pearlriver.com

Chinatown's Pearl River Mart is an amazing resource for weddings and parties. It's an enormous Chinese department store that has everything from cooking supplies to a huge assortment of paper lanterns, to embroidered silk slippers, and Chinese herbal remedies. Wander around and pick up fantastic guest books, photo albums, parasols, wrapping paper, and other atypical presents and favors. Their prices are reasonable and even though you can order online, the trip to Chinatown is always a blast.

Precious & Few

718-238-0782

kathleenlagas@worldnet.att.net • www.preciousfew.com

$: Prices vary

If you're interested in Irish heirlooms as attendant gifts or for guest favors, check out this online shop. Their stock includes ring-bearer pillows and bone-china keepsake cups, as well as monogrammed Irish linen, handkerchiefs, and garter belts.

Promotional World

888-556-PROMO

www.promotionalworld.com

If you want personalized favors, check out Promotional World. They have everything from coffee mugs to pens, caps, watches, paper fans—you name it.

Slam Bam Fun Merchandise

99 Gold Street • Brooklyn, NY 11201

718-858-1000

$: Prices vary

This fun shop offers wonderful wedding favors as well as silly gag gifts.

Weddingchannel.com

888 South Figueroa Street, Suite 700 • Los Angeles, CA 90017

888-750-1550 • Fax: 213-599-4180

The Wedding Channel is another enormous, well-respected online wedding resource that offers wedding planning tools, community features, articles, vendor descriptions, and a large store. The *Wall Street Journal* had high praise for a feature on the site that takes your wedding checklist and incorporates it into a calendar (and also sends you email reminders). The store carries a lot of the standard wedding favors, attendant items, and decorations, and it even provides a make-your-own CD service.

Wedthings.com

888-338-8818
info@wedthings.com

Wedthings sells an enormous array of amusing and tasteful wedding items. For favors, you can get everything from candy and personalized fortune cookies to picture frames, painted fans (perfect for June brides), and fabulous boxes and ribbons. They also have other wedding "essentials" including ring pillows, guest books, bridesmaid presents, and lots of items to fit holiday themes.

LONG ISLAND

The Favor Center

353 Merrick Road · Lynbrook, NY 11563
516-596-9765
$: Prices vary

This wonderful shop offers picture frames, candles, vases, and many more favor and gift ideas.

Have You Heard?, Inc.

2544 Merrick Road · Bellmore, NY 11710
516-409-0283
$: Prices vary

This shop sells almond sacks, picture frames, candles, and favors by Mikasa and Lenox, and will custom label everything from Hershey bars to wine bottles.

Make a Memory

22 Jericho Turnpike · Mineola, NY 11501
516-294-4503
$: Prices vary

This shop has invitations, gifts for the wedding party, and favors including candles, wine stoppers, embroidered throws, and even personalized ice cream scoopers.

Judy Paulen Designs

2 North Dean Street · Englewood, NJ 07631
201-871-1335
$: Prices vary

See New York City listing.

Mona Leesa

8 Mountain Avenue · Springfield, NJ 07081
973-467-9199
$: Prices vary

Find all sorts of wonderful favors at this Springfield store. By appointment only.

PARTY RENTALS & PROPS

If you're working with a wedding planner, you'll have no need to search for the perfect party tent or dining tables on your own. And even if you've chosen to plan your wedding yourself, most caterers are willing and able to help you round up any and all rentals you'll need. However, if you're still looking for stuff—tents, china, flatware, tables, chairs, interesting props— try some of these rental facilities.

Party Time

82-33 Queens Boulevard · Queens, NY 11373
718-457-1122 or 212-682-8838
and
532 Merrick Road · Lynbrook, NY 11563
516-599-8600

Party Time can provide every party item you need: china, silver, chairs, tables, and more.

Triserve Party Rentals/Just Linens Ltd.

770 Lexington Avenue · New York, NY 10021
212-265-7767
and
38 Nugent Street · Southampton, NY 11968
631-283-8808
$: Prices vary

This is simply one of the best sources for custom and stock linens, featuring an inexhaustible inventory of traditional and fashion forward tabletop items.

LONG ISLAND

Antique Costume and Props

709 Main Street · Port Jefferson, NY 11777
516-331-2261 · Fax: 516-331-9692

This shop not only rents period gowns, they also offer period furniture, props, and other items.

P. J. McBride

8 Lamar · West Babylon, NY 11704
516-694-1939

You'll find a complete selection of tent rentals here (up to 120 feet in width), along with dance floors, canopies, and even heating and air conditioning units.

Almar Party & Tent Rental

500 South Clinton Street · East Orange, NJ 07018
973-676-7777
www.almarparty.com · info@almarparty.com

Rent it all here: tents, linens, glassware, china, flatware, grills, and more.

Chair Hire

381 East First Street · Clifton, NJ 07011
973-772-4737

The name says it all: Rent your chairs here.

TOASTING HELP

The following listing defies categorization, but suffice it to say that if the groom (or best man, or father of the bride, or maid of honor) needs a little help in the toasting arena, don't hesitate—call Gladys Phillips right away.

Rhymes for Any Reason

516-764-7405
$: Prices start at $100

Gladys Phillips is known for her witty, right-on, this-is-your-life rhymes. They're perfect for a rehearsal dinner. Her toasts and roasts, along with her shower invites and unique shower ideas, are legendary. You can depend on her to come up with the perfect toast for a shy best man or maid of honor and she will even do pre-wedding coaching!

Notes

Mail-Order Bride

The Internet has become a primary resource for people getting married. You can do research, find bargains, and sell things, at all hours of the day or night, all without leaving your house. Of course there are drawbacks with doing all your ordering from online resources. Not every store has a sound reputation and you should always check to make sure that shops have a good record with the Better Business Bureau, particularly if you're spending a lot of money. Remember, if you're looking at designer dresses, sizes vary widely so try them on for size in a bridal salon before ordering online. Still, you should take advantage of some of the amazing deals and offers that you can only find online. If you're a smart shopper, you can do very well.

DRESSES: Bride/Bridesmaid/General

Aria Bridesmaid Dresses

Ariadress.com
213-629-3085 or 800-658-8885
inquiry@ariadress.com
Bridesmaid dresses from $175
Flower-girl dresses from $139

Aria Bridesmaid Dresses is a small Los Angeles design house that does elegant, sophisticated work in all-natural silk shantung, silk taffeta, and silk satin. Go to their website to see their wide range of designs and colors. They make dresses, separates, and some accessories (bags and wraps). They are a wonderful resource and are eager to provide advice about the fit of their dresses and the best choices to flatter figures. They even have a "Try-On Program" for out-of-state customers, where you can request that a favorite design be sent to you for up-close inspection. Dresses are usually ready 8 to 10 weeks after your complete order has been placed.

Bride Power

Lesley DiAngelo
www.bridepower.com
$: Gowns start at $399 on special clearance
but they average at about $1,000

Bride power is the website for the brick-and-mortar store Vows Bridal Outlet in Newton, Massachusetts. The store sells high-end designer samples or overstock at a 50 to 75 percent discount. Among the designers they carry are: Amsale, Angel Sanchez, Wearkstatt, Reem Arca, Richard Tyler, and Peter Langner. While the store does have a lot of New York brides who make the pilgrimage north, it is also easy to shop online, especially if you have a sense of the style and designer you're looking for. All the gowns are guaranteed to be in near-perfect condition and they are all cleaned and mended before they are sent out. The store also has an excellent return policy, but be sure to read the rules on the website FAQ.

Bride Save

www.bridesave.com
1-888-321-GOWN

Bridesave.com is the Internet incarnation of a brick-and-mortar store in Midland, Texas. The store provides one-stop shopping for most bridal needs from wedding gowns (the store only carries designers for whom it is an authorized dealer) to brides-maid and flower-girl dresses, accessories, and invitations, and it carries a complete range of sizes from 1-Petite to 54-W. Among the designers you can find at bridesave.com are: Diamond Collection, Maggie Sottero, Marisa, After Six, and Mori Lee. The site even has an online bookstore, in case you need some last-minute wedding planners. It is a member of the Better Business Bureau Online.

Bridesmade.com

www.bridesmade.com

Bridesmade.com is an online auction site where you can buy and sell wedding gowns, bridesmaid dresses, and accessories. Because it is an auction site, the inventory changes frequently, but you can often find bargains. The site also hosts celebrity auctions.

Net Bride

www.netbride.com

Netbride.com, a member of the Better Business Bureau Reliability Program, is a website that sells discount wedding gowns, bridesmaid dresses, flower-girl dresses, shoes, and accessories. Among the designers they carry are: Diamond, Marisa Bridals, Mori Lee, Regency, After Six, Watters and Watters, and Dessy. They also can easily handle the shipment of bridesmaid dresses to many locations. If you're a savvy shopper who doesn't mind taking your measurements and those of your bridesmaids (with help from the website), Netbride.com can be a great resource.

Pearl's Place

3114 Severn Avenue • Metairie, LA 70002
504-885-9213 • Fax: 504-885-814 • Store Fax: 504-780-1008
info@pearlsplace.com • www.pearlsplace.com

Pearl's Place is a huge brick-and-mortar bridal store in Louisiana that takes phone and Internet orders. They carry an enormous number of dresses by tons of designers including: Amsale, Anne Barge, Provincias, Vera Wang, and Melissa Sweet. Even their website doesn't give a complete listing of what they have, so the best way to work with them is to call them and ask about specific designers and styles. You can get a good deal if you know what you're looking for. They sell bridesmaid dresses too.

Simple Silhouettes

www.simpledress.com • inquiry@simpledress.com
$: Starting price: Knee length: $255, full length: $275

Designer Christina Dalle Pezze fell into the bridesmaid business by accident, designing elegant dresses for a friend's bridesmaids, and discovering the need for simple and wearable bridesmaid dresses. She works hard to keep her designs updated but classic, so that they have long lives and don't languish in closets. A benefit that Simple Silhouette offers is variety. Brides can come in and pick a color or palette of colors and then encourage her bridesmaids to select dresses or separates based on their own personal styles and what makes them comfortable. Customers can also shop through the website, which shows all of the designs, but it is recommended that someone visit the showroom to really get a sense of the styles. Simple Silhouettes also offers a small line of accessories including handbags, wraps, and some jewelry. They prefer for orders to be placed four months before the wedding.

SHOES

BridalShoes.com

1-800-575-7837
Fax: 516-569-4733

BridalShoes.com is a great Internet resource—especially if you're having trouble finding wedding shoes that come in wide widths. They have a large selection of shoes, organized on their website by heel height and in some cases by designer or style (they carry a lot of Kenneth Cole wedding shoes and a line of clear plastic "Cinderella" shoes) and it is very easy to order and do returns or exchanges. They also carry children's sizes in dyeable and "Cinderella" styles.

Discount Wedding Shoes

C/O Dyeable Shoes Online, Inc.
867 San Remo Drive • Weston, FL 33326
888-465-7330
dyeking@aol.com • www.discountweddingshoes.com
$: Shoes start at $30

A division of Dyeable Shoes Online (www.dyeableshoesonline.com), Discount Wedding Shoes carries Benjamin Walk "Touch Ups," in both dyeable and non-dyeable varieties and even stocks some Lucite shoes. They also carry a wide range of widths and some large-size shoes. DiscountWeddingShoes.com is also a great resource if you're looking for reasonably priced girl's shoes; they have dyeables and Lucite shoes in child sizes (kid's dyeables start at about $22).

Kenneth Cole
www.kennethcole.com
1-800-KENCOLE

95 Fifth Avenue · New York, NY 10003
212-675-2550

Grand Central Station
(42nd Street and Vanderbilt) · New York, NY 10017
212-949-8079

See page 142.

My Glass Slipper
423 King Street · Alexandria, VA 22314
703-838-8583 · Toll free: 866-WED-SHOE
Fax: 703-838-8926
www.myglassslipper.com
$: Sale shoes can start as low as $15;
non-couture shoes start at about $40

If you know what you want, My Glass Slipper is a terrific online resource. Their easy to-use website has shoes organized into "Couture Footwear" and "Shoes Under $100" categories. In addition they have a constant "Sale Shoes" section where you can find all kinds of treasures by great designers at a big discount. Some of the designers My Glass Slipper carries are: Kenneth Cole, Cynthia Rowley, Badgley Mischka, Fenaroli, Vera Wang, Richard Tyler, and Watters & Watters. The site also sells dyeable purses (couture and non-couture) and some jewelry, and provides a helpful FAQ section for shoe-seekers. If you're interested in their sales, you can sign up to get email notices that will let you know what's going to be discounted before it gets officially listed on the site.

Peter Fox
105 Thompson Street · New York, NY 10012
212-431-7426

www.peterfox.com
$: Shoes start at around $230

Peter Fox's classic white satin shoes represent an array of wedding archetypes. He makes everything from Cinderella slippers to chic slingbacks and ornate boots with embroidery. Julia Roberts wore a couple of different sets of Peter Fox shoes in *Runaway Bride*, and Kate Winslet wore a daring pair of red boots in *Titanic*. After your wedding, Peter Fox can dye your shoes for you for a small fee.

INVITATIONS

EInvite

www.einvite.com
888-346-8483
CustomerService@eInvite.com

If you want to take your bonanza of invitations, engagement announcements, and moving cards and order them all online, consider eInvite. This site uses a patented technology that lets you see a "proof" of your work online moments after you enter it. They provide almost 1,000 designs, ink colors, paper stocks, and graphics and the website even gives you tips for invitation etiquette, so you can make sure everything is kosher before you place the order. EInvite's invitations are printed using thermography.

EVERYTHING

E Bay

This incredibly popular online auction site is a terrific wedding resource. At any hour of the day or night you can shop for designer wedding dresses, shoes, veils, jewelry, accessories, even cake toppers. It's worth doing a few quick searches for the things you need, no matter how obscure you think they are, because they're probably on eBay.

CAKE TOPPER

It Figures Online

www.itfiguresonline.com
818-509-0200 • Fax: 818-761-0200
melanie@itfiguresonline.com
$: Two figures: $1,200; humans: $600 each, pets: $400 each

Many people save their cake toppers to give to their children and there is a booming trade in them on eBay, but if you want something original and personalized, think about It Figures Online. Artist Melanie Wynne Waldman will sculpt brides and grooms, pets, people, things—you name it—in polymer clay. Her figures are funny, lively, and completely customized to fit the interests, humor, taste, and style of her customers. You can order entirely through her site—she works from pictures, and it's wise to contact her for availability.

FAVORS

Candy Direct

5694 Mission Center Road #378 • San Diego, CA 92108
619-326-7215
www.candydirect.com
info@candydirect.com • orders@candydirect.com

This website offers great deals on bulk candy, hard-to-find candies, and candy favors and novelties. Check out their "candy bouquets" as fun presents for younger attendants. They also have great deals on enormous quantities of Jordan almonds.

Discount Photo Supplies

www.discount-photo.com

Order all kinds of photo equipment from one-time-use cameras to Polaroid film.

Economy Candy

108 Rivington Street • New York, NY 10002
212-254-1832 • 800-352-4544 • Fax: 212-254-2606
www.economycandy.com

Visit this Lower East Side emporium of delights; order by phone or off the website. Economy Candy has been in business since 1937 and sells almost every kind of candy you can imagine, in bulk or small quantities: fireballs, marzipan fruit, nostalgia items like Tootsie Rolls and candy corn. They also sell Jordan almonds (a popular wedding favor rumored to symbolize everything from luck to good fortune to fertility) in lots of colors, including gold and silver, and they always stock "conversation hearts," which are pretty scarce except around Valentine's Day.

The Knot

1-877-THE-KNOT (1-877-843-5668)
www.theknot.com

The Knot, an online wedding planning and information site, established in 1996, has a reputation for being the most comprehensive internet wedding resource. The site features: a wedding-gown catalog, searchable by style and designer; articles; hugely popular "community" features (bulletin boards and chat rooms), vendor listings (sorted by cities); an online registry (in partnerships with Fortunoff and Linens n' Things); and a store. The online store offers all kinds of wedding supplies, favors, and attendants' gifts. Some items like chocolate bars, napkins, one-time-use cameras, and matchbooks can even be personalized for your wedding.

Martha Stewart

Customer Service: 1-800-345-7795
www.marthastewart.com/weddings

You may as well check out Martha Stewart's site, after all, she did put wedding planning on the map. This well designed site is full of wedding information, interesting ideas, useful advice, and of course, gives you a chance to buy things or register. The Martha Stewart wedding registry is well organized and nicely set up (there's even a section called "petkeeping" so if you're not comfortable registering for yourself, at least your dog can get wedding presents).

Nature Perfect

1-888-328-8821
www.natureperfect.com

If you're looking to do something a little different for wedding favors, consider Nature Perfect's suggestions. They offer a range of botanical favors. Most of their wedding items are live lucky bamboo plants that you can use first as centerpieces and then break up as parting favors for your guests.

Oriental Trading Company

1-800-875-8480
www.oriental.com

Order all kinds of inexpensive party supplies and favors online from the Oriental Trading Company. They sell everything from candy to bubbles, confetti to votive candles, and they have latex and Mylar balloons in stock. They are a great resource for kitschy shower decorations and theme items.

Pearl River Mart

277 Canal Street · New York, NY
212-431-4770
Canal Street Branch is moving to:
477 Broadway, New York, NY 10013
and
Grand Street Branch: · 200 Grand Street · New York, NY
212-966-1010 · 800-878-2446
www.pearlriver.com

Chinatown's Pearl River Mart is an amazing resource for weddings and parties. It's an enormous Chinese department store that has everything from cooking supplies to a huge assortment of paper lanterns to embroidered silk slippers to Chinese herbal remedies. Wander around and pick up fantastic guest books, photo albums, parasols, wrapping paper, and other atypical presents and favors. Their prices are reasonable and even though you can order online, the trip to Chinatown is always a blast.

Promotional World

www.promotionalworld.com
888-556-PROMO · Fax: 877-9 USAFax

If you want personalized favors, check out Promotional World. They have everything from coffee mugs to pens, caps, watches, paper fans—you name it.

The Wedding Channel

888 South Figueroa Street, · Suite 700 · Los Angeles, CA 90017
888 750-1550 · Fax: 213 599-4180

The Wedding Channel is another enormous, well-respected online wedding resource that offers wedding planning tools, community features, articles, vendor descriptions and a large store. The *Wall Street Journal* had high praise for a feature on the site that takes your wedding checklist and incorporates it into a calendar (and also sends you email reminders). The store carries a lot of the standard wedding favors, attendant items, decorations, and it even provides a make-your-own CD service.

Wedthings.com

888-338-8818
info@wedthings.com

Wedthings sells an enormous array of amusing and tasteful wedding items. For favors, you can get everything from candy and personalized fortune cookies to picture frames, painted fans (perfect for June brides), and fabulous boxes and ribbons. They also have other wedding "essentials" including ring pillows, guest books, bridesmaid presents, and lots of items to fit holiday themes.

PRESENTS

Boucher Jewelry

9 Ninth Avenue · New York, NY 10014
212-807-9849 or 866-623-9269
www.boucherjewerly.com · info@boucherjewerly.com
Earrings or a basic necklace start at about $40

If you're looking for beautiful attendant presents, Laura Mady's beautiful jewelry designs, lively with color and light-catching shapes, can be made to order for an entire bridal party. Mady can design different pieces that use the same pearls or stones for each member of the bridal party (from mothers of the bride and groom all the way to junior attendants) so that the look is consistent, but people get to wear jewelry that matches their personalities. You can go into either of Boucher's two stores (in Manhattan and Cold Springs, NY) with swatches, or you can place orders online and have pictures of the pieces emailed to you. Boucher can work with any budget, offers discounts for large orders, and can even put together wonderful pieces in a rush.

VEILS and HEADPIECES

VeilShop.com

P.O. Box 32 • Mason, OH 45040-0032
513-336-6043
www.veilshop.com
$: Prices vary

VeilShop.com is an online-only store that sells more kinds of veils, headpieces, bun wraps, tiaras, and other hair ornaments than you can imagine. The site is easy to use and has all kinds of tutorials on everything from how to care for your veil to what sort of things you can do with short hair.

Feel-Good Bride

Weddings can provide wonderful opportunities for people to give to charities and seek out causes that are important to them. It isn't every day that you find yourself planning a huge party and this kind of event often lends itself, quite effortlessly, to various giving opportunities that you might want to take advantage of.

Below is a small list of interesting charitable organizations that accept everything from extra food from your reception to wedding dresses. Many of these resources are equipped to give you receipts for tax deductions in exchange for your donation. You can even extend the life of things like your flower arrangements by giving them to a hospital or nursing home. People often feel funny that they've spent so much energy planning and working on a wedding that will only last one day. Giving to these charities is a way of extending the good will and joy of your wedding to the world.

WEDDING CHARITIES

General

Married for Good

contact@marriedforgood.com • www.marriedforgood.com

Married for Good is a wonderful website that is full of information about how you can, in a number of different ways, do charitable work through your wedding. Their suggestions range from pointing out that if you have your wedding in a park or museum, the usage fee benefits the site to giving cash donations to charities in lieu of guest favors. Their website is full of interesting and creative ways for the bride and groom—and guests—to give to charity.

Dress Donations & Benefits

The Bridal Garden

Sheltering Arms Children's Services
www.bridalgarden.org
Bridal Garden at (212) 252-0661

The Bridal Garden, described in the Bridal Gowns section of this book, sells sample and "once worn" wedding dresses that have been donated to the organization. All proceeds go to children's support programs sponsored by Sheltering Arms Children's Services. If you would like to donate your wedding dress, contact the Bridal Garden. You'll get a receipt for a tax deduction in addition to peace of mind.

Bridesmaid's Ball

Sponsored by the Leukemia & Lymphoma Society
www.bridesmaidsball.org
610-776-8240

The Bridesmaid's Ball is an annual party, which the Leukemia & Lymphoma Society has sponsored since 1993. It is a huge wedding-themed bash full of dancing and contests and it is one of the few times you'll get to wear your bridesmaid dress again. They have garter and bouquet toss events and the highlight of the party is the "Dress From Hell" contest where top prize goes to the most horrific outfit. The Ball is traditionally held in Philadelphia, but people come from all over the tristate area to have fun for a good cause.

Glass Slipper Project

www.glassslipperproject.com

The Glass Slipper Project in Chicago hit the big time in its first year of operation when it appeared on the Oprah Winfrey Show in April 1999. The organization collects formal dresses and accessories (only current styles and in new or almost-new condition) in any size—they especially need size 16 and above—and gives them to underprivileged teenage girls to wear to their high school proms. Send them your dress, shoes, accessories, even unopened cosmetics and they'll give you a receipt for a tax deduction. Visit the Glass Slipper website to see when they are collecting. They are a fantastic organization.

Making Memories Breast Cancer Foundation

P.O. Box 92042 · Portland, Oregon 97292-2042
503 252-3955
www.makingmemories.org

The Making Memories Breast Cancer Foundation gives patients with metastatic breast cancer a chance to fulfill lifelong dreams. The organization accepts wedding and bridesmaid dresses, which they then sell. The proceeds are used to help make cancer patients' wishes come true. All donations are 100 percent tax deductible.

FOOD DONATIONS

America's Second Harvest

35 E. Wacker Dr., #2000 · Chicago, IL 60601
800-771-2303 · 312-263-2303
www.secondharvest.com

If you live outside New York City and want to donate food from your reception, America's Second Harvest can help you. They work with a network of food banks and you can use them as a resource to place your donation.

City Harvest

575 Eighth Avenue, 4th Floor · New York, NY 10018
917-351-8700 · Fax: 917-351-8720
www.cityharvest.org

City Harvest, founded in 1981, is a charitable organization that distributes leftover food from restaurants and catered events to a network of over 800 emergency food programs in New York City. They do accept food from catered events and weddings, so contact them if you'd like to donate. If you look through their website, you can find a list of caterers who are among City Harvest's "Top Donors," but you can also work with the charity directly.

Notes

Notes

About
the Author

Joan Hamburg dishes out the best advice on shopping, dining, entertaining, travel, and theater daily on WOR Radio's "The Joan Hamburg Show," and hosts the annual "WOR Bridal Show with Joan Hamburg." She has been a broadcast and print journalist for over twenty years and is the author of *Our Little Black Book of Shopping Secrets* and the *New York on $__ a Day Series*. She is a contributing editor at *Family Circle* magazine and writes for many other publications.

Joan and her husband Morton, a communications attorney and photographer, have two children, Elizabeth and John.

About
the Illustrator

Sharon Watts spent ten years illustrating for the "By Design" fashion column in the *New York Times*. She lives in Brooklyn with her two cats, Una and Rufus.

Other City & Company Guides Available from Universe Publishing:

CITY BABY:

The Ultimate Guide for New York City Parents
from Pregnancy to Preschool
2nd Edition
by Pamela Weinberg and Kelly Ashton
$18.95
ISBN: 0-789-308-320

LITERARY LANDMARKS
OF NEW YORK

The Book Lover's Guide to the Homes and
Haunts of World-Famous Writers
$16.95
by Bill Morgan
ISBN: 0-789-308-541

NEW YORK'S 50 BEST
PLACES TO TAKE CHILDEN

2nd Edition
by Allan Ishac
$12.95
ISBN: 0-789-308-363

NEW YORK'S 50 BEST
PLACES TO FIND PEACE & QUIET

3rd Edition
by Allan Ishac
$12.95
ISBN: 0-789-308-347

THE COOL PARENTS' GUIDE
TO ALL OF NEW YORK:

Excursions and Activities In and around
Our City That Your Children Will Love and
You Won't Think Are Too Bad Either
3rd Edition
by Alfred Gingold and Helen Rogan
$14.95
ISBN: 0-789-308-576

Coming Soon . . .

NEW YORK'S 100 BEST
LITTLE HOTELS

3rd Edition
by Allen Sperry
$14.95
ISBN: 0-789-308-592

HEAVENLY WEEKENDS

2nd Edition
by Susan Clemett and Gena Vandestienne
$14.95
ISBN: 0-789-308-584